STONES
OF DUBLIN

A HISTORY OF DUBLIN
IN TEN BUILDINGS

This book is for Ciaran

STONES OF DUBLIN

A HISTORY OF DUBLIN IN TEN BUILDINGS

LISA MARIE GRIFFITH

The Collins Press

First published in 2014 by
The Collins Press
West Link Park
Doughcloyne
Wilton
Cork

A CIP record for this book is available from the British Library.

Paperback ISBN: 978-1-84889-219-4
PDF eBook ISBN: 978-1-84889-871-4
EPUB eBook ISBN: 978-1-84889-872-1
Kindle ISBN: 978-1-84889-873-8

Photographs © the author unless otherwise credited.

Design and typesetting by Carrigboy Typesetting Services
Typeset in Berkeley

Printed in Malta by Gutenberg Press Limited

Contents

Acknowledgements

A GREAT NUMBER of people were prepared to give their time and energy to assist me with this book and I would like to take this opportunity to thank them. The publishers were hugely supportive of this project. They helped to develop the original idea and guide me from a list of 24 buildings to just ten.

Ciarán Wallace of Trinity College, Dublin was kind enough to provide advice, support and to recommend material for inclusion. He also gave up a large amount of time to read a draft of the book. A number of historians have provided me with assistance but I would like to single out a number of people in particular. I am very grateful to Dr Juliana Adelman (St Patrick's College, DCU), Eamon Darcy (NUI Maynooth), Suzanne Forbes (UCD and National Print Museum) and Léan Ní Chléirigh (Trinity College, Dublin) who volunteered their historical expertise and provided advice on buildings and sources.

Andrew Staunton, from St Patrick's Cathedral, was kind enough to meet with me and provide advice about Christ Church and St Patrick's Cathedral. Donal Fallon, from Come Here to Me (http://comeheretome.com/), provided information on the Guinness cartoon featured within.

We are blessed in Dublin to have a fantastic network of local libraries and archives. I would like to thank the staff at Dublin City Library and Archive at Pearse Street, and Rathmines Public Library for all of their assistance. Dublin history would be a very limited field without access to these repositories that provide not only wide-ranging sources but also the most up-to-date studies.

I was lucky enough to work as a tour guide for several years at Historical Insights, one of Dublin's best tour-guiding companies. During my time working for the company, I learnt a huge amount about the city's architecture, streetscape and history. Without the training provided by Tommy Graham and Peter Ballagh, as well as the rest of the team at Historical Insights, I could not have written this book.

I would also like to thank my colleagues and students at the National Print Museum for their patience and support while preparing this book including Carla Marrinan, Suzanne Forbes, Gretta Halpin, Mary Tobin and Conrad Devlin. Emma Arbuthnot, who has since left the museum, also provided assistance.

I had a huge amount of assistance selecting and gathering images. A number of repositories, archives and institutions, allowed me to reproduce images from their collection and I would like to thank them. They include Dublin City Library and Archives (DCLA), the National Library of Ireland (NLI), Guinness Archive, Hugh Lane Gallery, Irish Architectural Archive (IAA), Kilmainham Gaol, UCD Digital Archive, St Patrick's Cathedral and TARA Digital Repository (Trinity College Dublin). Niall Bergin (Kilmainham Gaol), Eithne Massey (DCLA) and Andrew Staunton (St Patrick's Cathedral) provided great assistance and helped me to find suitable images for the text. Some people were king enough to give me permission to use their own work, or images for which they hold the copyright, including Ciarán MacGonigal and Roger Stalley.

I would also like to thank those who helped me to complete and polish the book. John Gibney provided advice on the text and did a wonderful job copy-editing the work. Josette Prichard set the text and was extremely patient with the many last-minute changes made.

My family have provided enormous support while I researched and wrote this book. Thanks to my parents, John and Christine, also Sinead and Conor Pyne, Darren and Julie Griffith, and Jonathan Griffith. My friends have supplied very welcome breaks from the researching and writing process. Thanks to Denise Dwyer, Sinead Kelly, Margaret and Kenny Lynch, Nicholas Kelly and Michelle Behan. Finally, I could not have written this book without the support I received from boyfriend Ciaran Murray, who read chapters, gave feedback and provided encouragement.

suit their needs. Commentators and historians have ascribed symbolic values to these buildings too. These structures can tell us about our present, and not just our past. I have selected ten key buildings in Dublin that enable us to understand the city, its streetscape and its growth, its inhabitants and its rich and varied history from the Middle Ages to the twenty-first century.

CHRIST CHURCH CATHEDRAL

In the first chapter I will examine the Viking church that became Christ Church Cathedral. The population of the island of Ireland was fragmented in the Viking period, and different settlers would come to inhabit Dublin. Christ Church Cathedral was founded by a Hiberno-Norse king of the city, was located at the physical heart of Dublin, and was recognised by its inhabitants as an institution that was hugely important. Once Dublin was conquered by the Anglo-Normans, they seized the cathedral and made it their own. The English government also recognised its importance, and medieval lord lieutenants were sworn into office at the cathedral. During the Reformation, the cathedral's monastic order was due to be dissolved, and with this the cathedral would lose its purpose, but was saved by the protests of Dublin's inhabitants. It became a centrepiece of the reformation as the seat of the Anglican archbishop of Dublin. Although Christ Church began to decline in the nineteenth century, an expensive restoration undertaken by Henry Roe, Dublin's largest whiskey distiller, saved (as well as dramatically altered) the cathedral. The history of the cathedral shows us how diverse the city's inhabitants have been and brings us through the Viking, Anglo-Norman, English and Protestant periods in the city's history.

DUBLIN CASTLE

English power in Ireland was centred on Dublin Castle, which made it a hugely important building, and this is dealt with in the second chapter. The castle placed Dublin at the centre of the English colony

Introduction

I WORKED AS A WALKING tour guide in Dublin's city centre for several years. The tour I presented was a history of Ireland in two hours. One of the difficulties with giving an 'Irish history for beginners' tour is how to present information that is relatively unfamiliar to a group of visitors to the city. Dublin's buildings were important landmarks for people who were feeling their way around, and by telling the story of these buildings I could create a historical narrative. Through the buildings I could help the people on my tour to connect with events and people they might not have encountered before. The art and architecture of the buildings added rich detail to this narrative and allowed me to recreate a time and place. These details could be as small as a painting hanging on a wall, a tapestry, or bullet holes from a past rebellion. Pointing these out to visitors made me look at the buildings I passed every day in a whole new light. Buildings in the city set the stage for great events, influenced the people around them, and shaped and directed the growth of the city itself.

BUILDINGS AND THE HISTORICAL NARRATIVE

Buildings are a part of history. But they are often sidelined and appear merely as a stage upon which great events occur. In this book I have placed buildings at the centre of the historical narrative, so that a picture emerges of a city that was hugely influenced by the buildings themselves and the institutions they housed. The motivations of the men and women involved in creating the buildings examined in this book were manifold: religion, colonisation, education, trade, politics, and civic improvement. Although those behind the foundation of these buildings might have had clear motivations, this did not mean the buildings would retain their original purpose. The city, and its inhabitants, changed the meaning and purpose of the buildings to

1

in Ireland. The head of the English government, the lord lieutenant, resided at the castle, along with large numbers of the armed forces. During the infrequent occasions when British royalty visited Ireland, they resided at Dublin Castle, or used it as a venue for their receptions. Just one of the many ways that the castle benefited the inhabitants of Dublin was its influence on communications and infrastructure. Due to its importance for the English government, roads to Dublin had to be well maintained, and shipping to and from the city had to travel frequently. The downside was that the castle also tended to be the main focus for disaffected inhabitants, and rebellions often targeted Dublin Castle.

TRINITY COLLEGE DUBLIN

On its foundation in 1592 Trinity College Dublin, Ireland's oldest university, was seen as an important colonising tool. It was hoped that through the education of ministers, lawyers and doctors, English religion, law and civility would spread through Ireland. Trinity managed to shape the minds of those who were loyal to the English government but also many who questioned its authority. John Fitzgibbon, earl of Clare, was a firm advocate of the Act of Union and was educated in Trinity, but so too was Theobald Wolfe Tone, one of the leaders of the United Irishman's rebellion of 1798. The university's library is one of the most important repositories of Irish manuscripts and printed material in the world and houses the famous Book of Kells. The university shows how a Protestant institution, with strong government connections, could survive some of the most turbulent periods in Irish history and retain its place as one of the most important educational institutions on the island.

PARLIAMENT HOUSE (BANK OF IRELAND)

The imposing Bank of Ireland building on College Green might look like a monument to Irish commerce, but it was first a home to the Irish parliament and is investigated in the fourth chapter. As one of the earliest purpose-built parliament buildings in the world, the building was intended to make an important statement about power in Ireland. Nevertheless, the parliament was controlled by the British government for many decades. When 'patriots' within parliament began to wrest power from the British government, the assembly was seen as a threat to British power in Ireland, and, after the 1801 Act of Union, Ireland lost its parliamentary independence. Although taken over by the Bank of Ireland shortly after, in the nineteenth century, Irish nationalists repeatedly called for a parliament to return to College Green. They saw the building as an important symbol of what had been taken from them.

City Hall

This is the home of civic government in Dublin, and is the subject of the fifth chapter. The building was originally the Royal Exchange, and was constructed between 1769 and 1779. The building was funded by the Committee of Merchants, a group of Dublin traders from across the religious spectrum, for the purpose of promoting trade and commerce in Ireland. Although the group had honourable intentions, they became embroiled in a battle with property developers in the city who sought to move the city's Custom House to the east of the city, so that they could build additional bridges to access their estates. Although the merchants eventually lost out to the city's landed elite, the building's history highlights the politics behind Dublin's rapid eighteenth century expansion.

St James's Gate

Guinness is one of the most famous Irish brands, and the St James's Gate brewery where it is brewed is the dealt with in chapter six. Although the brewery was founded by Arthur Guinness in 1759, porter was not brewed there until 1778. The location of the brewery, in the centre of Dublin's Liberties, gave Arthur Guinness both a workforce and a market. St James's Gate expanded under each successive Guinness generation. It was Dublin's largest brewery in 1810, Ireland's largest in 1833, and the largest in the world by 1914. Guinness was also the city's largest employer. The Guinness family were hugely important outside the brewery too and used their money to develop Dublin's landscape through projects such as the Iveagh Trust development. The history of St James's Gate shows how one brand can shape a city, as well as how the drinking habits of Dubliners developed through history.

Kilmainham Gaol

The most famous jail in Dublin, Kilmainham, is looked at in chapter seven. Prison reform in Britain and Ireland was an issue that gained widespread support in the late eighteenth century and with an earlier jail in deplorable condition, a new Kilmainham Gaol was opened in 1796. Soon after, the 1798 rebellion broke out, followed by Robert Emmet's rebellion in 1803. Later came the foundation of the Young Irelanders, the Fenians, the Land League, and the 1916 Rising. From almost the moment the doors of Kilmainham opened, it housed some of the most prominent political prisoners of its day. The prison also housed thousands of Dublin's ordinary citizens, making the jail an important building in the social and political history of the city.

General Post Office (GPO)

This city-centre post office was the headquarters of the 1916 Rising, is arguably the most famous building in the city, and is the subject of chapter eight. The leaders of the rising seem to have chosen the building as their headquarters as the GPO was the centre of communications in the city. To seize the GPO was to seize telegraph and phone lines, and to disrupt post and communications across the city. Although the rebellion was short-lived and ended in the execution of 16 men, it gave birth to a stronger republican movement and led to the War of Independence. As such, the GPO is seen as the cradle of revolution, the birthplace of Irish independence. The events at the GPO have been celebrated in state parades, history books, documentaries and films. The history of the building tells us about one of the most important chapters in the foundation of the Irish state.

THE ABBEY THEATRE

In the late nineteenth century a Gaelic revival movement, which bemoaned the dominance of English culture in Ireland, sought to revive all aspects of traditional Irish culture including language, sport, folklore and literature. Two leading figures of the movement, W.B. Yeats and Augusta Gregory, felt that the spread of English books and plays had an adverse affect on Irish culture. With the aim of building up a 'Celtic and Irish school of dramatic literature' they founded the Abbey Theatre, the focus of chapter nine. The Abbey Theatre promoted the work of some of the most important early twentieth century playwrights including J.M. Synge and Seán O'Casey. Although the theatre suffered a creative decline in the middle of the twentieth century, it re-emerged in the 1970s to become Ireland's premier theatre. The Abbey Theatre helped to shape Irish identity, and the theatre's history can tell us about some of Ireland's most influential cultural figures.

CROKE PARK

The final chapter examines Croke Park, a site where people from all over Ireland came—and still come to this day—to celebrate Irish sport and culture. The Gaelic Athletic Association (GAA) made the Jones's Road site its home from 1913. All-Ireland finals are played at the stadium, making Croke Park one of the most important sites in Irish sport. Moreover, overlap in membership between the GAA and other nationalist organisations meant that the stadium was a site of huge political importance. In the aftermath of a civil war that tore apart Irish society and politics, Croke Park helped to unify the population in a way that no other building could. The *Aonach Tailteann* games were staged there in 1924, a type of Irish Olympic Games, and promoted the ideals of an independent Irish identity worldwide. In the opening decades of the new state the GAA flourished, and Croke Park was at the heart of the association. Although the stadium had begun to represent 'old Ireland' and was suffering declining numbers by the 1970s, the GAA fought back. A redevelopment of Croke Park from the 1990s turned Croke Park into one of the most modern stadiums in Europe, with a maximum capacity of 82,300. The stadium represents more than just sporting heritage, it tells us about the politics of Ireland too.

THE EXPANSION OF DUBLIN: POPULATION AND STREETSCAPE

The location of each of these 10 buildings also tells us about the growth and expansion of the city. The boundaries of the Hiberno-Norse city ran from the modern site of Dublin Castle and would have run along Castle Street, Werburgh Street, Christ Church Cathedral to Parliament Street. This medieval core expanded in two more phases, which we can trace through archaeological evidence and through the remnants of the city walls: it moved west as far as High Street and north as far as the River Liffey.[1] Looking at the development of the medieval city, we can see that, when Sitriuc Silkbeard founded Christ Church Cathedral in the eleventh century, he placed the cathedral at the heart of the city. When the Anglo-Normans conquered Dublin in the twelfth century they were well aware of potential threats to the city. The Hiberno-Norse population of the city had been expelled across the Liffey to Oxmantown, and although this was a substantial suburb (we know settlements developed outside the city walls as well), it would be several centuries before it became part of the core of the city. The new English government built a protective fortress, Dublin Castle, within the city walls to protect their regime. With little room for new development, the castle was placed in the southwest of the city. The river Poddle was diverted to run around the castle boundaries, creating a moat. This led to a double defence within the city. As the castle was a significant government centre, it encouraged growth in the east of the city. In the aftermath of the Anglo-Norman invasion, the city experienced economic expansion and the population increased. Although it is difficult to estimate the exact population

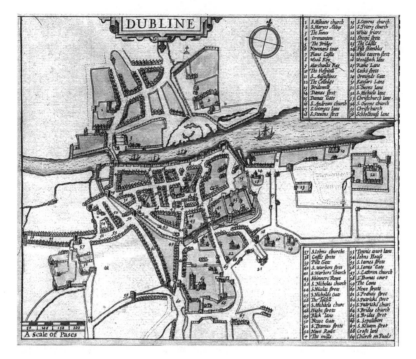

John Speed's map of Dublin, 1610 (Dublin City Library and archives)

numbers, some historians believe that by the fourteenth century about 11,000 people lived within the city walls and in the immediate suburbs.[2]

Unfortunately, the earliest extant map that we have dates to 1610. Nevertheless, this map was drawn at a time when the city was beginning to expand, and we can see how far Dublin had grown since the medieval period. The city had grown beyond its walls to the east and across the Liffey to the north. The map also allows us to guess what the city population may have been. The historian Louis Cullen has suggested 15,000 people lived within the city at this point.[3] We know that the population increased to about 40,000 people by 1680, and to 60,000 in 1700.[4]

Trinity College appears as part of the countryside on John Speed's map in 1610. Before the parliament house was erected, parliament resided in Chichester House (on the same site as the later building).

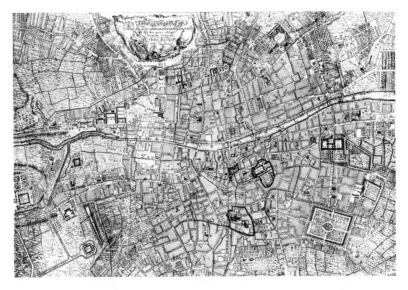

John Rocque's map of Dublin, 1756 (Dublin City Library and archives)

The house was located on Trinity Street, a prosperous part of the city outside the cramped medieval city. The locations of Trinity College and the parliament were advantageous. The development of Dame Street and College Green allowed an easy pathway to Dublin Castle and College Green, so these four institutions (Christ Church, Dublin Castle, Parliament and Trinity) were located on an east—west axis. While the castle and Christ Church were located in the old city, reflecting their medieval origins, Trinity College and the parliament house indicated where future growth would be, providing 'a focus for the capital city well to the east, complemented by the imposing extent of Trinity College'.[5] As we can see from John Rocque's map of 1756, growth in the north and east of the city ensured Trinity College and the parliament house were closer to the city centre.

Growth continued to the east of the city, and this can be seen on Rocque's map. The St Stephen's Green development can be seen on the outskirts of the city. This new type of estate had become hugely popular, and had been successfully developed in the northside of the city. Wealthy citizens wanted to live far from the noise and bustle of civic government and trade, and had begun to decamp to the northside. This led to increased traffic on the city bridges, which prompted proposals to build more bridges to the east of the city to ease congestion. This would cut off the Custom House, which was located close to the old medieval quarter. Merchants were angry. They built their Royal Exchange, now City Hall, in the older part of the city, hoping to halt this eastward movement. They failed, however, and the Custom House was moved to the northwest of the city.

Dublin's wealthy citizens may have moved north, but the poorer inhabitants had stayed in the old medieval part of the city. Linen, an important Irish export in the eighteenth century, created employment for many of the city's working poor. Weaving was concentrated in the Liberties (around St Patrick's Cathedral, High Street and Thomas Street), and so too were the linen-bleaching fields. It was in this industrial quarter of the city, with access to a clean water supply at the city reservoir, that Arthur Guinness established his brewery at St James's Gate. There were numerous breweries and distilleries located in the area from the medieval period to the nineteenth century.

Just three and a half kilometres west from this busy industrial part of the city lay the county jail, Kilmainham Gaol. Located outside the city when it opened its doors in 1796, the rapid population expansion of the eighteenth and nineteenth centuries meant that it was quickly subsumed into the city suburbs. In 1841, when the first reliable census was carried out in Ireland, the city's population was 233,000.[6] The boundaries of the city were marked by the Grand and Royal Canals. The Post Office map of 1852 shows the city boundaries within the canals, and hints at the suburban growth beyond the city limits. The upper and middle class inhabitants who had once lived in the city centre moved out to the suburbs which were springing up at an increasing pace. The tram and railway meant they had easy access to work and to shops in the city centre, while they also enjoyed the space and amenities of the suburbs. The poor of the city took up residence in the once-splendid Georgian mansions, and from here some of the worst slum conditions in Europe developed. The commercial heart of the city had moved with the new Custom House to the northside. When the Wide Streets Commission developed Sackville Street (now O'Connell Street), it became the busiest street in the city. The General

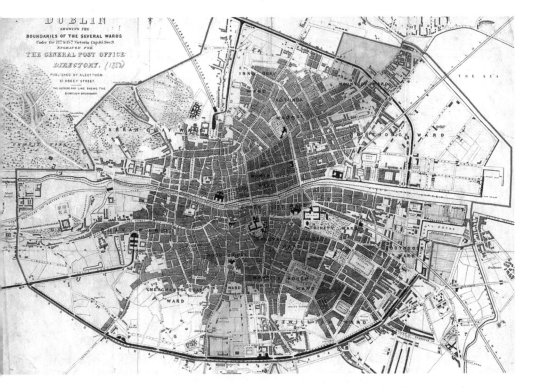

General Post Office Map of Dublin, 1852 (Dublin City Library and archives)

Post Office opened on the street in 1818, and when the tram system reached the street it became the centre of communications too. The area was the city's social and entertainment centre. Abbey Street, just off Sackville Street, was the location of the Abbey Theatre.

The expansion of the suburbs and the railway lines assisted the evolution of sports clubs and stadiums on the outskirts of the city. The Jones's Road stadium, which became Croke Park, grew in line with these nineteenth century developments. The suburbs continued to grow throughout the twentieth century, making transport networks even more important for Dubliners who travelled into the city for work and leisure. Croke Park, still in the suburbs, was a site that had to be well-serviced to cater for the tens of thousands of people who travelled to the stadium during match days, and today it is connected to the city centre and greater Dublin area by bus and rail links.

Dominating the skyline of the northside suburb of Drumcondra, Croke Park is indicative of the suburban growth of the nineteenth and twentieth centuries, which changed the landscape of the city irrevocably. The city limits have expanded beyond the canal lines that once marked the city boundary and now encompass suburban areas such as Drumcondra. The city population has grown to more than 525,000 inhabitants, while the population of city and suburban areas of Dún Laoghaire-Rathdown, Fingal and South Dublin was just over 1,273,000 in the 2011 census.

This book seeks to recreate a virtual walking tour of Dublin's history, so that the reader can imagine the events that shaped, and the people who influenced, the history of Dublin. It is not an architectural history, nor is it a potted history of Dublin; it provides biographies of ten of Dublin's most important buildings. Some of the sites discussed here, such as Trinity College Dublin, are not strictly 'buildings' any longer, and have grown beyond their initial limits to become complexes of buildings. This points to the success of the original institutions. This book sets out to look at how these buildings and institutions were founded, how they survived Ireland's turbulent history, the part they played in the great events of Dublin's past, and what they mean to us today.

For accessibility and consistency, anglicised versions of Irish names have been used throughout the book; unless otherwise indicated, all biographical details have been taken from the Royal Irish Academy's *Dictionary of Irish Biography*.

1

Christ Church Cathedral

CHRIST CHURCH CATHEDRAL has been at the heart of Dublin's religious community for almost a millennium. Nestled in the centre of the old medieval city, important civic and national institutions sprang up around the cathedral. Christ Church is one of the most important links to the city's medieval history and one of the oldest buildings in the city. This area of the city was inhabited long before the arrival of the Vikings. When Dublin's Viking community founded the church, in 1030, they placed it at the heart of their settlement. Many of Ireland's important medieval leaders, warriors and religious figures, including Dublin's patron saint (Laurence O'Toole) and the man who led the Anglo-Norman attack on Dublin (Richard de Clare, or Strongbow), are closely linked with the cathedral. The cathedral as we know it today is vastly different to the original site and the story of Christ Church is one of evolution and change. Once a monastic site and home to a Dublin order of Augustinians, it became a secular cathedral during the Reformation and, as the seat of the Anglican Archbishop of Dublin, it was an important institution of the Reformation. The cathedral also has a more obscure history. After the Reformation, the monastic buildings were used for a variety of purposes. For many years the city law courts were located within the cathedral complex. The cathedral precinct was also a busy commercial site, with stalls, shops and vendors attracting city shoppers. Rents within the precinct were a valuable source of income for the cathedral. Many of these medieval buildings were cleared away in the nineteenth century, leaving the cathedral building visible. Consequently, many people do not know the part that the cathedral played in the commercial, civic and legal life of the city.

THE ORIGINS OF SETTLEMENT IN DUBLIN: ÁTH CLIATH AND DUBH LINN

To understand how the cathedral came to be built we must examine the early city settlers. Dublin is one of the oldest capital cities outside the boundaries of the Roman Empire, and had grown long before the arrival of the Vikings. The early settlement developed in two distinct phases—around, respectively, a secular and a monastic site—and it is from these early settlements that the city takes its modern name. Áth Cliath, or 'Hurdle Ford', is believed by historians to have been on a ridge that facilitated fishing on the river Liffey. It is thought that a farming settlement grew up around it. We cannot be sure exactly where this community was, but we know that one of the early roads from the ancient royal site of Tara led to it.[1] The Irish name for Dublin, Baile Átha Cliatha, has evolved from this early settlement. We can't be precisely sure when this community first came into being. The second site, Dubh Linn, was a monastic settlement. The name for this settlement in English, 'black pool', is said to be derived from its position. A pool was created when the river Poddle, which flows underneath the city today, met the river Liffey. It is probable, then, that this village was around the present-day site of Dublin Castle. Archaeological excavations have confirmed that the Liffey tide would have flowed as far as the castle's northern boundary. The Poddle was re-directed and used to create a protective moat defence on the southern and western side of the castle. With little material evidence we cannot date the settlement and must work on scant information.[2] Nevertheless, details from Irish texts and archaeological digs have allowed us to build up a likely scenario for how the settlement evolved.

We know that Norse Vikings were undertaking raids in the Dublin area, and along the Irish coast, from 795 to 836. By 841, according to the Annals of Ulster, there was a *longphort* at Dublin that lasted until 902. The *longphort*—a type of temporary settlement which the Vikings used to winter at Dublin—was known as *longphort oc Duibhlin*. There is much debate about its exact location. By 902 the Irish in the area managed to defeat the Vikings, who were by now using the longphort as a more permanent residence. The Vikings then fled the

Christ Church Cathedral, 1968, from O'Donovan Rossa Bridge
(Dublin City Library and archives)

city, some going to the Isle of Man, England and southern Scotland.
This exile did not last long, and within 15 years they had returned to
Dublin, where they established a second settlement in the area after
917. This would grow into the modern-day city. Their exile abroad
had probably encouraged them to emulate some of the characteristics
of urban settlements they would have seen in other countries. The
Vikings were turning from raiders to traders, and they set up trading
networks throughout the Viking world.[3] We know from excavations at
Wood Quay that they traded not just agricultural goods like food and
hides, but also jewellery and combs. We also know Dublin was part
of the extensive European slave economy.[4]

Hiberno-Norse Dublin

While the Vikings at Dublin certainly looked out towards the rest of the Viking world, that did not mean they were isolated from the Gaelic population. There was cultural and economic exchange, which has led to historians identifying the period between 980 and 1170 as 'the Hiberno-Norse' period in the city. This was a time when the inhabitants of Dublin would have spoken Norse, English and Irish. It was also during this period that Christ Church Cathedral came into being. The medieval historian Howard Clarke describes Dublin in this period as 'Ireland's first genuine town'.[5] As a successful trading port and a busy settlement, Dublin was seen as an attractive prize. Several Irish kings from the late tenth century managed to bring Dublin under their jurisdiction.[6] The medieval city occupied only a fragment of the territory that is the modern-day city, and only a few medieval buildings have survived. These include the two cathedrals of Christ Church and St Patrick's, the churches of St Michan's and St Audeon's, and Dublin Castle. Interest in the medieval city blossomed due to discoveries at Wood Quay, in the heart of the medieval city. The Wood Quay site ran from the existing cathedral boundary to the Liffey. Excavations, which took place between 1962 and 1981, uncovered a Viking settlement that was practically intact and revealed extensive settlement in this area of the city.

Unfortunately, the excavations were taking place so that Dublin City Council could build their new headquarters. A protest movement campaigned against the new building and sought to preserve this part of the city, and to create a protected site at Wood Quay (there were few protective laws in place for sites of this nature). When the case came before the Irish High Court, the Wood Quay group lost and archaeologists were given just five months to extract as many finds from the area as they could before Dublin City Council built on top of the area. This was a great loss to not just Irish heritage and history, but to medieval studies internationally, as no comparable site (in terms of size, and the number of objects so well-preserved) has been discovered before or since. Nevertheless, the fight to protect Wood Quay ensured that the need to safeguard urban history and

Archaeological excavations at Wood Quay in 1974 (Dublin City Library and archives)

geography from rapid development was highlighted.[7] If a silver lining is to be found, it is that 'these stormy events prompted new research, which is reflected in the growing number of publications that are now available on different aspects of medieval Dublin'.[8] The Friends of Medieval Dublin, a research group of archaeologists and historians, has been central to our understanding of medieval Dublin. By exploring the stories of the medieval buildings that have survived, like Christ Church, we learn a great deal about the early inhabitants of Dublin.

THE FOUNDATION OF CHRIST CHURCH CATHEDRAL

The Church of the Holy Trinity (informally and then later known as Christ Church Cathedral) was founded by Sitriuc Silkbeard, who came from a strong Hiberno-Norse background. His father, Olaf, was a Norse man who had made a failed claim for the title of king of York before settling in Dublin, while his Gaelic Irish mother, Gormlaith, was a daughter of a future king of Leinster, Murchad. Their marriage highlights the continued connection between the Gaelic and Norse communities in Ireland. Sitriuc came to the kingship after Glúniarainn, king for a brief period, was murdered by one of his slaves in 989.[9] While Sitriuc ruled during the Battle of Clontarf (1014), his reign is generally considered to be peaceful, and a time when the city was more closely connected with English trade, culture and politics.[10] A large horde of English coins found in the city, dating from 991–97, confirms the importance of English trade during this period. One of Sitriuc's greatest achievements was the creation of a Dublin bishopric and the foundation of the Church of the Holy Trinity. The coming of Christianity to Ireland in the early fifth century had led to development and settlement along the Liffey, and we know of four churches along the Poddle river bank: St Brigid, St Kevin, St Patrick and St MacTaill. While it can't be proved conclusively that they were pre-Viking churches, it is very likely.[11] This points to the existence of a lively Christian church, but the establishment of a bishopric in Dublin was significant as it created a position of power, from which Dublin could lead and effect changes within the Irish church. Sitriuc made a pilgrimage to Rome in his seventies and it was during this trip that he gained permission to have Dublin established as an episcopal base, along with permission to found a cathedral dedicated to the Holy Trinity. While historians are not certain of the date for the foundation of the cathedral, it is believed to be *circa* 1030 when he returned from Rome.[12]

The foundation of the cathedral was not merely a religious matter, though, and the location within the confines of the Viking walls (which were made of wattle and built up with silt from the Liffey), where land was at a premium, shows the significance that Sitriuc placed on the new cathedral. The medieval historian Stuart Kinsella has said that 'in one move Sitriuc gave the Hiberno-Norse town a new heart, embracing its westward expansion by situating the cathedral in the western edge of Duiblinn's old *dún,* and unifying the Viking settlement of Átha Cliath and the older Irish Duiblinn'.[13] The cathedral unified two distinct parts of the city and became the centre of the town. While it has been suggested in the past that this new church was made of wood, it is now thought more likely that it was made of stone.[14] This would have been quite expensive, but would have added a permanency to the building and would have made the cathedral stand out from the other buildings in the Viking town.

THE ANGLO-NORMAN INVASION

The cathedral was rebuilt when a new ruling elite in the city, the Anglo-Normans, came to power. Traditionally the king of Leinster claimed that the town was within his jurisdiction but it was directly governed by Ragnall Mac Torcaill, a member of the Ostman family of Hiberno-Norse descent. When Ragnall died in 1166, he was succeeded by his brother Hasculf, who submitted to Rory O'Connor, the over-king of Connaught, effectively ousting Dermot McMurrough, the over-king of Leinster, who had been acknowledged as overlord of Dublin in 1162. Dermot moved to build up an army to reclaim his jurisdiction but was forced across the water to England to do so.[15] While Henry II was not in a position to grant Dermot an army, he gave Dermot permission to raise a force of mercenaries. In 1169 an Anglo-Norman army from Wales under the command of Richard de Clare, Earl of Pembroke (Strongbow), sailed to Ireland to support Dermot. Together they captured Waterford. With an army of about 5,000 they marched on Dublin. Hasculf called on Rory O'Connor to defend the town. O'Connor had just been installed as high-king of Ireland and had a larger army than Strongbow and Dermot.[16] As O'Connor moved to defend Dublin, Dermot and Strongbow took a route through Glendalough, bypassing his forces stationed at Clondalkin. Those left to defend the city sent the archbishop of Dublin, Laurence O'Toole, to negotiate with the approaching army. O'Toole was an important political figure in his own right. He was the son of Muirchertach O'Toole, who had been king of North Leinster. As a child he had become a hostage to McMurrough, over-king of Leinster, to ensure his father's good behaviour.[17] O'Toole's sister, Mor, was married to McMurrough, and Aoife was his niece. O'Toole had introduced the Augustinian order to the monastery at Christ Church

Cathedral, and on his death was elevated to sainthood for his good deeds. On 21 September, 1170 O'Toole submitted to McMurrough and Strongbow, recognising Dermot (his brother-in-law) as king of Dublin once more.[18] O'Toole would have sought a speedy handover of the city to protect its inhabitants, but during the negotiations two knights breached the walls and slaughtered most of the townspeople.

Dermot, happy to have retaken the city, retired to his capital in Ferns, Co. Wexford, and died in the spring of 1171, leaving Strongbow to inherit his title of Lord of Dublin. On his way back from the funeral, Strongbow encountered Rory O'Connor and a pan-Gaelic force that had been sent to recapture the city in his absence. Strongbow defeated them and returned to his seat at Dublin. By now, however, Henry II was concerned about Strongbow's activities in Dublin. With Rory O'Connor defeated for a second time, and as Strongbow was Dermot's legitimate successor, Henry was worried that Strongbow could seize the rest of the island independently of the English crown. Henry had been encouraged to take Ireland by the only English pope to occupy the papal see, Pope Adrian IV (he was pope from 1154 to 1159). Under his papal edict (known as a bull) *Laudibiliter*, the King of England would be known as Lord of Ireland if he brought Ireland under the authority of the Roman Catholic Church. While Ireland was a Christian country, the church in Ireland diverged from Roman Christianity in some practices, as well as the dating of Easter. This has led to the title 'Celtic Christianity' being applied to the church in Ireland. Adrian wanted Henry to conquer Ireland in order to impose the rules and jurisdiction of the Roman church. Adrian's request was not unusual. His papal bull was issued just 60 years after the first Crusade, when the papacy was seeking to reclaim as many Christians as possible.

Henry sailed to Ireland in 1171 with a fleet of 400 ships, the largest foreign force to land in Ireland up to this point. On 11 October he landed at Waterford, took control of the city and proceeded to Dublin, where the city capitulated. He built himself a palace in the 'Irish style' beside the Thing Moate, the old Viking assembly, and from here received the submission of Irish kings.[19] These kings submitted to Henry for a variety for reasons. The size of Henry's army certainly would have prompted many to submit in order to avoid war. As the Irish system of kingship dictated that kings be elected, rather then being succeeded by their sons, they may have thought they could replace Henry once he had died. It is also possible that they favoured Henry over Strongbow and his supporters after the terrible attack on the city. Henry threw a lavish Christmas banquet and left Dublin on 2 February 1172. The invasion, and Henry's assertion of power, radically changed the ethnic make-up of the city. The Hiberno-Norse who remained crossed to the north bank of the Liffey and settled at Oxmantown (Ostmantown), where they established a community (now modern-day Stoneybatter). The new town would be populated by Anglo-Normans, and later English settlers, who did their best to keep other ethnicities and influences out. Dublin may have appeared to be a conquered city, but Henry did not completely trust Strongbow. While he allowed Strongbow to keep the title of king of Leinster, and granted other lands to Anglo-Normans in his army, he denied him Dublin. He made Waterford and Dublin royal cities; territories that were now under royal control. Under his first charter to the city he gave the city and port of Dublin to the men of Bristol. Bristol was a busy trading port and a powerful city. This would have ensured the support of Bristol's government and merchants for Henry's monarchy. It also reminded Strongbow that he had lost to Henry. City charters became the way that successive monarchs granted certain rights to cities. For instance, Henry's second charter in 1174 declared Dublin free of all taxes. This helped the city to grow economically.[20] Charters were an effective way of ensuring that towns and cities remained loyal to the English crown.

Christ Church during the twelfth century

The Anglo-Normans were eager to put their stamp upon the city. The construction they carried out throughout the twelfth and thirteenth century was heavily influenced by their own domestic architecture.[21] This was a trend that would continue throughout the history of the Irish colony as Irish architecture was shaped by English style and

Decorative capitals at Christ Church Cathedral (copyright TRIARC.
Image available from TARA)

tastes. While the crypt in Christ Church Cathedral probably dates
to 1171, more extensive rebuilding, in a Romanesque style, was
undertaken some time between 1181 and 1212.[22] We do not have
plans of this early medieval building. Centuries of rebuilding and
alterations, and damage to the church through natural disasters,
has meant significant loss to the fabric of the original church. Some
fragments of the original building are still visible, 'fossilised into a
monument that was largely reconstituted by George Edmund Street
in the late nineteenth century'.[23] They are to be found in the 'quire'
and transepts of the cathedral. Medieval churches took on the pattern
of a crucifix. The top of the crucifix was known as the quire, while
the transepts were the side wings. The medieval features include two

Grotesque head from the medieval period at Christ Church Cathedral (copyright Roger Stalley. Image available from TARA)

original archways, decorative capitals (a type of Corinthian pillar) with English stiff leaf details, pictured on facing page, and other decorative scenes depicting clerics, noblemen and pastoral scenes.[24]

Not all of this medieval detail has remained in situ. The above is an image of one of these details, a 'grotesque head', that has remained within the cathedral collection but is no longer in its original place. The excellent condition of some of this stonework highlights the craftsmanship of the stonecutters used by the Anglo-Normans, who would have encouraged English craftsmen to come to Dublin to carry out projects like the rebuilding of Christ Church. Art historian Roger

Stalley tells us that 'a huge amount of experienced craftsmanship was invested in the details'.[25] About 1234, work started on a new nave, allowing them to lengthen and widen the cathedral. This nave has been described as 'the most distinguished piece of Gothic architecture in Ireland', and brought the nave to its current size.[26] The quire was further extended in the 1280s, to a length of 100 feet. There are a number of chapels around the nave and quire which are dedicated to St Nicholas, the Holy Trinity, Lady Chapel, St Edmund and St Laurence (although this was later re-dedicated to the Holy Ghost).[27]

THE MEDIEVAL CATHEDRAL PRECINCT

The church precinct was larger during the medieval period. The cathedral boundary was well defined, and has been described as follows:

> There was a gateway opening into Fishamble Street, which by the late Middle Ages was fortified within a tower. From this gate, the wall ran in a southerly direction, close to the line of Fishamble Street, before turning west along the backs of houses in Skinners' Row (now Christchurch Place) ... The wall itself continued towards Christ Church Lane (not necessarily in a straight line) ... It then continued north along the east side of Christ Church Lane before reaching the cathedral. The west gate, the so-called 'great gate', was situated in this area, but its position has been [the] subject of some confusion.[28]

Unlike today, where the only whole and functioning building within the precinct is the church itself, the medieval precinct contained a number of additional buildings that were central to the monastic life of the cathedral. Excavations undertaken in the Wood Quay area of the city in the 1960s and 1970s show us that 'the area around the cathedral was densely populated, with tightly packed houses, well-defined property boundaries, workshops and narrow pathways'.[29]

As a monastery, the Christ Church precinct would have had a number of buildings in the complex, including the prior's chambers, a kitchen, refectory, dormitory and toilets. A chapter house was added

24

Christ Church
Cathedral nave
today

to the grounds *circa* 1220.[30] This chapter house was used until the eighteenth century, but was abandoned and filled in with rubbish in the nineteenth century, after which point it was lost, only to be rediscovered during excavations later in the century.[31] The bottom half of the building is exposed today and can be seen while standing in the cathedral grounds. The craftsmanship of the stonework is of a high quality and shows that, in rebuilding Christ Church, the Anglo-Normans not only influenced Irish architectural styles, but also the techniques and quality of Irish craftsmanship. The discovery of the chapter house, seen in the image opposite, was very important as it helped historians and archaeologists to piece together what the original monastery looked like. We know that the original gateway to the Abbey was underneath the present south porch door, which is adjacent to the chapter house today. Early accounts tell us that the gateway was seven feet from the chapter house.[32] The exposed chapter house, as well as the excavations in Wood Quay, give us an idea of where the original church stood and the extent to which the city level has risen since medieval times.

CHRIST CHURCH CATHEDRAL AND ST PATRICK'S CATHEDRAL

The history of Christ Church Cathedral could not be told without referring to its rival, St Patrick's Cathedral, which was founded under the new Anglo-Norman regime in 1191. Unlike Christ Church Cathedral, St Patrick's was situated outside the city walls. It is said that a church was founded as early as 450 to mark the spot where St Patrick baptised Dubliners from a well.[33] There are wells throughout Dublin, however, that claim the auspicious title of St Patrick's well, including one near Trinity College.[34] It was not very common to have two cathedrals in a city, but St Patrick's was a collegiate church (where priests could study) when it was created, and it fell outside the jurisdiction of the city. It was elevated to the status of cathedral some time later, when Henry de Loundes was elected to the chapters of Christ Church and St Patrick's, thereby promoting him to archbishop and placing him as head of both churches. The medieval cathedral was rebuilt after Henry III granted permission to collect money for a

Remains of the medieval chapter house in the precinct of Christ Church Cathedral

building scheme in 1215. Once rebuilt it became the largest structure in Ireland, and remained so for many centuries.

The two cathedrals have a long-standing rivalry made worse by their close proximity. St Patrick's may have been 'outside' the city in 1191 but the Anglo-Norman city thrived in the late twelfth and thirteenth century and quickly spilled beyond the walls into the growing suburbs. Today the two cathedrals are connected by Patrick Street and are a ten-minute stroll from each other. By 1300, it was necessary for rules to be laid down for the two cathedrals operating within the city. The *Pacis Compostio* was agreed upon, which stated that Christ Church Cathedral had precedence as the seat of the archbishops of Dublin. They were enthroned in Christ Church, but would be buried alternately in the two cathedrals. Today St Patrick's still has no archbishop associated with it, which is very unusual for a cathedral. When the power of the Church of Ireland was dwindling in the nineteenth century, the two cathedrals were amalgamated for a short period, but they were soon separated again. In order to balance the two cathedrals, St Patrick's Cathedral is the Church of Ireland's national cathedral, while Christ Church is the capital's cathedral. As the two cathedrals struggle to survive financially in a period where religious congregations are shrinking rapidly, competition remains for visitor numbers, with Christ Church losing out. On an annual basis it attracts roughly half those of its competitor St Patrick's Cathedral (*circa* 350,000 visit St Patrick's while 170,000 visit Christ Church Cathedral).[35] The choirs of both cathedrals are well renowned, and both tour nationally and internationally, as well as holding a number of very popular annual events. The choirs performed Handel's 'Messiah' together when it premiered in Dublin in 1742.

RELIGIOUS RELICS AT CHRIST CHURCH CATHEDRAL

Christ Church was a site of pilgrimage for many Irish people, and a number of relics were housed in the monastery. In 1180 the cathedral acquired the *Baculus Jesu*. The *Baculus* was a staff reputedly owned by St Patrick and was gifted to him by a hermit. The staff was kept at Armagh but it was seized by Anglo-Norman knights and gifted to

Christ Church Cathedral. The staff attracted many visitors. In 1461, during a storm, the eastern window was blown down damaging the chest which housed the staff. While the other contents of the chest were badly damaged the staff remained unharmed, which was considered a miracle.[36] By 1310 there was also a relic of St Catherine of Siena in the cathedral.[37] In 1404 the shrine of St Cybis was taken from Wales and brought to Christ Church.[38]

The church also had relics in its own right, the most curious of which was the talking cross. Our most thorough account of the cross comes to us from Giraldus Cambrensis, the Anglo-Norman chronicler. He recounted the first miracle that the cross performed 'not many years before the arrival of the English': one of the citizens of Dublin 'invoked the crucifix as the sole witness' in a loan agreement.[39] The loan was reneged upon and the case was tried in the cathedral in front of the cross and, being a peculiar case, it drew a crowd. The cross was called to give its testimony, which it did 'in the presence of many persons who heard the words'.[40] The second and third miracles that the cross was said to have performed occurred during the invasion of the city in 1171 by the Anglo-Normans. Knowing that Strongbow's army was approaching the city, some citizens who were preparing to flee went to the cathedral and tried to seize the cross, but the cross refused to leave. The third miracle concerned an archer in the Anglo-Norman army, who had sacked the house of an archbishop (the account does not make clear if it was the archbishop of Dublin). After the city was taken he went to the cathedral to pray, and offered a penny to the cross. When his back was turned the cross threw the penny back at him.[41] The story was perhaps intended to suggest that the sins committed during the invasion would not be forgotten.

THE IMPACT OF THE REFORMATION ON THE CATHEDRAL

During the Henrican reformation (discussed more fully in chapter three), Archbishop George Brown was sent to Ireland to oversee the implementation of new church reforms, to dissolve the monasteries, and to seize church lands. Christ Church Cathedral, being a monastery, was due to be dissolved along with the other Dublin monasteries of

St Mary's Abbey, All Hallows and St Patrick's Cathedral. When moves were made to dissolve Christ Church, there was a general outcry from the civic leaders and prominent citizens. It was decided that the cathedral would not be dissolved but instead would lose its 'monastic' charter and would be reissued with a 'secular' charter to make it a church for the citizens of Dublin.[42] The extensive network of buildings used by the monastery, such as the refectory and dormitories, were rented out, providing an important source of income for the church. Dublin's law courts moved into the precinct, adding prestige to the area. While the institution managed to survive, the relics were not so lucky. The new reforms claimed that relics had no healing properties and were simply superstitious nonsense and a way of making money for the church. Archbishop Brown oversaw the public burning of the relics in the cathedral, including St Patrick's staff. One relic that survived these changes was the heart of St Laurence O'Toole which was on display in the cathedral until March 2012, when it was stolen.[43] The 'wooden heart-shaped container' was protected 'within a small iron-barred cage in St Laud's chapel in the cathedral', but the thieves cut the bars of the cage in order to get at the relic, which Gardaí reported thieves had specifically targeted.[44] To date no one has been apprehended for the theft, but there are suggested links between this theft and the theft of other relics, including a relic of the True Cross stolen from Holycross Abbey in County Tipperary in October 2012, and the theft of a relic of St Manchan from St Manchan's church in County Offaly.[45]

CHURCH REVENUE AND COMMERCE

Revenue from property was an important source of income for the cathedral, and Christ Church had vast properties throughout Dublin, including Clonkeen, Deansgrange, Glasnevin and Grangegorman. The cathedral did not just profit from land outside the city, however, and its immediate surroundings had been rented out by the cathedral as far back as records go. The 'Liberties' is the name given to the area around St Patrick's Cathedral that was exempt from the laws and taxes of the city. There were, however, originally four 'liberties', which had evolved out of royal grants. They belonged to, respectively, the dean and chapter of St Patrick's, the dean and chapter of Christ Church, the earl of Meath, and the archbishop of Dublin. These 'liberties' were in effect small principalities, exempt from tax, and with the right to hold their own courts. By the nineteenth century, however, the city corporation had undermined the liberties and brought these areas under their control.[46] Up to this point, property within each of these liberties had been very valuable, as the governors of each area (such as the earl of Meath and the deans of Christ Church and St Patrick's) set their own tax rates and rents. As the liberties sought to attract tenants to their area, they kept rates low and fixed rents as they saw fit. We know from cathedral records that an address in this area was highly sought after by one group in particular: merchants. Those who lived within the liberty were exempt from city taxes and merchants had much to gain from this as they avoided paying city taxes. In 1631 the dean and chapter made regulations for the management of the Christ Church liberty, which were signed by forty-one heads of household who resided or held leases in the liberty. Half of these were merchants, although others on the list represent different trades or shopkeepers of various types. Nevertheless, about a quarter of these heads of household were illiterate, suggesting perhaps a poorer class living within the cathedral liberty.[47]

Some interesting stories emerge of those who lived and traded within the precinct and the liberty at large. We know that by the fourteenth century the crypt 'had no religious value' and was being used as commercial premises.[48] In 1332–33 it was used to store wine shipped from France, the final destination of which was the household of the king of Scotland.[49] When Thomas Wentworth took up his post in Dublin Castle as lord lieutenant of Ireland in 1632 he was horrified to learn that the crypt held 'tippling rooms for beer, wine and tobacco'; Wentworth insisted the cathedral shut the taverns down but 'commerce ... won out over morality and some forty years later identical criticisms were voiced by the earl of Ormond'.[50] It is, perhaps, not surprising to find taverns listed among the businesses within the cathedral precinct and in the church crypt. Fishamble Street and Castle Street, very close to the cathedral, were two busy

Eighteenth-century watercolour depicting domestic buildings built alongside the west front of the cathedral (image reproduced by the UCD Digital Library from the original held in UCD library Special Collections)

city drinking spots. The Tholsel (the equivalent of the modern city hall) was located on nearby Skinner's Alley. In the aftermath of the Reformation, the cathedral was left with a number of monastic buildings it could rent out. The city law courts took up residence in some of these buildings and remained there until they were moved into the purpose-built Four Courts across the Liffey, designed by James Gandon, in 1796. The grounds of the cathedral would have been a busy commercial spot where merchants vied to sell their wares to the civic officers and lawyers who worked within the grounds. It is difficult to imagine what the grounds of the cathedral would have looked like with this hive of buildings and businesses. Roger Stalley has pointed out that 'amidst the warren of commercial and legal activity, the cathedral, in its semi-ruined condition was scarcely visible'.[51] A water-colour from the early nineteenth century by Gabriel Berenger, which depicts the west front of the cathedral, shows the extent to which the building had become part of the ordinary fabric of the city.[52]

Houses are built right up against the cathedral. It is difficult for us to imagine the cathedral in such a built-up area as it is situated in open, relatively empty grounds today. But many of these buildings were cleared away in the late eighteenth and early nineteenth century when the Wide Streets Commission were affecting to improve the city. A small gated laneway that led off Christ Church Lane, was nicknamed 'Hell' during the seventeenth century.[53] Wine merchants were located in the area throughout this period and the name may have come from their deep cellars, so deep that they were close to hell. Equally, the name may have come from the fact that the laneway was on a lower level to the rest of the city, and was therefore so low that it was closer to hell. One of the legacies of the laneway is that advertisements can be found in eighteenth and nineteenth-century newspapers for 'rooms to let in Hell'. The street was demolished along with some of buildings in the Christ Church precinct.

THE CATHEDRAL DURING THE JACOBITE-WILLIAMITE WAR

The cathedral remained in the hands of the Anglican Church of Ireland, which had been created in the course of the Reformation. For a short period during the 'War of the two kings' (1689–91), the church was seized by Catholic Jacobites who supported the Catholic King James II, whose claim to the thrones of England, Ireland and

Scotland was being challenged by his daughter Mary and Protestant son-in-law William of Orange (see chapter four). The position of lord deputy was given to the Catholic Richard Talbot, earl of Tyrconnell, and James even resided in the city for a short time. Seeing how the tide was turning, the dean and many of the senior church figures fled to England in 1688, which was securely held by the supporters of Mary and William.[54] The church plate was also removed from the cathedral to protect it from being sold or melted down by James, who was desperate for ways to fund his army. By February 1689 the order was given that any Protestant with arms (swords, guns, bayonets) had to give them up, and in February 1689 the cathedral was used as the official site for the relinquishing of such arms.[55]

A further sign of the change of power in the city was the arrest of the cathedral bellringers, Flood and Wolfe, in July 1688 by the lord mayor, as he 'fancied they did not make the bells ring merrily enough' on the birth of the Prince of Wales, James's Catholic successor.[56] They were released, but not for long. In August 1689 they were re-arrested for being in possession of a sword and a case of pistols, which they had hidden in the cathedral grounds. Up until this point, Anglican churches and cathedrals had not actually been seized by the authorities. James was hoping to keep the support of Protestants in the city, but Catholic pressure proved too great as they sought to reclaim institutions like Christ Church that had remained in the hands of the Protestants. On 6 September the king finally gave permission for the cathedral, along with many other churches and cathedrals in Dublin, to be taken. On 26 October a Catholic priest, Alexius Stafford, was appointed dean of the cathedral. He celebrated mass according to Catholic rites in Christ Church the next day. In November the Protestants of Dublin presented a petition to James asking him to return the churches to them. His reply shows the pressure he was under to retain the support of Irish Catholics. He stated that 'his own clergy had obliged him so much that he could deny nothing and that the churches were taken away unknown to him, but he must not disoblige'.[57] The cathedral remained in the hands of Catholics for the next eight months, until after the Battle of the Boyne (1/12 July 1690), when James was defeated by William and fled Ireland.

THE REBUILDING OF THE CATHEDRAL

From the late eighteenth century the penal laws, a set of oppressive laws put in place from the 1690s that limited the civil, economic and political rights of Catholics, and some Protestants, were being dismantled, and, in a goodwill gesture towards the Catholic community, the government supported the foundation of a Catholic seminary at Maynooth in County Kildare. With the passage of the Catholic Emancipation bill in 1829, and the Disestablishment Act of 1869 (which stripped the Church of Ireland of its status as the official, 'established' church) the Church of Ireland received substantially less state funding and was thereby weakened. The Catholic Church went from strength to strength and began to assume a more prominent place in Irish political and social life. Dublin historian Michael Barry says that 'the emergence of Catholic power was made manifest in a physical way in the streets of Dublin. As the repression of the penal times faded away the Catholic Church began building'.[58] The first of their major building projects pre-dated Catholic Emancipation. The Pro-Cathedral, the first Catholic cathedral built in Ireland since the Reformation, was begun in 1816. This was followed by a flurry of building projects throughout the nineteenth century, with prominent city churches like St Francis Xavier's on Gardiner Street being added in 1832, St Andrew's Church on Westland Row in 1883, St Paul's on Arran Quay in 1844, St Audeon's on Cornmarket in 1846 and St James's Church on James's Street in 1859.[59] These churches were large, bombastic statements of the Catholic Churches position in Irish society. As Barry has stated, this building 'asserted the new reality: the Catholic Church had arrived and was no longer the church of the side streets'.[60]

These new Catholic churches stood in sharp contrast to the condition of the two Protestant cathedrals. The medieval fabric of the buildings had been improved and restored over time, but both were in poor condition by the early nineteenth century. The Wide Streets Commission, which was established to create wide and convenient streets in the city (see chapter 5), may have enhanced the aesthetics of the vista between Trinity College and Christ Church, but it also reduced the size of the church precincts and removed the boundary walls. The church's appearance in the nineteenth century did not match its prestige and importance. It was decided to embark upon a programme of restoration, but money was tight. The two figures who were central to the preservation and restoration of Christ Church Cathedral were Henry Roe, a whiskey distiller who gave a generous grant of money to have the church renovated; and the English architect George Edmund Street, the architect responsible for carrying out that work and adding the General Synod Hall and connecting bridge across Winetavern Street. St Patrick's Cathedral had been given a major facelift in the 1860s when the Guinness family donated £150,000 to it (see chapter six), and its new appearance contrasted sharply with that of Christ Church. When it became clear just how expensive the renovation of the cathedral would be, patrons were sought. Rev. Edward Seymour, of the cathedral, contacted his wealthy cousin, distiller and philanthropist, Henry Roe, who donated £160,000.[61]

Street suggested extensive changes to the fabric of the building, including tearing down much of the medieval and Tudor interiors. A rare photograph from the 1860s or early 1870s shows what the original fourteenth-century 'quire' of the cathedral looked like before it was removed.

The current layout is more open, less cluttered, and the organ is tucked discreetly to the side of the choir rather than holding pride of place as it is here. The walls of the cathedral had to be periodically white-washed throughout its history, as candles provided an important source of light in the cathedral and the smoke blackened the walls. The effect of these white-washed walls can be seen here too. While Street proposed some drastic changes to the cathedral, 'his plans were accepted because of the generally unsightly and unstable nature of Christ Church at the time'.[62] While the cathedral was being renovated, a General Synod Hall for Church of Ireland meetings was needed. Synod meetings were usually held within the cathedral nave, but this was deemed wholly unsuitable. It was proposed that the abandoned church of St John's, close to Christ Church, could be used while the cathedral was being renovated. Roe, very generously, offered to provide

Dublin City coat of arms, which has been in use for over 400 years, displayed on a pew in Christ Church Cathedral. The three towers on the crest are representative of the city walls. The towers appear on fire to represent the zeal of the citizens in the defence of the city, rather than to reflect a real event.

further funding to pay for a synod hall, stating that 'it is my earnest desire that this cathedral (when restored) may prove useful to the Church of Ireland at large'.[63] Instead, Street proposed ambitious plans that would convert St Michael's church, directly across the road, into the new synod hall, with a linking bridge between the two buildings. Roe granted a further £60,000 for the project.[64] This was not his final donation; he provided funding for new church plate (silverware, chalices and candlesticks used during the service) as well, making him 'the cathedral's supreme benefactor'.[65] While the renovations produced a stunning cathedral, they caused a lot of controversy. As well as moving quite a few of the cathedral monuments, including Strongbow's tomb, Street banished the monuments of some well-known personalities to the crypt. Many of these had to be brought above ground later due to complaints. Street had an impressive knowledge of medieval architecture. The building can be seen as a Victorian interpretation of a medieval cathedral. His work on the fabric of the building can not be wholly described as 'restorative'; it was more of a re-design and rebuild. Street believed that 'it was the task of the restorer to recover and recreate the intended design of the original architect which at times required the sacrifice of later additions or alterations'.[66]

IRISH FIGURES LAID TO REST OR COMMEMORATED IN CHRIST CHURCH

The cathedral has a significant legacy in terms of religion in the capital. Laurence O'Toole, patron saint of Dublin, was the second man to hold the position of archbishop of Dublin at Christ Church Cathedral. George Brown, who directed the Reformation on behalf of Henry VIII, did so from Christ Church Cathedral, and the Catholic James II installed his personal chaplain there when he tried to win Ireland to his cause. The cathedral was connected with many powerful groups in the city, including with Dublin Castle. It acted as the chapel for the Merchants Guild, the wealthiest city guild, as well as being the place for religious worship for the city corporation. It is perhaps

Nineteenth-century stereoscope showing the duke of Leinster's monument in the
cathedral (National Library of Ireland)

because of these powerful connections that a religious institution like
Christ Church had not just civic importance to Dublin, but was also
of national importance. Parliaments were held there in 1297 and in
1560, and the chief governor of the island was often sworn in within
the cathedral.[67] This importance is recognised by those who chose
to be buried within the cathedral, as well as the monuments erected
to them, including those to Strongbow (d.1176), Gerald Fitzgerald
(d.1513), Robert Fitzgerald, duke of Leinster (monument pictured
above), nineteenth earl of Kildare (d.1743), and the former lord
chancellor John Bowes (d.1767).

Successful and prominent Protestant businessmen like Henry Roe
were not prepared to let Christ Church Cathedral fall into disrepair,
and his extensive investment led to renewed interest in the Cathedral.
It also ensured that the fabric of the building was not just restored
but reinvigorated, so that it could be enjoyed well into the twenty-
first century. While Christ Church's congregation is tiny today, it
still enjoys support and patronage from Dublin citizens and visitors
to the city. Perhaps the most important legacy it provides relates to
the city's origins. The excavations that took place in the 1960s and
1970s confirm that this was one of the earliest sites inhabited within
the city. The foundation of the Abbey of the Holy Trinity, the extant
features of the twelfth-century church within the modern cathedral

and the exposed thirteenth-century chapter house within the grounds connect us to the the Vikings and the Anglo-Normans who established so much of the original city. For these reasons the cathedral remains a significant landmark in the streetscape of the modern capital. The cathedral successfully re-established itself as an important civic site in the 1960s and today the church is one of the most iconic buildings in the city. It is linked with the civic calendar; it is a central part of the St Patrick's Day parade route and the ringing of the cathedral bells each 1 January marks the beginning of the new year for many Dubliners. The synod hall is now home to Dublinia, a heritage site that explores the history and archaeology of medieval Dublin and is a very popular site during Culture Night, when Dubliners get an opportunity to ring the bells.

2

Dublin Castle

IN 1204 KING JOHN, youngest son of Henry II, ordered that a castle be built in Dublin, and Dublin Castle remained central to the day-to-day running of the colonial administration in Ireland until 1922, when British forces withdrew from the new Irish Free State. While the fortunes of other civic and national institutions have peaked and declined over time, the castle was been at the heart of the conquest and colonisation of Ireland throughout its existence, so much so that the term 'Dublin Castle' is often used interchangeably with 'English/British government'. For most of its history the castle was the residence and office of the lord lieutenant. The lord lieutenant ruled Ireland in the absence of the king, but this position was given to princes of the blood throughout the medieval period, and they rarely travelled to Ireland to take up the position. In their place, the lord deputy—the second-in-command—ruled. This changed during the seventeenth century when the lord lieutenant was in the country more frequently. In the eighteenth century it became mandatory for the lord lieutenant to come to Ireland to take up his office. In the nineteenth century the term viceroy—which is the same position as the lord lieutenant—was favoured.

During its long history Dublin Castle has also housed the parliament, the exchequer, the mint, the Irish Privy Council, and the Irish Constabulary, all of which placed it at the centre of Irish politics, finance and power. The prisons contained within the grounds were an important reminder of the real power of the state which ruled from the castle and over the centuries many Gaelic leaders, and later nationalist rebels, were held within their confines. Also contained within the castle walls were the state apartments, where royalty stayed on their infrequent visits to Ireland. Despite the importance of the building, it was often let fall into decay and received only occasional renovations. As a result, many visitors were puzzled by the layout and look of the castle. A French visitor to the city in 1890, Madame de Bovet, described the castle as 'an irregular pile of heavy and sombre-looking buildings'. She complained it has 'no particular style', and was 'without character or grandeur. It is cold, ugly, and melancholy'.[1] Despite its neglected and haphazard appearance, Dublin Castle remained the centre of government in Ireland, for good or for ill, for over seven centuries.

The origins of Dublin Castle

A settlement like Dublin was very prone to attack. Indeed, in its early history the city had succumbed to invasion by the Gaelic Irish, the Vikings and the Anglo-Normans. We know from contemporary accounts of the invasion by the Anglo-Normans that the city was encircled by a 'wall' built up from wattle and estuarine mud from the Liffey (the latter was used as a bonding agent).[2] Archaeologists believe that this wall was built as early as *circa* 936.[3] After the Anglo-Norman invasion (see chapter one), these new settlers further strengthened the defences by building a stone wall and expanding the physical boundary. The new Anglo-Norman settlers built fortifications in the style known as 'motte and bailey' in the countryside to defend the territories they had been granted by Henry II. These were stone or wooden structures built on top of a large mound, surrounded by wooden fencing. They were perfect for the countryside, as the settlers could view the surrounding area and protect themselves and their growing communities from Gaelic Irish attacks. By the early thirteenth century, Dublin also needed a fortified structure with which the growing English administration could protect itself. In August 1204 King John wrote to the head of this English administration in Dublin and requested that a castle be erected 'to curb and defend the city, making it as strong as you can with good ditches and strong walls'. The castle would be built in two phases, first as a tower, and later a 'castle and bailey and other requirements may be suitably made'.[4]

This early castle occupied what is today the upper yard. Over time the castle sprawled out to occupy a greater space. It is believed to have been completed in 1215, but the records show that workmen were being paid until 1228.

Very little of this medieval castle survives today; most of it is hidden underneath the modern castle. No images survive of this early structure, and, as the earliest map of Dublin to survive dates to 1610, we are forced to piece together fragmentary accounts and archaeological evidence to establish what the early castle might have looked like. We know that the castle was built close to the site known as 'Dubh Linn' ('black pool'), because the River Poddle runs underneath the castle today. As we saw in the last chapter, archaeologists believe that the Poddle was re-directed to skirt the walls of the castle and act as a moat. The castle would have provided the ultimate defence. While the complex itself provided fortifications, it also lay within the city walls, which were enlarged and strengthened by the Anglo-Normans when they took over the city. Inside the castle complex a mint, a mill, the exchequer, a hall (a multi-functional room for dining and where parliaments and other important assemblies met), and a kitchen could be found. There were two sally ports, or secure gateways, that allowed access in and out of the castle and led onto Castle Street and Sheep Street (now Ship Street).[5] The castle was expanded further by Henry III who added a very decorative new 'Great Hall' in 1234 which featured glazed windows, probably the first on the island.[6] Economic growth in Dublin during this early phase of the colony was brought about by an increased population and greater trade links. This building in Dublin Castle was in line with developments in the rest of the city. Along with markets like the Corn Exchange, a number of civic and religious buildings were added to Dublin in the thirteenth century but the medieval historian Anngret Simms believes that 'the most significant was Dublin Castle'.[7]

THE DECLINE OF THE ANGLO-NORMAN COLONY

By 1330 the Great Hall was lit by stained-glass windows; again, these were probably the first in Ireland. It was rebuilt in 1361 by Lionel, duke of Clarence, the king's lieutenant, with more work taking place in 1372. But by the late fourteenth-century the castle, much like the colony, was beginning to fall into decay. The clerk of the castle works was called in to look at the building and in 1381 there was an enquiry into the state of the premises. In 1411 the Bermingham Tower was added, as the English began to show more concern for the state of the colony, but by 1430 there were further reports that the castle was falling into disrepair, and that the state records were being badly housed and damaged as a result.

The decay of the colony was a real concern for the English government by the late fourteenth century. The Anglo-Normans who accepted English rule and had been given land to govern on behalf of the English monarchy were becoming more Irish than the Irish themselves, and the English government worried about the cultural assimilation of the Anglo-Norman community with the Gaelic Irish. They summoned a parliament in 1366, which met in Kilkenny, to try to turn the tide. There they passed a series of laws to reverse this assimilation. The Statutes of Kilkenny forbade intermarrying of the English and Irish, speaking the Irish language, wearing Irish dress and pursuing Irish customs, or adhering to the Gaelic Brehon laws. Dress, in particular, was seen as an outward display of political allegiance. It was a clear way of assessing if someone had adhered to the English way of life, or if they had rejected it. Four Irish kings who submitted to Richard II in 1394–95 were made to shed their Gaelic style of clothes, which consisted of a mantle (a type of cloak often lined with fur), in favour of English-style drawers with a fur-trimmed silk gown. A historian of Irish clothing, Mairéad Dunlevy, has noted that this adoption of English dress would have been a humiliating experience for these kings.[8] The English administration was still complaining a century later that Irish dress was too visible on the streets of the capital. In 1462 they imposed a fine of six pence on any man found wearing a mantle within the city limits.[9] The English colony had retreated, culturally, linguistically and geographically, and this continued throughout the fifteenth century.

By the late fifteenth century the English colony in Ireland was in a state of severe decay. The English government in Ireland could only claim jurisdiction over the Pale, which consisted of land in what are now the counties of Dublin, Meath and Louth, but some of this territory was often in a state of unrest. Cities such as Cork, Waterford, Limerick, and Galway held royal charters, which gave them rights and liberties to trade and protection and thus made them loyal to the English government. The English also claimed jurisdiction over the territories ruled by the Anglo-Norman families like the Fitzgeralds (who held extensive land in modern-day Kildare and Wicklow), the Butlers of Ormond (who held land in modern-day Kilkenny and Tipperary) and the Fitzgeralds of Desmond (whose land sprawled across modern-day Kerry, Cork and Limerick). If constant raids by Gaelic clans were creating headaches for the administration, the in-fighting of these old Anglo-Norman families was catastrophic. The English needed loyal families in Ireland to govern on their behalf and the position of chief governor was held alternately during the sixteenth century by the Fitzgerald earls of Kildare, or the Butler earls of Ormond. The reality was that the English monarch was far away, and the civil war in England—the 'War of the Roses'—was his main focus. In 1478 the Yorkist King Edward IV tried to curb the power of Gerald Fitzgerald, earl of Kildare, by revoking his seal of office and appointing an Englishman, Henry, Lord Grey, as lord deputy. Kildare refused to stand down. Sir James Keating, the castle constable and a Kildare supporter, 'strengthened the garrison, destroyed the drawbridge and refused entry to Grey'.[10] Grey moved to Meath and called a parliament from there instead, but when Richard III came to power he reversed his brothers' order and placed Kildare back at the centre of power. The Kildares were too powerful to be challenged from war-torn England, which presented a problem for successive kings who struggled to control them. When the Yorkist claimant to the throne was defeated by the Tudors, Kildare found he had backed the wrong side. The new Tudor king, Henry VII, wanted stability, and he allowed Kildare to remain in power. In 1487 Kildare conspired against Henry and Lambert Simnel, a pretender, was crowned King of England and Lord of Ireland in Christ Church Cathedral. Simnel's bid for power failed and Henry knew that he had to move to weaken or eradicate the Kildare house.[11]

THE TUDOR CONQUEST OF IRELAND

The Tudors had to wait until the eight earl died and his son, Garret Óg, took power as the ninth earl of Kildare. In 1533 Henry VIII summoned the earl to London to answer charges of mismanaging his office and armaments. He was charged with taking armaments from Dublin Castle and distributing them to his supporters and to his own castles. Kildare (Garret Óg) left his twenty-one year old son Thomas—known to history as Silken Thomas—in charge, to make sure that the Butlers did not seize power. Henry spread rumours that Kildare had been executed in the tower. When Thomas heard these rumours on 11 June 1534, he rode to St Mary's Abbey (outside the city on the northern banks of the Liffey) where a meeting of the king's council was being held. He flung down his sword of state as an open act of defiance, and embarked upon a rebellion. With a force of 140 armed horsemen he tried to seize the castle, but the city inhabitants had closed the gates against him. Thomas's forces seized people who were trying to escape the siege as hostages, and he began to negotiate with the city. He also cut off the water supply, which forced their hands. The city gates were opened to him and he tried to attack the castle, but was unsuccessful. Henry sent promises of aid, and when this news reached the city, many of the inhabitants turned on Thomas's soldiers and killed them. Henry's aid reached the city and Thomas fled, falling back on his family stronghold in Kildare. His supporters were defeated or fled and Thomas eventually surrendered on 24 August 1535. Thomas and five of his uncles were brought to London, executed as traitors and their heads displayed on spikes at London Bridge.

With the Kildare dynasty out of the way, Henry moved to implement his own programme of reform. For the rest of the century (and most of the history of the office) the viceroys or chief governors—those who held the rank of lord lieutenent, or the slightly less prestigious title of lord deputy—would be Englishmen. As these new governors did not normally reside in Ireland, the castle became their residence. Sir Henry Sidney (lord deputy from 1565 to 1571 and again from 1575 to 1578) became the first chief governor to reside in the castle

Detail from John Derricke's *Image of Irelande* (1581), depicting Lord Deputy Sidney leaving Dublin Castle

in two centuries. He undertook a building campaign to improve the defences and to make the castle habitable once more. Under the Tudor monarchs the castle became the centre of the re-colonisation of Ireland as they attempted to re-conquer the country. This was done slowly, and it was not until after the Flight of the Earls in the early seventeenth century that the island was fully brought under English control.

The Irish parliament frequently met in the castle along with the Court of Exchequer. Both of these institutions were central to the most effective method of reclaiming Ireland: plantations. The Tudors moved to take tighter control of Ireland, and when Gaelic families rebelled, the crown reacted by moving armies in, crushing the rebellions, and seizing their land, which was then redistributed to loyal Protestant settlers from England. The most famous of these plantations took place in Munster after the Desmond rebellions, from the 1560s onwards and in Ulster after the Flight of the Earls in 1607. Planters and Tudor government officials settled in Ireland and brought with them a firm belief in the Protestant faith. These new settlers made up only a small percentage of the population and were surrounded by Catholics who were embittered that their lands had been seized.

When rebels were captured on the battlefield, or tried and executed for treason, often their heads were displayed on spikes outside Dublin Castle. A contemporary etching shows Lord Henry Sidney leaving Dublin Castle after a recently suppressed rebellion. The heads of the rebels are displayed above the drawbridge. The caption says 'Those trunkless heads do plainly show/ each rebels fatal end/ and what a heinous crime it is/ The Queen for to offend'.[12] A fourteenth-century Gaelic Poet, Angus O'Daly, wrote a lament after seeing his chieftains headless body outside Dublin Castle:

> O Body which I see without a head,
> It is the sight of thee which has withered up my strength.
>
> Divided and impaled in Ath-Cliath [the Irish name for the city],
> The learned of Banba [a personification of Ireland] will feel its
>   loss. Who will relieve the wants of the poor?
> Who will bestow cattle on the learned?
> O Body, since thou art without a head,
> It is not life which we are to choose after thee.[13]

The sight of these slain rebels often provoked more bloodshed, rather than prompting loyalty.

DUBLIN CASTLE AS A PRISON

In 1537 the Act of Supremacy was passed, which declared that Henry VIII, not the pope, was head of the church in Ireland. The act also necessitated all members of a religious community to take an oath stating they accepted Henry as head of the church (see chapter 3). A number of clergy, including priests and friars, were imprisoned in the Castle for refusing to take the oath. Archbishop George Browne was charged with the responsibility of forwarding the reformation in Ireland. In 1585 a parliament that sat in Dublin Castle declared Catholic priests and seminaries traitors if they remained in Ireland and refused to conform. Those found guilty of recusancy (not attending services of the new Church of Ireland) could be imprisoned in the castle. One of the most striking stories of recusancy is that of Margaret Ball, a former lady mayoress and aristocratic widow. Margaret made her home outside the city a shelter for Catholics who wished to hear mass in their own faith. During raids in the 1570s, Margaret was arrested, and priest's vestments were found in her home. She was released because of her aristocratic standing, but her home was raided on numerous occasions. In 1580 she was re-arrested by her own son, Walter, a Protestant, the serving lord mayor and a member of the Court of High Commission. Her known Catholicism and refusal to convert would have been extremely problematic for his political career. By the time of her final arrest she was so ill that she had to be carried through the streets on a 'wooden hurdle' to Dublin Castle, where she was imprisoned. The poor state of the castle prison proved too much for her and she died in 1584.[14] She has been commemorated in a statue outside the current Catholic Pro-Cathedral on Cathedral Street, along with Francis Taylor, a former lord mayor of Dublin who was also imprisoned in the castle as a recusant and died there in 1621.

Security in the castle, which was not always a secure prison, was a major concern in the sixteenth century. Between 1583 and 1588 thirteen prisoners managed to escape. One of the most prominent political prisoners of the day was the Gaelic chieftain, Red Hugh O'Donnell. In 1588 Red Hugh was lured on board a ship to purchase wine. He was kidnapped on the instructions of Lord Deputy John Perrot, and imprisoned in the castle. It was hoped that this would

Sculpture of Margaret Ball
and Francis Taylor outside
Dublin's Pro-Cathedral

encourage the good behaviour of his father Black Hugh. Red Hugh escaped in 1591 by climbing through a window and down onto the castle drawbridge. He sought refuge with Phelim O'Toole, who had also spent some time in the castle prison. Fearful of being returned there if Red Hugh was discovered, O'Toole handed him over to the authorities, and Red Hugh found himself imprisoned once more, this time in the more secure Record Tower.[15] In January 1592 Red Hugh escaped a second time. He headed for the Wicklow mountains, managed to evade capture and became head of the O'Donnell clan.[16] After the war that broke out in Ulster between Hugh O'Neill and the crown, Gaelic forces were defeated. Unable to live under the conditions imposed on them by the new king, James I, Red Hugh and Hugh O'Neill fled Ireland for the continent in 1607, in what became known as the Flight of the Earls. Their lands were declared forfeit and made ready for plantation.

DUBLIN CASTLE IN THE SEVENTEENTH AND EIGHTEENTH CENTURIES

During the seventeenth and eighteenth centuries, the castle went through a complete transformation from a 'medieval' fortress to the complex of early-modern offices and state apartments, with some nineteenth century additions and alterations, that we see today. This work was due to a number of fires that broke out in the late seventeenth and early eighteenth century; these destroyed much of the medieval fabric of the complex and meant that sections of the castle had to be rebuilt. As usual, there was little revenue to spare, so this renovation was piecemeal. We can tell something about what the castle looked like in 1673 before the most destructive of these fires.[17] There were numerous ways that the building could have gone on fire. The Powder Tower and coal yard are located directly beside one another. Ovens in early modern kitchens were difficult to control. The Great Fire of London in 1666 was started at a bakery and swept through the city, consuming 13,200 houses. Thankfully, Dublin never suffered a fire on this scale, but the many fires that broke out in the castle were a reminder that the city remained vulnerable to them.

View of Dublin Castle from Dubh Linn gardens. Visible are the Tower Record, the only medieval tower to have survived intact, the eighteenth-century apartments and Chapel Royal completed in 1814 and used as the Lord Lieutenant's personal church.

A large-scale fire that broke out in the complex in 1671 'marked the end of the old medieval castle'.[18] William Robinson, the surveyor general, was brought in to restore the building. A further fire in 1684 made this restoration even more important. Part of the old structure was pulled down in 1687 to allow for this work to proceed. Gunpowder was originally stored in the towers, but had to be moved to a powder house in the gardens. This powder house exploded in 1689 and a new magazine was built in the Phoenix Park to replace it. A Castle munitions store was built near Ship Street, but this too went on fire and blew up in 1764. During this explosion the ballroom lost its roof and the Bermingham Tower nearly burned down. It was stripped down to its first floor and rebuilt.

A number of important additions were made to the castle throughout the eighteenth century, but the construction continued to be piecemeal. It was during this time that the castle was extended into the Lower Castle Yard. By 1720 the Treasury Block in the lower courtyard was completed, along with offices for the Linen Trustees (linen was one of the Ireland's largest exports in the eighteenth century).[19] While a chapel was added to the Lower Castle Yard in the eighteenth century it was demolished to make way for the current Chapel Royal which was opened on Christmas day 1814.[20]

In 1737 George I had ordered that the Great Staircase, Battleaxe Hall, chaplain's apartments and castle entrance be demolished. In 1745 Philip Dormer Stanhope, the new lord lieutenant, discovered that these instructions had not been carried out and that this part of the castle was in danger of falling down. He had these rooms demolished, and he initiated the construction of the current State Apartments, which were completed by 1761 and which included the present entrance, a new suite of bedrooms, the throne room, the picture gallery and the Great Hall or Ball Room (which was later renamed St Patrick's Hall). A new gateway was erected in the Lower Castle Yard in 1769. Around this time land was purchased on Cork Hill where a new guard house was built. Robinson's work is not generally admired. Peter Costello has said of this phase of rebuilding that 'none of this work was particularly distinguished, and does not compare with the domestic works to be found elsewhere in the city and country'.[21]

State banquets and socialising at Dublin Castle in the eighteenth century

A large number of staff was needed at the castle to cater for the constant rounds of social occasions and state dinners. There were usually one hundred people employed in the kitchen to undertake cooking for the lord lieutenant and his family, with additional staff being hired for special banquets. The duke of Shrewsbury reorganised the staff and running of the Dublin Castle household when he took up the office of lord lieutenant (1713–14). His model for the castle household remained in place until 1922, although it was enlarged and made grander as various lord lieutenants saw fit.[22] Shrewsbury has been noted for keeping a good table, and his grocery bills included 'Westphalia ham, sturgeon, anchovies, mangoes, caviar (at 2s. 6d. per lb.) Jordan almonds, Holland cheese, 'Italian vermicelli', orange flower water and 'Best Bordeaux Vinegar', as well as larks.[23] In 1737 a state dinner included a course of thirty-four dishes, accompanied by six removes (side dishes that are topped up throughout the meal) and fourteen dishes of sweetmeats.[24] Less important functions had fewer dishes, but nonetheless, copious amounts of food were prepared by the kitchen staff. Dinner was served in the State Room, later replaced by St Patrick's Hall. The Battleaxes, or the lord lieutenant's ceremonial bodyguards, were sometimes involved in presenting the dishes, accompanied by trumpets. Some state dinners were described as 'largesse days' when the leftover food would go to the poor.

The Order of St Patrick

The round of annual state banquets was added to with the formation of the Order of St Patrick in 1783. The English had the Order of the Garter for centuries; a special award for nobles. This was an attempt to create an Irish equivalent. Membership of the Order of St Patrick could not, however, be held alongside membership of the Order of the Garter and some Irish nobleman turned down the Irish order in the hopes of joining the more prestigious English one. The banqueting hall, or ballroom, was renamed St Patrick's Hall after the order. At the time there was a strong 'patriot' movement in Ireland. As well as arguing for greater parliamentary independence from Britain, they sought to encourage and expand Irish trade and manufactures (see chapter four). In creating the order of St Patrick, the British administration was recognising the distinct identity of Ireland, thus Patrick was honoured in the name of the order and St Patrick's blue was a central part of the clothes worn by those in the order (green was not associated with Irish nationalism and republicanism until the 1790s, when the United Irishmen adopted the colour).

The new order prompted the creation of the Irish crown jewels, which were to reflect the patriotic nature of the order and to encourage Irish manufacture. A strong 'buy Irish' campaign had existed in Dublin throughout the eighteenth century, although it was more prominent in the later eighteenth century. The art historian Sarah Foster has investigated this trend and noted how widespread it was throughout the social elite: 'Gentry support for Irish manufacture took the form of wearing Irish silk and poplins, and nobility like the earl of Charlemont and duke of Leinster made a point of buying Irish goods; a ball at Leinster House was usually catered for by Irish cooks. The viceregal court stipulated that guests at Her Majesty's birthday ball "be dressed in the manufactures of the kingdom". Theatres also participated, by kitting out their casts in costumes of Irish cloth'.[25] The new order prompted the monarch to create Irish crown jewels for the first time. The jewels were made up of 394 stones given by Queen Charlotte from her personal jewellery along with one of the diamonds from the order of the garter crown jewels.[26] The jewels were then made into a 'king-size, eight-pointed star … and a gold ceremonial knight's badge, with each leaf of shamrock', with the badge worn on the collar.[27] Those initiated into the order were to wear special clothes, as in the Order of the Garter; in keeping with the ongoing trend of buying Irish goods, the clothes and jewels were to be of Irish manufacture, however, there was such a rush on the orders that, while the fabrics were purchased in Dublin, 'Clements the jeweller had to rush to London', as he could not purchase the gems needed for the collars and medallions at such short notice in Dublin which was 'quite a loss to Dublin jewellers'.[28]

The chapel of the order was St Patrick's Cathedral, while the Castle Ballroom, renamed St Patrick's Hall, was where new members were installed. The office was invested for the first time on 14 March 1783 with the *Freeman's Journal* reporting on the occasion that the scene was 'magnificent beyond description'. The proceedings started at six in the morning:

> The drums of the regulars and volunteers beat to arms, and a little after the corps to their respective stations. His Excellency

the Lord Lieutenant, with a princely retinue of the Knights of St Patrick, accompanied by their esquires, and with the great officers of the order, arrived at the Cathedral at a quarter before eleven o'clock, and after a short delay in the Chapter room, they made their procession through the western or Great Nave into the choir headed by all its members ... the installation took up about two hours, when the procession returned in the same order, but with additional grandeur as all the knights appeared with their hats on and collars of their order, their esquires wearing their caps.[29]

The lord lieutenant and knights then proceeded to the castle for a ball.[30] The painting opposite depicts the order dining at St Patrick's hall on 17 March 1785, in full regalia, including hats embellished with ostrich feathers. The inauguration of the new order in the eighteenth century can be considered the pinnacle of Dublin Castle socialising.

Dublin Castle after the Act of Union

After the Act of Union which saw the dissolution of the Irish parliament in favour of a combined British and Irish parliament (see chapter four), the day-to-day government of Ireland fell to the chief secretary, usually a young politician seeking to enhance his career, assisted by an under-secretary, normally an Irish civil servant, who were stationed at Dublin Castle. The viceroy, a term that was increasingly used instead of lord lieutenant, was by now more of a figurehead position, with real power being held by the chief secretary.[31] The castle also became home to the offices of the Irish Constabulary, later the Royal Irish Constabulary, which served to consolidate the opinion of nationalists that the castle was the seat of British rule and oppression. The castle administration received much blame for the poor British government response to the Famine. In 1867, after the short-lived Fenian rebellion, arrested rebels were imprisoned there. The castle became the antithesis of nationalist hopes.

From the nineteenth century onwards the Viceroy divided his residence between Dublin Castle, where he tended to reside during

John Sheyes Kirwan, *The banquet held in the Great Hall of Dublin Castle for the installation of the first Knights of the Order of St Patrick*, 1785.

the winter months, and the Viceregal Lodge in the Phoenix Park, now Áras an Uachtaráin, the residence of the Irish President. The Viceregal Lodge impressed Queen Victoria and she stayed there on each of her visits to Ireland (1847, 1853, 1861 and 1900). The lodge suffered from the same problems of poor financing as the castle and the lord lieutenant found himself having to personally pay £2,500 for the alterations that were deemed necessary to make it suitable for the queen's visit.[32] Victoria's first visit to Ireland was in the midst of the Great Famine, and she was criticised for the round of socialising that her visit entailed.

DUBLIN CASTLE'S SOCIAL SEASON IN THE NINETEENTH CENTURY

Attendance at Dublin Castle balls was considered to place those invited in the highest rank of Ireland's social hierarchy. The castle season started in February and ran for six weeks until St Patrick's Day. It began with the viceroy's levee (an intimate social occasion where guests could socialise with the Viceroy) and included balls, banquets and drawing room levees. Although these occasions were supposed to be restricted to the most important peers and nobility of the realm, after the Act of Union there was a slow but steady exodus of the gentry from Ireland. Increasingly the military, politicians and wealthy businessmen moved to fill the vacancies left by the departed nobility. Elizabeth Grant, a very wealthy Scottish lady who was in her mid-fifties when she came to Dublin, described the social season in her journal. It gives us an idea of how many people attended these events. She estimated that there were 1,700 people at one of the lord lieutenant's levees in March 1852 adding that just 40 of those present were peers.[33] In April 1855 she reported that Dublin was 'very busy with its levee and drawing room'; 1,400 attended the levee and 3,000 were present at one of the lord lieutenant's drawing rooms.[34] In 1856 she tells us that a levee was 'crowded beyond measure', with about 2,000 in attendance.[35] It is difficult to imagine so many people tightly packed into the reception rooms at the castle, particularly as the gargantuan size of ladies' dresses ensured they took up a lot of space. It must have been a wonderful sight to behold so many people in full court dress, particularly at balls, which took place at night and ensured that the rooms were, at great expense, lit by candlelight. Grant was quite critical of the 'court' at Dublin Castle, and at the outset of the social season wrote in her journal that 'I don't like ... all that rubbish of nobility, and court fudge, and entertainments with horse riding etc. which from the very style of people sent here will of course be all the go again'.[36] She added that she thought these entertainments were 'folly' and should be discouraged 'among the idle, semi-barbarous people'.[37] Grant was often critical of what she observed touring the balls, levees and drawing-rooms in Dublin, but, as an outsider who had experienced court life and the social season of other cities, she makes some shrewd and witty observations about what she saw in Dublin.

Grant was not the only critic of the Dublin social season. Percy Fitzgerald wrote a scathing account of his time working in Dublin Castle that was published in 1902. Fitzgerald said of the St Patrick's ball that it 'was always supposed to be a highly rollicking affair. Every one who had been at a levee or drawing room was entitled to go, and had to go and dance too in court costume'.[38] Balls of this kind were places to see and be seen. They were also important events for those on the marriage market. Members of the military were an important addition to society events at the castle. Fitzgerald highlights this throughout his account. He mocks the attempts of some families to have their daughters married off to officers at these balls:

> In Dublin the officer is looked on much as the peer ... he is admired, worshipped, followed; he is the only partner worth having, the only admirer, the only husband. It was truly astonishing to see a whole family, father, mother, and daughter all in eager chase of some small boy, who had little more than his pay, simply because 'he was in the army' and still more surprising what a number of marriages, some really advantageous, were brought off.[39]

Grant also commented on the marriage market in Dublin. She wrote that 'Irish girls are really queer. Marriage is with them a necessity. If they can't get the man they prefer, they set to work to attract another, systematically manoeuvring mothers are said to ... think it no harm'.[40] In Ireland, these social events were considered to be the perfect setting for manoeuvring daughters into the right company, and amongst eligible young men.

Even the lord lieutenant did not escape criticism in some of these accounts. One of Fitzgerald's most scathing stories centred on the period in office of Lord Carlisle. He recounted a story of Lord Carlisle's insulting attempts to administer charity to some of Dublin's poor who came from the Liberties and gathered at the castle every St Patrick's day to hear the bands:

As the band played Irish airs specially designed and ordered to humour the natives 'Patrick's Day' over and over again some ragged fellows, going out into the middle, set up a sort of jig to the music, more by way of burlesque than anything else. Lord Carlisle, stooping over the balcony, his mouth opening wider and wider with enjoyment, encouraged these ragamuffins with gesture and voice ... Then he rushed into the room beyond and reappeared laden with cakes, bread, &c., which he actually threw down to the mob amid the yells and shouts of the rest, who struggled and fought for the morsels. This humiliating scene went on for a long time. All in authority really believed that the way to treat the lower Irish was to approach them much as Captain Cook did the savages, with glass beads, etc.[41]

The awkwardness with which Carlisle distributed his gifts shows an upper class wholly at odds with the poverty in the city, and yet highlights in what close proximity the upper class and the poor of Dublin lived and worked. While there were critics of the Dublin court, and nationalists rallied against the behaviour of English government officials like Carlisle, the social season was significant for a number of reasons. It was supposed to remind the Irish peers who stayed in Ireland that they had lost nothing through the union with Britain, and that the castle and its supporters would continue court life. It was also an important way for Irish peers, grandees, government officials and lord lieutenants to highlight that, as Dublin was the second city of the empire, it deserved special ceremonies and to have its own court. It was a way of ensuring that loyalty was maintained and that the prestige and privileges of the upper class in Ireland were upheld.

THEFT OF THE IRISH CROWN JEWELS

One of the biggest scandals to hit Dublin Castle broke in 1907 when the crown jewels of Ireland were stolen from the castle offices, under the nose of the King of Arms, Sir Arthur Vicars, who was charged with their safekeeping.[42] Vicars' office was moved in 1903 from the Bermingham Tower to the Upper Yard and in accordance with the statutes of the order, a new strong room had to be built to hold the jewels and other appendages of the order. A problem arose, however, when it was discovered that the new safe that had been ordered to house the crown jewels, could not actually fit through the doorway of the strong room. As an intermediate solution, the safe was to be kept, in the library, until a new one was purchased. While seven members of staff held keys to the office, just two keys existed to the safe that housed the crown jewels, and these were both in the possession of Vicars, one of which he kept on him at all times.

The last recorded sighting of the crown jewels was on 11 June 1907, when Vicars showed them to John Hodgson, a librarian to the duke of Northumberland. The strong-room door was found to be unlocked several times in July, with no explanation give by Vicars, and, on the afternoon of 6 July, when Vicars requested that his messenger deposit the collar of a deceased knight in the safe, it was discovered that the jewels were gone. But some of Vicar's own personal effects were also missing, as he had deposited his mother's jewels in the safe. A police investigation, which included expert testimony from a locksmith, confirmed that the safe had not been forced. Investigations into the theft heavily implicated Francis Shackleton, brother to the famous explorer Ernest, and a close friend of Vicars. Shackleton had lived with Vicars for over two years, and during the investigation it was uncovered that Shackleton was gay. This was thought to give him further motive as the investigators believed he could have been blackmailed into stealing the jewels.[43] While suspicion about Vicars' own sexuality was raised, this was soon dropped, probably because it would have incriminated the administration at large who appointed him.[44] What we can be certain about is that Vicars was known to unwind in the castle at parties where homosexual activity was known to occur. According to Myles Dungan, during the investigation, Harrel, the assistant commissioner of police, told Viceroy Aberdeen that 'after office hours, it was the habit of Vicars to offer hospitality in the Bedford Tower to his acquaintances. There he would unwind, along with some of the junior heralds and many of the leading civil servants working in the Castle. Harrel stopped short of depicting Babylonian orgies, but gave Aberdeen to understand that, among the guests at Vicar's soirees in the castle, were some of Dublin's leading homosexuals'.[45] Even more worrying for the Viceroy, it became clear that Aberdeen's own son, Lord Haddo, was a frequent guest at these parties. At one of these gatherings, Haddo stole the crown jewels from a drunken Vicars as a 'joke'. When Vicars was interviewed after the theft he supposedly stated 'I would not be a bit surprised if they would be returned to my house by parcel post tomorrow'.[46] While he was not in the country at the time of the theft, Shackleton was implicated. He was in debt and had a motive for stealing the jewels. Shackleton had injudiciously commented at a party in July 1907 that he wouldn't be surprised if the jewels were stolen.[47]

Progress in the case was slow, and once the news was leaked that the jewels had been stolen, it was of much public interest, leading to great embarrassment for Dublin Castle. In August 1907 the *Freeman's Journal* reported that the theft had been mentioned in parliament. Jeremiah McVeagh, Nationalist MP for South Down, announced that he intended to speak directly with the chief secretary and asked 'whether the gems have been traced, recovered or redeemed and if the latter under what circumstances?'[48] By January 1908 the scandal had not abated, and the *Freeman's Journal* hinted that it was not just the loss of the crown jewels that made King Edward VII angry: 'Gossip about the Dublin Castle mystery is as busy as ever ... His majesty is more angry about the incidents connected with the lost Irish Crown Jewels than about anything since his accession, seven years ago'.[49] Nationalists used the theft to suggest that the administration in Dublin Castle could not keep order in their offices, never mind run the country.

At least part of the reason that the jewels were not discovered seems to be that officials within Dublin Castle were fearful of what a full investigation would uncover and the difficulties they would have in hushing up any scandalous findings. The gay activities in the castle seem to have gone as far as Aberdeen's own family, which would have raised questions about Aberdeen as well as bringing shame on the royal family. Myles Dungan has investigated the theft and concludes that, as 'the office of Arms was directly answerable to the King', there was concern about how any link to this gay Castle circle might affect his public image. This was something that the king was directly aware of, and Edward VII 'did not want a homosexual controversy erupting into the open'.[50] The investigation to find the jewels seems to have been sacrificed to cover up the scandalous goings on in Vicars' chambers. The lord lieutenant, Lord Aberdeen, formed a commission to investigate Vicars' conduct, and it concluded that he 'did not show proper care in his handling of the safe keys' which should have been kept at a bank, not about his person. The report was highly critical of Vicars and he was dismissed from office in disgrace on 30 January 1908. The king was furious and criticised the police for their inability to solve the crime and insisted that the whole staff of the chief herald's office resign. The scandal rumbled on and in November 1910 the chief crown solicitor, on behalf of the attorney general, claimed that the jewels were still in Vicars' possession, but Vicars sued for libel and was awarded £5,000 in damages.[51] While myth and rumour have abounded that the jewels were sold, or were hidden and waiting to be discovered, they were never found. It is most likely that they were broken up and sold quickly after the theft.

DUBLIN CASTLE DURING THE 1916 RISING AND THE WAR OF INDEPENDENCE

The Castle acted as a military garrison and red cross hospital throughout the Great War; it housed offices of the Royal Irish Constabulary, as well as the plainclothes detective force of the Dublin Metropolitan Police. It was usually well-manned and armed. Despite this, it was attacked during the Easter Rising of 1916 (see chapter eight). Due to last-minute confusion over when the rising should take place, when the Irish Volunteers and Irish Citizen Army (ICA) rose on Monday morning 24 April 1916, their numbers were significantly less than originally anticipated. The main plan behind the rising was to capture significant buildings and to knock out or take-over government offices and services. As such the Castle was one of the first buildings to be attacked. Although in use as a military garrison at the time, many of the forces stationed in the castle were on leave for Easter. The rebels seem to have had a good opportunity to take the complex.[51] On Easter

Monday morning as buildings were being seized through the city a battalion headed by Seán Connolly, an Abbey actor, approached the Castle Street entrance and tried to seize the castle. Constable James O'Brien, the on-duty policeman, tried to shut the gates against them Connolly tried to stop him by opening fire. O'Brien was mortally wounded and became the first fatality of the rising. Connolly and his forces fell back to Dublin City Hall. The failure to take the Castle was a huge disappointment and 'almost everyone involved agreed that the Castle should have fallen'.[52] Helena Moloney, a member of the ICA, believed that they had failed to seize the Castle because of the confusion within the battalion; 'it appeared that the men behind Connolly did not really know they were to go through … there was hesitation on the part of the followers'.[53] Once they had taken Dublin City Hall the battalion moved to secure their position. Connolly went up to the roof to view the surrounding area but he was shot and killed by a sniper in the castle's clock tower.[54] The part that the castle played in the rising was not over yet. James Connolly, who was badly injured during the fighting at the GPO, was moved to the castle and hospitalised after the rising, before his execution at Kilmainham Gaol.

The republican fight for Irish independence focused on Dublin Castle throughout the later War of Independence as well. Government spies had traditionally been successful in infiltrating Irish republican movements and bringing them down. During the War of Independence the tables turned, and the republican leader Michael Collins was successful in gaining the services of several members of the British Intelligence Service based at Dublin Castle, and getting them to spy for him. One of these spies, David Neligan, wrote an account of his time working for Collins called *The Spy in the Castle*, which gives us a vivid account of the Castle during the War of Independence. Born in rural Limerick in 1899, Neligan wanted to get out of the countryside and to see Dublin. The Dublin Metropolitan Police (DMP) were recruiting so he joined up. In 1919 he joined the G-Division, the intelligence branch of the DMP.

As the War of Independence advanced, Neligan tells us, they were desperate for recruits to work in the castle as republican attacks on the force 'had made this service unpopular'. Neligan was 'heartily tired of

Armoured vehicle near Dublin Castle during the War of Independence (National Library of Ireland)

uniform and beat duty, I applied and was accepted'.[55] He described the network of police buildings, located primarily in the lower yard, as follows: 'The lower yard contained the HQ's of the D.M. Police and the R.I.C.; the British Army's Dublin Command, the Bermingham Tower containing state archives, and the Chapel Royal ... [there] was also a police station of the uniformed DMP., a central telephone exchange, and the house of the chief superintendent'. Security within the castle was understandably tight and was strengthened throughout the period: 'The castle had a military garrison that manned each gate, strengthened by steel plates since 1916. When things got hot, a pass was necessary to enter. Later, a company of Police Auxiliaries arrived and took up quarters inside the lower gate at Exchange Court'. The picture above from this period shows an armoured car stationed outside Dublin Castle. Those who were known to work for the castle were threatened by the IRA, who pressurised them to leave. Those who stayed were fearful for their lives and many moved into the castle seeking as much protection as possible. Neligan says that 'the police offices were cramped and shabby. Space was at a premium owing to the disturbed state of the country. This situation grew worse as time

Civic Guard lining up for inspection in Dublin Castle's lower yard, 1922
(image reproduced courtesy of NLI)

went on, for hordes of officials lived in terror of their lives, and had to be accommodated there, never leaving the place day or night'.[56]

Neligan quickly realised that he did not enjoy working for the British government. He met with Michael Collins, one of the leaders of the Irish Republican Army (IRA), who clearly impressed him, and he agreed to work for the republicans. The work that Neligan and other spies undertook was invaluable to the republicans. By the time Neligan signed up to undertake work for Collins there were a number of British 'Auxiliary' units stationed within the castle. The Auxiliaries were British paramilitary forces who had little understanding of the Irish situation and little patience for civilians. They ran amok in Ireland and succeeded only in gaining more sympathy for the republican cause. Neligan describes them as 'hard-drinkers' and 'terrorists'.[57]

While Neligan provided general information about what went on in the castle, Collins also sent requests to Neligan for information on specific Auxiliaries and 'G-Men' (members of the DMP's 'G' division) who were involved in killing or ambushing republicans. Neligan also assisted in compiling a list of British secret-service men active in Dublin. This information was reported to Collins at regular meetings which Neligan attended with another colleague, Joe McNamara. Spying was a very dangerous game, and Neligan, and many others like him, risked their lives for the republicans on a daily basis. Collins appreciated the dangerous nature of the work that these men and women undertook for him. When one of Collins' DMP spies, Ned Broy, was arrested, Collins was desperate to break him out of prison. Rumours spread that Broy would be executed, a likely sentence for a spy in a conflict in which violence was escalating by the day. Neligan warned Collins that Arbour Hill prison where Broy was being kept, was 'a military dungeon equivalent to the Tower of London, and that he had little hope of breaking him out'.[58] In the end Broy was protected by passing threats to anyone involved in his case to ensure that he be left alone. This worked, and Broy was allowed out on bail until the end of the war. The British never discovered Neligan and he survived the war undetected. His account of his time spying for Collins is an invaluable account of life in Dublin Castle during this turbulent period as well as a colourful recollection of the risks many took for Irish independence.

Dublin Castle in independent Ireland

One of the most symbolic acts for the new Irish Free State was the handing over of Dublin Castle to Michael Collins on 16 January 1922. While the Anglo-Irish Treaty had been ratified, this was only by a small minority and the treaty still had to be accepted by the country at large. With uncertainty about the future of the new state, the castle was taken over with little ceremony, as Michael Collins did not want the new state to look as if it was simply replacing the hated British administration. The Castle remained home to the police force. The image opposite shows the Free State's Civic Guard, later named An Garda Síochána, lining up for inspection in the lower yard.

In more recent times the castle has continued to be an administrative centre. The offices are used by the Revenue Commissioners. The State Apartments are used today for presidential inaugurations and visiting heads of state, such as the visit of Queen Elizabeth II to Ireland in 2011. The castle was also used as the seat of the Irish presidency of the European Union in 2013 and, earlier, EEC presidencies. The castle apartments are a popular tourist attraction, and entertainment events are often hosted there. Despite all of this, the castle is still strongly linked with the legacy of British colonisation in Ireland and stands as a reminder of seven hundred years of British occupation. One clear reminder of this, and one that Dubliners relish pointing out, is the statue of justice that was erected in the Upper Yard over the Castle Street gate. The statue is a poor representation of justice as she wears no blindfold and holes had to be made in the scales of justice to stop rain water unbalancing them. The statue is used to indicate that the justice meted out by the British administration while it was housed at Dublin Castle was neither impartial, nor balanced. Perhaps the most obvious manifestation of this is that as the statue faces towards the castle, it looks as if she has turned her back on the people, whom she is supposed to oversee and protect, in favour of the British administration.

3

Trinity College Dublin

TRINITY COLLEGE DUBLIN is the oldest university in Ireland and has survived over four centuries of political, religious and social change. It was founded as part of the Tudor reconquest of Ireland. The government in Ireland believed that the university could be an effective tool with which to instil English law and civility, as well as the Anglican faith, in the Irish population. Indeed, many Irish people still associate the university with colonisation and the Reformation. As a centre of learning the university has left a far greater legacy, one that is often overlooked. Trinity houses some of the most valuable manuscripts, books and artefacts relating to Ireland's history and culture in existence. Its treasures include the Book of Kells, the Book of Armagh and the Book of Dimma.

Throughout its history, the university made important contributions to a range of areas in Irish life and some of Ireland's most celebrated theologians, philosophers, politicians, scientists and writers studied or taught at Trinity. It was diverse enough to have had a hand in the education and formation of such disparate political personalities as the staunchly conservative supporter of the Act of Union, John Fitzgibbon, and the nineteenth-century unionist leader, Edward Carson, as well as one of the founding fathers of Irish republicanism, Theobald Wolfe Tone, along with the Young Irelander and leader of the 1848 rebellion, Thomas Davis. The contributions and breakthroughs which Trinity's academics and graduates made within their fields prove that Trinity was just as likely to shape Irish cultural and political life as to be shaped by it.

THE REFORMATION IN IRELAND

One of the prime concerns of Henry VIII from early in his reign was producing a male heir to inherit his thrones. Henry's wife Catherine of Aragon was unable to produce male heirs for him, and, unable to gain a divorce within the Catholic Church, Henry split from Rome and founded the Anglican Church of England. He subsequently gained a divorce, and in January 1533 married Anne Boleyn and began trying to conceive a male heir again. The establishment of a new church necessitated both a legislative framework to establish it, and changes to religious doctrine. It was not until 1534 that the Act of Supremacy was passed by the English parliament. This act made Henry, not the pope in Rome, the head of a reformed English church. The Reformation gathered pace in 1536, when an act was passed through the English parliament to dissolve the monasteries.

The acts passed in England were not simply followed up by corresponding acts in Ireland. Henry did not turn his attention to Ireland until July 1536, when George Browne was appointed archbishop of Dublin. Browne had been a loyal supporter of Henry's marriage to Anne Boleyn and an advocate of his reforms. This appointment meant that Browne was now responsible for implementing and directing the reformation on the ground in Ireland. The reformation here was never going to be introduced easily. In the sixteenth century Ireland was a divided society both politically and in religious terms. Browne's first move was to have the clergy within his own dioceses swear the oath of supremacy. This oath stated that Henry, not the pope, was head of the church. In 1538 Browne issued guidelines to each congregation on doctrinal changes, which covered what each parish could pray for within the new religion. Pilgrimages, prayers to saints, beliefs in shrines and relics, patterns and other 'superstitious' practices were banned.[1]

Browne was supported in his work by a leading Anglo-Irish nobleman, Piers Butler, earl of Ormond, who promoted the reformation in his own territories and throughout Munster. Two archbishops and eight bishops took the oath of supremacy in 1538. By the end of 1538, however, news had arrived in Ireland of the complete suppression of religious houses and orders in England. Full-scale dissolution of the monasteries began in the areas under crown control from 1539. The forfeited lands were used to enrich the king's coffers and also to curry favour with powerful leaders who were quick to petition for some of the confiscated land. Some of the most powerful and important religious houses in the vicinity of Dublin city (which was still within the city walls at this point) were shut, including All Hallows monastery and the Augustinian friary of St John's of Newgate. The city fathers did not miss the opportunity to present a petition to the king requesting the grant of both of these houses and their lands as compensation for losses incurred during the rebellion of Silken Thomas. They were duly granted both. The civic government would, later in the century, give the land of All Hallows for the establishment of Trinity College, and it is on this land that the college stands today.[2] Two of Henry's successors and children, Edward VI and Elizabeth I, continued his work of spreading the Anglican faith, but this proved difficult in Ireland. The turbulent nature of Irish politics, particularly successive wars that broke out in Munster and Ulster and the plantations that followed, diverted attention and resources from a large-scale and organised attempt to convert the population. The Reformation in Ireland needed a central institution. In order to be successful it needed educated clergy who understood the precarious nature of Irish politics and who could speak the same language as the people. Trinity College was conceived to fill this gap.

THE FOUNDATION OF TRINITY COLLEGE DUBLIN

It is surprising that it took so long for a university to be formed in Ireland. We have seen that George Browne had mentioned that a university should be established in 1547. When Elizabeth came to the throne in 1558 her lord deputy in Ireland, Sir Thomas Radclyffe, earl of Sussex, revived the idea, suggesting that the revenue from St Patrick's Cathedral could be used to endow a new college on the grounds. As St Patrick's Cathedral was then outside the city walls, this would presumably give the cathedral room to expand while remaining close to main routes in and out of the city. The archbishop of Dublin, Adam Loftus, was concerned about the financial impact this would have on the cathedral and was eager that another site be found.[3] Dublin's civic leaders, however, realised that a university would be good for the prestige of the city, and for commerce, so in 1591 they offered the site of All Hallows monastery and the surrounding lands for the project, which they had been granted during the Reformation. The gift of land was probably orchestrated by Loftus to protect St Patrick's Cathedral. But more than a site was needed to establish a university, so the Anglican Church sent James Ussher, the archibishop of Armagh, to London in November 1591 to petition for a charter from the queen. The charter bears the date 3 March 1591 which pre-dated the deputation headed by Ussher. The bulk of the charter was probably drawn up in Dublin. Interestingly, it is this date of 3 March 1591 which the college takes as its foundation date, rather than November, when Elizabeth signed her name to it and allowed the university to come into being.[4]

Elizabeth I is remembered as the founder because she provided the charter, but she gave no money to assist in establishing the college. Money for the first buildings was raised by the lord deputy, the Irish privy council and the aristocracy of Ireland. This shows there was a broad support-base for its foundation across the Anglo-Irish elite. Elizabeth gave the college confiscated estates amounting to 3,000 acres in Kerry and Limerick in May 1597, and the revenue from this greatly assisted with the expansion of the college.[5] Further endowments of land made by the monarchy, and those connected with the college, gave Trinity an important source of rental income in rent from land. Elizabeth's heir, James I, also acted as a patron to the college and granted it 20,000 acres of land between 1610 and 1613.[6]

The first provost (chancellor) was Adam Loftus, then lord chancellor of Ireland. This appointment was probably to reward his assistance in encouraging the scheme. The charter states that the college was 'mother of a university'. It was not initially intended to be as large a structure as the multi-collegiate Cambridge or Oxford, but this stipulation allowed it to confer degrees and ensured that if there was a demand for smaller colleges, these could be born under

Front of Trinity College Dublin from Charles Brooking's 1728 map of Dublin

the University of Dublin. As early as January 1594 the college was preparing to receive its first students, and in August 1594, the second provost, Walter Travers, took up his post. He described Trinity in a letter to the English government as 'a quadrant of bricks of three storeys, and on every side within the court, it is 120 feet broad, the west side which is of chambers, and the north side where are the chapel, hall, buttery and kitchen, are orderly finished. The other two sides are only walls, saving some little beginning of chambers, which for want of further means, it [is] yet imperfect'.[7] We know this original quadrant corresponds with the modern Parliament Square, although the quadrant was enlarged with the addition of the Old Library in the eighteenth century. Unfortunately none of the original buildings have survived, but there are some early depictions of the university (above). On John Speed's 1610 map of Dublin (p. 8), Trinity is located far from the centre of the city in the 'suburbs'. The Liffey was wider at the time, and the university was much closer to the water.

The idea to establish a university may have been supported and promoted by the Anglican hierarchy, but the college charter and the nature of its early degrees was surprisingly open. The charter states that the university was 'for the education, formation, and instruction of youths and students in the arts and faculties'.[8] The university did not just want to produce ministers. It aimed at educating men to become lawyers, doctors and gentlemen. All of these graduates would assist in trying to impose a more anglicised (and Anglican) government and society on the island of Ireland. The turbulent nature of religious affiliation in Ireland, however, after decades of upheaval, ensured that theology became a dominant subject within the college.

Catholics were quick to voice their concerns about the college, showing an awareness of the potential damage that a Protestant seat of learning could do to the Catholic faith in Ireland. Traditionally, Irish Catholic clerics were educated in Europe. This was something that the original college charter touched on, and it was used to justify the need for a college where the Anglican faith could be taught: 'many have usually heretofore used to travel into France, Italy, and Spain, to get learning in such foreign universities, where they have been infected with popery and other ill qualities, and so become evil subjects'.[9] The return of these clerics from European Catholic countries had helped to strengthen the Catholic Counter-Reformation movement in Ireland. In 1595, fearing the impact that Trinity could have on the religious beliefs of the population, Irish exiles in Europe wrote to the pope outlining their fear of the college and claiming that 'from this college a great danger threatens the Irish'. They described the political and religious situation in Ireland at the time. The letter first discusses the invasion of Ireland by the English and states that they 'deliberately contrived to keep the natives in the gloom of barbaric ignorance, so as thus to retain them like slaves in abject obedience'. It also discusses the conversion of some Irish to the Protestant faith: 'the Irish, though full of genuine love of the Catholic faith, were not educated enough to detect and repel that corruption of religion which for some decades of years the English have sought by fraud or force to introduce into Ireland'. A trap was being laid for the Irish through 'the building of a certain ample and splendid college beside Dublin, in which the Irish youth shall be taught heresy by English teachers'.[10] Perhaps surprisingly, despite the university's clearly Protestant ethos, there was no religious qualification for entry to the college until 1641 and some Catholics were educated in the college during this period.[11] But Trinity had to shelter from ongoing political and military upheaval throughout the seventeenth century, and Protestant communities throughout Ireland, increasingly suspicious of Catholics, began to systematically exclude them from public and political life.

POLITICAL TURBULENCE AND THE UNIVERSITY

By the early seventeenth century the confessional faith of the population of Ireland seemed to have been settled, but not in the way the English government had wished. The majority of the population, both the Old English who had settled in Ireland before the reformation and the Gaelic population, remained Catholic. Wars of religion engulfed the country in the seventeenth century and impacted on Trinity's development, affecting the relationships between Catholics and Protestants for many centuries. In 1641 a large rebellion broke out in Ulster when Catholics rose up against Protestant settlers in the province. This violence spread quickly throughout the rest of the country and plunged Ireland into one of the bloodiest civil wars in its history. This cut Trinity off from its estates in Ulster and from one of its most important sources of income. Admissions to the college fell off; no students entered Trinity between 1642 and 1652, while there was no provost between 1641 and 1645.[12] As the war continued to rage, the fate of the college looked uncertain. The government appointed Anthony Martin, bishop of Meath, to the position of provost in 1645 and he tried to steer a middle ground between the two opposing sides. His vice-chancellor was Henry Jones, then bishop of Clogher. While initially the conflict had been controlled by Ulster leaders like Phelim O'Neill and Rory O'More, it had descended into a popular sectarian violence with Catholics attacking Protestant settlers and seizing their lands and goods in retribution for land that had been seized from them a generation earlier during the plantations.

The conflict was chaotic and confused, and resulted in many thousands abandoning their homes, making their way to Dublin, and fleeing abroad. In December 1641 the 'Commission for the Despoiled Subject' was set up to take accounts of the losses endured by these refugees. It was headed by Henry Jones, who began his work in March 1642, assisted by seventy other commissioners. Many thousands of testimonies ('depositions') were collected from all parts of the country and they detail various levels of violence, chaos and loss. They help to create a clearer picture of one of the most controversial and divisive events of Irish history, but they are an incomplete source, in that the vast majority were taken from members of the Protestant community. While the depositions have been studied by scholars, only a handful of people have had access to them until very recently, when the whole collection was transcribed, digitised and put online. They are among one of the most important manuscript sources for the history of seventeenth-century Ireland, and they detail not only this conflict but relations between the new settlers and the Gaelic population before the rebellion broke out, the material wealth of people, and the types of farming and commercial practices that were common at the time. Nevertheless, Jones himself was a controversial figure. He edited some of the most violent and graphic depositions, depicting the Irish rebels at their worst, into a collection called *A remonstrance of divers remarkable passages concerning the church and kingdom of Ireland* (1642). Accounts like this did much to stir up anti-Catholic sentiment in England. Other pamphlets and books reprinted these accounts, and they were used by English leaders such as Oliver Cromwell to justify dealing with Ireland severely.

In England the civil wars ended with the execution of King Charles I on 30 January 1649. The following August Cromwell was sent to Ireland to end the war there and to bring Ireland under the control of the English parliament. Cromwell's armies ravaged the country for the following nine months, earning him the reputation of one of the most brutal English leaders to ever step foot in Ireland. In 1650, in the midst of this second wave of conflict, the college closed.[13] It did not stay shut for long. The new government in England, now headed by Cromwell and known as the Commonwealth, set about restoring normal life within its borders, and Trinity was reopened in March 1652.

James Ussher and the Book of Kells

Some of the most important early Irish Christian manuscripts came into the possession of the library in the seventeenth century, including the Book of Kells, an early transcription of the Christian gospels. One of the first students to study in Trinity when it opened its doors in 1594 was James Ussher, who became vice chancellor of the university in 1615 and vice provost in 1616. He was elevated to the role of bishop of Meath in 1621, one of the most senior positions in the Church of Ireland at the time.[14] Ussher, an expert in early Christian manuscripts and an avid bibliophile, first came into contact with the Book of Kells during his posting in Meath, although the manuscript was not in fact a book when he initially came to study it. The loose manuscript sheets that today make up the Book of Kells would have originally been kept in a *cumdach*, or book shrine. This is a type of manuscript casing unique to Ireland. These were heavily decorated with gold and precious stones, and are beautiful examples of Irish Christian art. Thanks to the Annals of Ulster we know that the manuscript and book shrine, which was originally called the Gospel of Colum Cille, was stolen in 1007. While the majority of the manuscript sheets were returned, the golden shrine was not. When the book was returned it was missing the front pages which would normally describe where the transcription took place.[15] As the *Annals of Ulster* describe the manuscript as the Gospel of Colum Cille, we know that it was transcribed in one of two monasteries associated with Colum Cille: at Iona off Scotland or at Kells in Meath *circa* 800. Ussher, assisted by Henry Jones, began to collate the pages into several volumes. Six hundred pages from the original manuscript have survived. The Book of Kells is uniquely ornate amongst Irish manuscripts of this kind, and this is why it is the best known of all the extant early Irish Christian manuscripts. George Otto Simms, an art historian, explains that it is the sumptuous and playful illustrations of animals and monks that makes the Book of Kells so special: 'Unparalleled in the other manuscripts of this Irish family are the writhing, chasing, struggling, frolicking creatures, now hiding, now scampering between the lines'.[16]

Ussher himself was a renowned scholar, particularly of early Irish manuscripts. By the time of his death in 1656 he owned over

10,000 volumes, which he had intended to bequeath to the college. Unfortunately, his poor financial position meant that his library had to be passed on to his daughter who had to sell it. This meant that the vast and intellectually significant collection would most likely be broken up when sold by private auction. Oliver Cromwell had a keen interest in Ussher and his work, and insisted that Ussher be given a full state funeral in Westminster Abbey, which took place on 16 April 1656.[17] He also intervened in the sale of Ussher's books. The Commonwealth government purchased the collection on Cromwell's behalf, with the intention of using the collection to open a second university in Dublin. The sale proceeded at a very slow pace and by the time the collection was acquired, the Commonwealth regime had fallen and Charles I's son had returned from exile to take his place on the throne as Charles II. The plans to open a new university were abandoned and the collection went instead to Trinity. It was a very significant addition to the library, as the collection included a number of important medieval manuscripts.[18] At the same time, Trinity acquired the Books of Kells when Henry Jones, now bishop of Meath, presented the manuscript to the college. In 1688 he also gave Trinity the Book of Durrow, another important early Christian manuscript, which is also on display today in the Old Library.[19]

Narcissus Marsh

Another interesting college figure of this period was Archbishop Narcissus Marsh, an expert in maths and languages, who took up the position of provost in 1679. During his tenure he worked to raise the standard of scholarship of the staff and students, undertook a revolutionary programme to promote the Irish language, and oversaw the building of a new chapel and college hall. In 1681 he produced a university textbook, probably the first textbook written specifically for Trinity students. During a review of the college statutes, Marsh discovered that 30 of the 70 scholars had to be natives of Ireland and fluent in the Irish language. While Trinity took on scholars that could speak Irish, few of these could write the language. He employed Paul

Marsh's Library, founded by Narcissus Marsh and opened in 1701

Higgins, a former Irish Catholic turned Protestant minister, to teach Irish to the students and preach in the language once a month. Marsh also ordered that Irish students had to both speak and write the language.[20] This was a popular move, and attendance never dropped below 300, with about 80 students attending lectures. We know that

Marsh led the way, learning the language and attending lectures and sermons.[21] This encouragement of the language was not always well recieved and he was criticised in some circles.[22]

Marsh was particularly interested in Trinity's library. During building work the college library was used as a dining hall, and the books were moved into storage. When they were moved back into the library he set about trying to improve the organisation of the library: a time-consuming and difficult task. Muriel McCarthy, former keeper of the famous public library that Marsh founded, described the rigorous work: 'Marsh checked and revised the regulations; he ordered tables to be drawn up and hung at the end of each classis (division) of the books, containing the shelves and numbers and names of all the books on every shelf, the books likewise being numbered and figured'.[23] This seventeenth-century library would have appeared very odd to us. The books were placed on shelves with the spines to the wall and the pages facing outwards. The classification and shelf number was noted down the side of the pages on display, rather than on the spine of the book. Some of the books on the library collection still have their original classifications printed in this way, they look remarkably odd, although this was the standard way of storing books across Europe.[24] As college provost, it is hard to understand where Marsh found the time for so many rigorous tasks such as reviewing the college statutes, taking up Irish, reorganising the library, writing textbooks and running the college. His reforms went even further. There was no library keeper at the time but he managed to raise £6 annually to pay a junior fellow to take care of the library, insisting that all the books undergo an annual check to be accounted for and replaced if necessary.[25] During this period an unfortunate statute stated that students who wanted to use the library had to be accompanied by the provost or a fellow. Marsh wanted this statute repealed and for the library to be free to all students, but despite his attempts he was unsuccessful in having it overturned.

Marsh fled Ireland in 1688 when war looked likely, but he returned afterwards and became the dean of St Patrick's Cathedral. He wanted Dublin to have a library that could be used by the public and, in 1701, with funds from his own pocket, he began erecting a library

View of West Front of Trinity College Dublin from Front Square

on the grounds of St Patrick's Cathedral. It is a testament to Marsh's commitment to promoting scholarship that he is responsible for the establishment of the first public library on the island. It must be pointed out, however, that 'public' in the eighteenth century meant something very different to today. In this case the new city library was for 'all graduates' of Trinity College and 'gentlemen' of Ireland.[26] Nevertheless, Marsh's library was used by countless Irish scholars over the centuries, including James Joyce, and can still be visited today as a wonderful example of an early eighteenth-century library.

TRINITY COLLEGE IN THE REIGN OF JAMES II

In the late 1680s Ireland once more became a battlefield. Charles II failed to produce a legitimate heir which brought his brother, James, duke of York, to the throne as James II. James had converted to Catholicism but his heirs, his daughters Mary and Anne, were both firm Protestants, and so while there were objections when he ascended the throne in 1685, it was believed that this Catholic reign would be short lived. When James's wife produced a male heir in 1688 who was subsequently baptised a Catholic, England's protestant elite panicked. Fearing a restoration of the Catholic faith, they invited James's elder daughter Mary and her Dutch husband William, prince of Orange, to take the thrones of England, Ireland and Scotland. James fled to France, William and Mary were declared to be the new monarchs, and were celebrated as saviours of the Protestant faith. Mary's and William's accession became known as the 'Glorious Revolution', and while it was relatively peaceful in England, it dragged Ireland into war. Believing that Ireland would be easier won than England, wooed by Irish Catholics eager to use his cause to reassert their own supremacy, and backed by the French who saw an opportunity to harass William, with whom they were at war, James decided to make a stand in Ireland. He landed in Cork on 12 March 1689.

The Jacobite period was a very difficult time for the college. James and his French army made their way to Dublin and took the city on 24 March. He visited the college and was waited on by the vice chancellor. James promised to protect Trinity, but on 6 September the college was seized for use as a military garrison. Five days later the college was turned into a prison, and Protestant citizens were imprisoned within the walls. It was recorded by one of the college staff that 'a great number' of Dublin's Protestants 'were confined to the upper part of the hall' and that on the 16 September 'the scholars were all turned out by soldiers, and ordered to carry nothing with 'em but their books. But Mr Thewles and some others were not permitted to take their books with [them] ... but the bishop of Meath, our vice-chancellor, interceded with the King, and procured the last order to be stopped'.[27] With the staff and fellows ejected, there was no one on hand to protect the college and its contents. On 28 September the chapel plate and mace were seized to be melted down to finance James' campaign. One of the revenue commissioners managed to save the plate from being destroyed. The following month the chapel was broken open and consecrated as a Catholic chapel (see chapter one). It was later used to store gunpowder. The library was broken into but the books were put under the protection of a Catholic priest called Macarty, who 'preserved them from the violence of the soldiers but the chambers and all other things belonging to the college were miserably defaced and ruined'.[28] By 3 October 1691 James had been defeated in battle and had fled back to France, the Treaty of Limerick had been signed, and the war was over. The Protestant faith was now secured as the state religion in England, Ireland and Scotland.

THE LIBRARY

By the 1690s the college library, positioned in the old Elizabethan quadrangle in rooms above the scholars' chambers, was in a poor state and had suffered badly at the hands of Jacobean soldiers. The library was not an inviting place to be. George Berkeley, who served as librarian from 1700 to 1710, described his day there in a letter to a friend: 'I am lately entered into my Citadel in a disconsolate mood, after having passed the better part of a sharp and bitter day in the damp and musty solitudes of the library without either fire or anything else to protect me from the injuries of the snow that was constantly driving at the window and forcing its entrance into that wretched mansion'.[30] Berkeley persuaded the college to ask for public funding to build a new library, and, in 1709, £5,000 was granted for a new library building. Two more grants of £5,000 were given in 1717 and 1721 to finish the building. To thank parliament for these generous grants, the college named the front square 'parliament square'. The plans for the building were drawn up by the surveyor general, Colonel Thomas Burgh, a notable architect who left a significant legacy.[31] His first known building was the Royal Barracks (now Collins Barracks), and he was also responsible for Dr Steeven's Hospital; both fine examples of his work. He also designed the original Custom House near Temple Bar and the Linen Hall near Constitution Hill, neither of which have survived into the modern age.[32] The new library building was completed in 1733, although he did not live to see his masterpiece finished. The length of the building doubled the size of the original square and must have dwarfed the other buildings. It was, however, a grand addition to the city's architecture. Throughout the eighteenth century a number of significant buildings followed, such as the Parliament Building, the Four Courts, the Custom House, the West Front of Trinity, the Rotunda Hospital and City Hall. Despite being one of the earliest of these Georgian public buildings, the library managed to keep pace with them all.

The Long Room is the name given to the main reading room within the library. It is one of the most celebrated interiors in Ireland, but the Long Room has not survived in its original state because of a number of alterations being made to the fabric of the building to make room for books. In the original design, the ground floor that we see today was open colonnades with an arcade. A wall that ran the length of the building prevented access between Library Square and the Fellows Garden. The land that the college was built on is exceptionally marshy, so it made sense to place the library and books on a raised floor, away from damp ground. These colonnades were converted in 1892 into a reading room and for library storage.[33] The interior of the library chamber also looked quite different when it was first opened. Books were shelved on just one floor in alcoves, while the roof of these alcoves was used as a walkway.

Space has been an issue in the library for much of the building's history. When the library building originally opened, the shelves would have looked sparse enough as the college owned fewer than fifteen thousand books.[34] The collection steadily grew through purchases at auctions or through bequests. In 1801, after the Act of Union combined the Irish and British parliaments, a copyright act was introduced into Ireland, making the library of Trinity College a copyright library. This meant that a copy of every book, pamphlet and periodical printed legally in Britain and Ireland had to be deposited in Trinity's library.[35] This copyright act is still in force today and was a great coup for the library. It meant that it received a huge number of books each year for free, which vastly improved its collection at no extra cost. But it also had disadvantages. By the early nineteenth century the library was running out of space. By mid-century the library took 1,500–2,000 books a year, so the shelves were filling up fast.[36] Alterations had to be made to the building, and the gallery was altered by adding bookcases, providing the easiest way to make

Long Room after the
Dean and Woodward
alterations

room. These adjustments were made to create the maximum amount of space. The overall look is beautiful, and the sliding shelves are ingenious, as the walkways between the stacks cannot be seen from the ground floor, giving the effect of uninterrupted shelves of books.

As can also be seen from James Malton's depiction of the Long Room, the ceiling of the building was flat and was lower than it is today.[37] The roof was in a bad condition by the middle of the nineteenth century, almost collapsing at one point. This would have been disastrous for the books and manuscripts stored in the library. In November 1856 the bursar was directed to get the assistance of the architect Sir Thomas Deane. Deane and his partner, Benjamin Woodward, had won the contract to design Trinity's museum building in 1852, a superb addition to the campus. Progress on the Long Room was slow, as opinion in the college was divided as to how they should proceed. Deane and Woodward proposed a far more radical solution to the problem of the roof than the college expected. They wanted to underpin the whole building with stone columns (remember that the building was set on a swamp), increase the roof line and install a double-vaulted wooden ceiling. While some believed that this was a step too far, the ceiling was rapidly deteriorating and the college finally moved to allow the architects to carry out their proposals. They used stained Canadian white oak for the roof, and it was a stunning addition to the Long Room, creating neat and seamless continuity between the ceiling and the alcoves. It has been described as 'a daring transformation that has undoubtedly enhanced the grandeur of what is still one of the largest single-chamber libraries in the world'.[38] It was, unfortunately, the last building that Deane and Woodward worked on.[39]

TRINITY COLLEGE FROM THE EIGHTEENTH CENTURY TO THE FOUNDATION OF THE FREE STATE

Trinity's reputation increased throughout the eighteenth century as, increasingly, the Anglo-Irish gentry sent their sons there. Trinity men filled the ranks of the professional classes across Ireland, as they graduated to take up positions at the bar, as doctors and as clergymen.

By 1775 the college had over five hundred students a year.[40] Some of the most important political, literary and intellectual figures to emerge in Ireland during the eighteenth century were students at the college, including Jonathan Swift, Oliver Goldsmith, Edmund Burke (statues of Goldsmith and Burke stand outside the college today) and Theobald Wolfe Tone.

The college improved its campus and appearance throughout the eighteenth century. A new west front was added in 1759. This building altered the face of College Green and the city centre itself. The focus of the city was shifting eastwards from the old medieval quarter around Christ Church Cathedral and Dublin Castle, and with the Parliament House positioned opposite Trinity, the college was no longer in the suburbs, but was now located in the heart of Georgian Dublin. The Provost's House was added in 1760 to provide a private residence for the college president. The role was becoming more prominent in Irish political life throughout the course of the eighteenth century, thanks to provosts like John Hely Hutchinson who also acted as MP and who made the Provost's house a political salon. The college exam hall was designed in 1780 by Sir William Chambers, who also designed the chapel (completed in 1798). Both buildings are almost mirror images of each other. Many of these buildings were funded by parliament with the profits from the economic expansion that Ireland enjoyed in the eighteenth century.

The eighteenth century can be considered something of a golden age for the college as well as for the city. But if anything this was a 'gorgeous mask'. Ireland remained a divided country in many ways. This can be seen clearly in Trinity's intake of students during these years. In the aftermath of the Glorious Revolution, the penal laws prevented Catholics from having access to education and to Trinity College. In 1793, when Catholics were allowed access to university education once again, sons of Catholic businessmen and landed gentry entered the college. Suspicion fell, however, on Catholic entrants to the college after the 1798 rebellion. John Fitzgibbon, Lord Clare, was college vice-chancellor during the rebellion, and had purged the college of its United Irish members or sympathisers in early 1798. Eighteen students were expelled, including Robert Emmet; five of these students were Catholic, the rest Protestant.[41] It would be incorrect to say that Catholics no longer entered the college: Daniel O'Connell, the famous Catholic politician (see chapter four), sent his sons there.[42]

Nevertheless, in the aftermath of Catholic emancipation in 1829, Catholics began to create their own identity within the state in a new and visible way. There were calls for a Catholic university to be established. Sir Robert Peel pushed forward the funds for the foundation for three 'Queen's Colleges' in Ireland in 1845. These were at Cork, Galway and Belfast. The colleges did not promote any religion, and so they were unpopular with Catholic bishops who called them 'godless colleges' and repeated their calls for a seperate Catholic college. These repeated attacks on Trinity and the Queen's Colleges were followed up by a ban on Catholics entering Trinity, which did little to improve inter-denominational relations. The ban was not lifted by the Catholic Church until the 1970s, and, although Trinity did not openly encourage Catholics to enter the college, a small number of liberal Catholics continued to enrol. It was not until 1854 that the Catholic College, under the direction of Cardinal Newman, was founded, later evolving to become University College Dublin. This new college catered for the vast majority of Dublin's Catholics. Despite the foundation of these new universities, Trinity's numbers continued to increase steadily throughout the nineteenth century. The college continued to have a hand in the education of some of Ireland's foremost literary, political and intellectual figures. Several members of the Young Ireland group (a cultural and political movement who called for Irish separation from Britain) attended Trinity.

Library space became a pressing issue once more in the late nineteenth century. It has been mentioned that, by the 1850s, the library was taking in 1,500–2,000 books a year.[43] The copyright privileges were extended and the number of books received on an annual basis increased. The library was rapidly running out of space. The conversion of the colonnades into a ground floor in 1892 was just a stop-gap measure and, by 1908, there were more than 300,000 books and no further ways to alter the Old Library. The college favoured building a new reading room and using the old colonnade space for book storage. Discussions on this new reading room and its location were interrupted during the Great War but were taken up again when the Irish Free State was established in the 1920s. It was decided that a Hall of Honour in Front Square (formerly Parliament Square) marking those students and members of staff that fell during the war, should be combined with a reading room. It is estimated that 210,000 Irishmen enlisted in the British army during the war, approximately 3,500 of whom were Trinity students, graduates and staff. Over 450 of them were killed.[44] Many, but not all, had been unionist in their politics. Trinity staff had come out against the 1916 Rising, with some veterans of the Boer War shutting the gates and arming themselves to defend the college.[45] Students were enlisted to man the roof of the West Front, looking on to College Green, to pick off republican dispatch riders cycling between the GPO on O'Connell St and St Stephen's Green during the fighting. Many of the staff and students remained loyal to the British crown during the subsequent War of Independence, although the college accepted the Irish Free State when it was established in 1922.

TRINITY COLLEGE IN INDEPENDENT IRELAND

The Hall of Honour was opened on Armistice Day, 11 November 1928, and featured inscriptions in gold of all the names of the men who fell in the Great War. Armistice Day was celebrated throughout Ireland very publicly for years and on the tenth anniversary of the end of the war large crowds gathered in the Phoenix Park to mark the day. Masses and church services were held throughout Ireland. James Campbell, Lord Glenavy, the vice-chancellor of the university, officially opened the hall and commented that 'there was a growing conspiracy of silence as to the deeds' of Irish soldiers who had helped to gain 'victory at a cost in life and treasure which had brought bereavement and privation to many a home, but had enriched their history with an imperishable inspiration and example of duty and devotion'.[46] It is unfortunate that in future years the sacrifice that these men made during the Great War would be eclipsed by republican commemoration, but the War of Independence had made the two conflicts seem incompatible.

89

This was evident on Armistice day as well. Republicans marked the tenth anniversary of the end of the war with their own protest. On Sunday morning, 11 November 1928, they detonated explosives at a number of symbolic sites around the city, including the statues of King William III on College Green, King George II in St Stephen's Green and the King Edward VII memorial fountain in Herbert Park, Ballsbridge. The statue of William III by Grinling Gibbons, unveiled in 1701, had traditionally been a centrepiece for public displays of loyalty to the Protestant monarchy and establishment. It had also been a target for earlier attacks. It was said that Trinity students in particular did not like the statue, deeming it disrespectful, as the horse and rider faced up Dame Street while the horse's large backside faced the college front. It was defaced by two trinity students in 1710. A guard was sent to watch the statue but this did little to protect it. In 1806 the bronze statue was painted black on the eve of the anniversary of King William's birthday. The culprit explained to the guards that he had been sent by the corporation to paint it to prepare it for the celebrations. In March 1836 there were three attempts to blow up the statue. In April 1836 it was blown up but was pieced back together and restored.[47] On this occasion 'the hoof of the left hind leg had been blown off and a corner of the pedestal damaged'.[48] There was little appetite to restore the statue after the 1928 attack and, the government decided to remove it as the constant attempts to destroy it made it a threat to public safety.[49]

The reading room at the back of the Hall of Honour was finally opened in 1937 by Taoiseach Éamon de Valera, who had once been registered as a student in Trinity. By the 1960s the college had run out of space here too and even after the addition of the Arts Building (1966) with a library in the basement (the Lecky Library), and the the Berkeley Library, the college has had to acquire additional storage space for its books. The ground floor in the Old Library (the former collonades) remained in use for book storage until the 1990s when the space was converted into a permanent exhibition for the Book of Kells. The library was on the tourist trail for visitors to Dublin as early as the 1820s, and during the Irish Industrial Exhibition in 1853, over 18,000 people visited the Long Room.[50] King George VI and Queen Victoria both visited the Long Room and viewed the Book of

Kells. The Old Library now contains more than 500,000 books, and it receives as many visitors each year to view the Book of Kells and the Long Room.[51]

With Trinity being viewed throughout most of the twentieth century as effectively an English Protestant institution, relations between the students and the wider city were sometimes poor. The Belfast-born historian R.B. McDowell recalled nearly causing a riot by strolling through the city while wearing a poppy on Armistice Day in 1932. Poppies were often snatched from jackets by those who felt that it was a symbol that disrespected those who died in the struggle for independence. McDowell recalls that one response to this was to place a razor blade behind the poppy so that when it was snatched the assailant was wounded in the process.[52] While small numbers of Catholics continued to attend Trinity throughout the twentieth century, it was only in 1970, after years of mounting pressure, that the Catholic Church backed down and allowed Catholics to freely enter the university.

The Republic of Ireland now has seven universities (three in Dublin) and numerous third-level institutions, but Trinity has maintained a national and international reputation as the foremost university in Ireland. This is in part because of its long history and the countless number of Trinity graduates and staff who made a significant contribution in their fields of learning. Some of Ireland's brightest and best attended Trinity College, such as Ernest Walton, a college professor who shared the Nobel Prize in 1951 for splitting the atom, and Samuel Beckett, who won a Nobel Prize for literature in 1969 and who had both attended the university and lectured in French there. But University College Dublin, the largest university in Ireland, emerged in the twentieth century to produce a generation of writers, politicians, broadcasters and public figures who also shaped and influenced the country. In a bid to reduce government spending, there have been proposals to amalgamate the two institutions since the 1960s. This has been fiercely resisted by both universities. In fact it seems the competitive spirit between the two helps to drive the high standard of their education and outputs. Trinity College Dublin remains as independent as ever, quite an achievement for an institution that has survived on this turbulent island since the sixteenth century.

4

Parliament House (now Bank of Ireland)

THE COLLEGE GREEN building where a major branch of the Bank of Ireland now resides was the world's first purpose-built bicameral parliament house. It is one of the finest Georgian buildings in Ireland and marked out the man responsible for the building's design, Edward Lovett Pearce, as the finest architect in Ireland. It has been singled out for much praise; the architectural historian Christine Casey has stated that 'its scale and magnificence vividly evoke the confidence and sense of purpose of the eighteenth century parliament, while the potency and sophistication of its form establish Edward Lovett Pearce as an architect of the first rank'.[1] The building made an impact outside Ireland too. When Sir Robert Smirke was employed to design a building for the British Museum decades after Pearce's building had been completed, he borrowed heavily from the parliament house, with the result that the two buildings look quite similar. The building also inspired the Capitol Building in Washington, although a large dome was added to the top of that parliamentary structure. Dublin's parliament house was intended to make an impact. When it was opened in the first half of the eighteenth century, the ruling elite who sat in parliament were making a clear statement of their own intentions; Protestants ruled Ireland and were a permanent fixture in the political landscape. They would express their power through parliament. With these intentions clear in their mind it is surprising to think that the Irish parliament sat in the building for just sixty-nine years before it dissolved itself.

The building was vacated by parliament in 1801 after the Act of Union, combining the British and Irish parliaments at Westminster, came into effect. The Bank of Ireland purchased the building in 1804,

Masthead of *The Freeman's Journal*, featuring the parliament house on College Green

and has occupied it for over two hundred years. The building did not lose its significance though. It became an important symbol of the desire for parliamentary independence and was used as a backdrop for rallies by the nationalist movement led by Daniel O'Connell and, later, by Charles Stewart Parnell and the Home Rule movement. The building became an important element of Irish nationalist iconography. A sun rising over College Green, to represent a return of the Irish parliament, became a popular nineteenth and early twentieth-century nationalist imagary. The *Freeman's Journal*, the longest-running news-paper in Irish history, had a strong nationalist slant. It used the image of the sun rising behind College Green as its masthead, above the slogan 'Ireland a nation', so readers were regularly greeted with the building and its association with Irish independence.

PARLIAMENT IN IRELAND

Parliament did not always have its home in College Green. Some early political assemblies had met in Dublin, including the Viking assembly known as the 'Thing Moate' (see chapter one) which was a large mound adjacent to the present site of O'Neill's pub on Suffolk Street. It was not until the thirteenth century that the Anglo-Normans created a political assembly that claimed jurisdiction for the whole island when an official parliament met in Castledermot, County Kilkenny, in 1264. This Irish parliament drew its legal status from the English Magna Carta, which was extended to Ireland in 1217 under 'the great charter of Ireland'. The Irish parliament developed along the same lines as the English parliament; it had two chambers: an upper house for members of the aristocracy who inherited their seat and sat for life and a lower house for those commoners elected to parliament. In the medieval period the parliament frequently sat at Dublin Castle, and also, as we saw in chapter one, at Christ Church Cathedral. But the Irish parliament had less power than its English counterpart; until the eighteenth century the real power to govern the country was vested in the lord lieutenant and the English administration at Dublin Castle. In fact, the Irish parliament had quite a patchy record until the eighteenth century. When William III called a parliament in 1692, just four parliaments had met in the preceding century.[2] Until then parliament was not dissolved and MPs would remain elected until a king died and a new parliament was called. The only other time that an election was called was when an MP died and vacated a seat.

Parliaments may have been called intermittently, but Irish parliaments sat for a lengthy period of time each time they assembled. Nevertheless, unlike in England, central government at Dublin Castle did not need a parliament to effect changes in how the state was run. During the eighteenth century the Protestant ruling elite—or Protestant 'Ascendancy'—became increasingly focused on parliament and used it to control and run the state. But Dublin Castle maintained ·a guiding hand within parliament through 'undertakers', or MPs who 'undertook' to carry out the government's business in parliament for them. This system was very successful at first, but over the course of the eighteenth century the parliamentary system became more developed, and a 'patriot' faction seized more and more power from these undertakers. Parliament met on average every two years, 1692 and 1785, and every year from 1785.[3] When Benjamin Franklin visited Dublin in 1771, he reported that the Irish parliament 'makes a most respectable figure': high praise from one of the founding fathers of republicanism and the United States.[4]

CHICHESTER HOUSE

Parliament had usually assembled in Dublin Castle, but by the seventeenth century the castle was in poor repair and overcrowded. When parliament assembled in 1661, just after the fall of the Cromwellian regime and the restoration of the monarchy in 1660, it met in an aristocratic house in College Green called Chichester House. The building itself was originally intended as a hospital, but by the time of its completion in 1605 it was redesignated for use as law courts. As the government did not seem willing to spend money on acquiring the building, it passed to Sir Arthur Chichester. The building was described as 'a large mansion, with a gate-house, a garden, and plantation'.[5] In the Viking period this part of the city was used for burials, and it developed as a public green, Hoggen Green, just outside the city walls by the Middle Ages.[6] By the seventeenth century this city suburb (outside the walls), called College Green, was mainly populated by gentry town houses. By Chichester's arrival into the area, Trinity College was established and had served to make the district more attractive. Chichester had actually served as lord deputy of Ireland from 1604–1615 and lord high treasurer of Ireland from 1622 until his death in 1624. But he owed money to the crown when he died, and his heir sold the property to pay these debts.

The building had a curious connection with national events before it ever became parliament. The house was taken over by Sir John Borlase, a veteran soldier, who was lord justice from 1640 onwards. During the 1641 rebellion powerful Catholic families undertook co-ordinated uprisings across Ulster, usurping local sheriffs and other authorities and taking control. Their plan had been to seize Dublin Castle on 23 October 1641 which would have been a major victory. The night before the planned rebellion, Owen O'Connolly, one of the Dublin conspirators, was seized at Chichester House and drunkenly revealed the plan to those present in the house. O'Connolly was interrogated and, with more details provided on the plan, the city managed to defend itself.[7]

After the restoration, Chichester House became the temporary home for parliament, and in 1685 this arrangement was made permanent when the house was purchased by the king for use as a parliament. When the assembly convened for its first sitting after the restoration, on 8 May 1661, the whole body of MPs were Protestant except for one Catholic and one Anabaptist, a clear indication of what was in store for Catholics.[8] Anglicans had returned to power and would do everything to hold on to it. Anti-Catholic laws were passed within this house, all with the aim of 'defending' the Anglican faith and ensuring its supremacy. The laws passed undermined Catholic rights to land but also to power. In this period land 'was the key to political power, locally as well as nationally'.[9] Each time land was taken from Catholics and given to Protestants, Catholics lost more power. Charles II had promised to return lands seized by Cromwellian settlers to those Irish Catholics who could prove their innocence during the 1641 rebellion. He also promised land in Ireland to those who had supported him in exile. One politician quipped that you would need another Ireland to provide all of the land that had been promised by Charles—there just was not enough to go around. In an attempt to settle the land question, parliament passed the Acts of Settlement and Explanation, which ultimately saw many Cromwellian settlers, who had taken land from Catholics during the Cromwellian period, hold onto their land while Catholics lost out once more.

There were more anti-Catholic laws to follow. When Charles's Catholic brother James succeeded him in 1685, the Protestant elite were prepared to accept him as long as they knew that he would be succeeded in turn by his eldest Protestant daughter, Mary. James's increasingly pro-Catholic policies, followed by the birth of a son who was baptised a Catholic, meant that his reign proved intolerable to Protestants. In June 1688, a group of Protestant nobles invited Mary's husband, William of Orange, to invade England to take the throne. James fled and this 'Glorious Revolution' turned Ireland into a battleground, as Irish Catholic's supported James's claim to the throne. Once the Catholics were defeated, the Protestant victors set about ensuring that those who rebelled were punished by dispossession of their lands. Forfeited Catholic lands were sold off wholesale in the 1690s by parliament. This had a huge impact on the extent of Catholic landowning and it led to a huge reduction in Catholic power. It has been estimated that Catholic land ownership, which had been approximately 70 per cent in 1641, was reduced to just 14 per cent in the aftermath of these land confiscations.[10]

THE PENAL LAWS

The Protestant victors went one step further; in order to protect the Anglican faith, and Anglicans themselves, a series of laws were enacted between the 1690s and 1730s, which became known as the 'penal laws'. These laws protected the place of Anglicans in Irish life by limiting the rights of Catholics, Presbyterians and 'Dissenters' (those Protestants who did not accept the canon of Anglican beliefs). While it is difficult to estimate accurately the size and make-up of the population at this time, Catholics made up approximately three-quarters of the population, with Anglicans, Presbyterians and other Protestants making up the remaining quarter.[11] Being a minority of the population, Protestants were insecure.

There were four 'types' of penal law. The first type of legislation enacted was military, aimed at disarming the large number of Catholics who had taken up arms for James II. These laws were intended to ensure that Catholics would not re-emerge to pose a military threat again, and so they stayed in force for most of the eighteenth century. From 1695 Catholics were prohibited from owning weapons, or owning a horse worth more than £5 (a horse of this value was a military-standard horse). The second type of law related to religious practice. These laws had initially banned the Catholic faith, hoping to turn people to the new religion. They had then imposed financial and other penalties on those who had refused to adhere to the new Anglican faith. Suspicion of Catholicism had later led to the passing of laws intended to diminish the status Catholics in public life. The anti-Catholic laws enacted in the aftermath of the Glorious Revolution were the most comprehensive and systematic to date. In 1697 the Bishops Banishment Act stated that all members of the Catholic Church hierarchy discovered on the island would be banished. In 1704 an act was passed to register Catholic priests, which allowed the government to monitor those clergy returning from the European continent and their movements around the country. This effectively allowed priests to carry out their regular duties but under surveillance. Catholic schools were prohibited, and Catholics could not become schoolmasters.[12] Catholics were also banned from intermarriage with Protestants. The third type of law was economic, and was 'aimed at the destruction of the Catholic landowning classes'.[13] Catholics could not buy land, could not own leases for more than thirty-three years, and, when a Catholic died his land had to be subdivided between each of his sons. This last act was aimed at breaking up large parcels of land to further weaken Catholic land-holding. By 1776, Catholics in Ireland, still about three-quarters of the population, owned approximately five per cent of the land.[14] The final type of law was political, prohibiting Catholics from any say in the politics of the country. The historian Ian McBride has observed that 'while restrictions on landholding and religious worship could sometimes be evaded, the exclusion of Catholics from the public world of Irish politics was complete'.[15] In 1728 Catholics were excluded from parliament because they could not take the oath which stated the king was head of the church. Their exclusion from the political arena of the country was complete.

On the whole, there is little within these laws to suggest that the new 'Protestant Ascendancy' were interested in converting the Catholic population. The laws were reactionary. There had been two large and sustained rebellions in Ireland in the previous fifty years, and, as the minority of the population Protestants sought to weaken the Catholic position while enhancing their own. Just 5,500 Catholics converted between 1704 and 1798; a very low number considering conversion had to take place if a Catholic and Protestant were to marry.[16] It must be added that Catholics were not the only losers in the aftermath of the Glorious Revolution. These 'penal' laws were intended to protect the Anglican faith. While many religious dissenting groups such as Presbyterians had fought alongside William of Orange to uphold Protestantism, they too would be persecuted in this new 'Anglican' Ireland. Any Protestant who did not subscribe to Anglicanism, such as Presbyterians or Quakers, were effectively blocked from public life. Under the Test Act of 1707, dissenters were required to take an oath that was unacceptable to their religious beliefs.

The political philosopher, English MP and native of Ireland, Edmund Burke, said that the penal laws were 'well fitted for the oppression, impoverishment and degradation' of Catholics.[17] These laws were in place throughout the eighteenth century, and, while they were dismantled in a slow and piecemeal fashion from the 1770s onwards, they would not be fully repealed until the Catholic Emancipation Act of 1829. In eighteenth-century Ireland power was contained in Protestant hands. The great irony is that, although these laws were exceptionally severe, Catholics remained peaceful throughout the period and only a relatively small number became involved in the rebellion of 1798, the leadership of which was overwhelmingly Protestant.

BUILDING A PARLIAMENT HOUSE

By the early eighteenth century Chichester House was in poor condition. In 1709 the house had undergone extensive and expensive repairs to fix some of its many problems. The banqueting hall had collapsed, the floors throughout the house were uneven and there were holes in the ceiling. The repairs, however, only slowed the process of decay.[18] In 1723 a parliamentary committee sat to assess the condition of the house, but progress was not made until 1727, when the house was in such a bad condition that 'the outer walls of Chichester House overhung dangerously in several places ... the rafters were so decayed ... but for timely repairs the roof must have fallen in'.[19] In 1728 parliament voted in favour of an initial subsidy of £6,000 to build a new house. Thomas Burgh, the surveyor-general, or chief engineer to the army, was employed to design a new building on the same site. The old house was demolished in December 1728. The foundation stone of the new building was laid on 3 February 1729, with a silver plate bearing the names of the lords justices as well as silver coins inscribed with the names of George I and George II being buried in the foundation.[20]

Between 1728 and 1729 Sir Edward Lovett Pearce took over the design of the building.[21] The architectural historian Edward McParland says 'it is not clear how Pearce superseded Burgh. Burgh, as surveyor-general, was the obvious choice as architect'. Pearse was 'less experienced' but 'better informed of current fashions'. He had also undertaken work in the 1720s for William Conolly, speaker of the Irish House of Commons and arguably the most influential politician of the period, on his country estate of Castletown in Co Kildare.[22] This political patronage may have gained him the job. Nevertheless, the change of architect is curious, and rumours circulated after the event that Pearce had stolen the designs for the building from his architectural rival Richard Castle. Castle designed Leinster House (built between 1745 and 1748) and was a popular architect well into the 1740s. Pearce had died by the time these rumours appeared in print, and so could not defend himself, but they continued to resurface from time to time. Rumours about Pearce circulated for other reasons too. He had a reputation as 'an energetic adulterer', and apparently had an affair with 'the sexual contortionist Lady Allen'.[23]

When a parliamentary committee surveyed the progress in November 1729 they were very happy and reported that the building displayed 'an uncommon beauty, order, and contrivance', and that the work was 'carried on with unusual expedition and diligence'. The committee added that money for the project was 'laid out with the greatest frugality, and the accounts thereof kept in a most regular and orderly manner'.[24] This is not strictly true: the building ran over budget. By 1735 the total spent on the building, including the money paid to Burgh, was £28,471. The work was completed in 1739, with an additional £5,461 being spent. While parliament was very happy with his work, Pearce had not lived to see it completed. He died in 1733. His successor as surveyor general, Arthur Dobbs, oversaw the remainder of the project.[25] McParland praises Pearce's talent, saying 'nothing in the earlier architecture of Ireland … made the advent of Edward Lovett Pearce predictable … By the time of his death he had designed, and built, in the parliament house one of the finest buildings of the time in Europe'.[26] The building was recognised as one of the finest in Dublin, even though the city had seen important contributions to its public architecture throughout the eighteenth century. The English painter Thomas Malton, who specialised in architectural views, said that the parliament house is 'the noblest structure Dublin has to boast; and it is no hyperbole to advance, that this edifice, in the entire, is the grandest, most convenient and most extensive of the kind in Europe … It derives all its beauty from a simple impulse of fine art; and is one of the few instances of form only expressing true symmetry'.[27] Many commentators were struck by the beauty of both the Parliament House and the west front of Trinity College (completed in 1759), and the overall effect these had on College Green. Malton added that 'the contiguity of two such structures give a grandeur of scene that would do honour to the first city of Europe'.[28]

The building had two chambers, for the House of Commons and the House of Lords, with a number of offices for administration, committee meetings and dining surrounding these two central structures. One of the radical aspects of Pearce's design was to place the House of Commons chamber at the centre of the building and to locate the House of Lords behind it. The House of Commons would thus become the centre of political life, whereas the House of Lords had previously taken precedence. Pearce was placing the commons, as voted by 'the people' (Protestant male freeholders), at the heart of Irish politics. Some alterations were made to the original building during its life as a parliament. In 1785 extensions were made to the House of Lords, according to designs by James Gandon, the architect of the new Custom House and Four Courts. These alterations saw new committee rooms and offices being added as well as a grand new entrance on Westmoreland Street. Not to be outdone, the House of

Commons too sought enlargement. In 1787 Robert Parke undertook additions to the House of Commons and additional offices, an enlarged hallway and an enlarged facade at Foster Place.[29] A fire devastated the commons chamber in 1792, which was largely rebuilt as a result. We have a description of the chamber of the House of Commons from Malton, who viewed it before the fire:

> The commons-room is truly deserving of admiration. Its form is circular, 55 feet in diameter, inscribed in a square. The seats whereon the members sit are disposed around the centre of the room in concentric circles, one rising above another. About 15 feet above the level of the floor, on a cylindrical basement, are disposed 16 Corinthian columns supporting a rich hemispherical dome, which crowns the whole.[30]

The chamber included an upstairs public gallery behind the speakers' chair upstairs, which ran in a half moon around the chamber and allowed members of the public (men and women) access at the invitation of an MP. Students of Trinity College were allowed access to the gallery as of right as it was believed it would assist their education.

The gallery made an impression on Malton, who recalled that 'the appearance of the House assembled below from the Gallery corresponds with its importance, and presents a dignity that must be seen to be felt; the strength of the orators' eloquence received additional force from the construction of the place, and the vibration in the dome'.[31] While the MP Jonah Barrington claimed in his memoirs that the gallery could seat up to 700 people, this figure has been contested.[32] In his *Ireland Sixty Years Ago*, John Edward Walsh complained that 'the greater number who were admitted were squeezed together behind the high partition between it and the wall, where they could neither hear nor see'.[33] In Francis Wheatley's portrait of the Irish House of Commons, painted in 1780, the people in the gallery do not look particularly uncomfortable but neither does the gallery look like it could facilitate seven hundred people. As the gallery no longer exists we can only speculate. It was significant in that it allowed the public to view the law-making process in Ireland. Michael McDonagh believed that the gallery 'was six or seven times

Francis Wheatley's 'House of Commons', 1780

as large as the gallery in the contemporary House of Commons at Westminster ... No place for strangers was specially provided in the English House of Commons'.[34] When Benjamin Franklin sat in the gallery of the Dublin parliament, he was the first American on record to do so, and this required a special invitation from the speaker, which was supported with 'ayes' from the floor.[35]

The chamber of the House of Lords was described 'a noble apartment ... 40 feet long by 30 feet wide, in addition to which, at the upper end, is a circular recess 13 feet deep, like a large niche, wherein the throne is placed, under a rich canopy of crimson velvet; and at the lower end is the bar, 20 feet square'.[36] Another remarkable feature of the room are two large tapestries commissioned by parliament, and which were manufactured by Robert Baillie, of Dublin. The tapestries depict the Siege of Derry (1689) and the Battle of the Boyne (1690), and are still on display today. These battles were two of the most

Robert Baillie's tapestry depicting the Siege of Derry

significant Catholic defeats during the Glorious Revolution. The tapestries are large, running almost half the length of the chamber, and hanging opposite each other, making a clear statement. The depiction of James II outside Derry shows a great Catholic loss, while the strong image of William at the Battle of the Boyne shows a great Protestant victory. Protestant power and dominance, as well as the landholding of those Protestant peers who sat in the chamber of the House of Lords, depended on the Catholic losses of the previous century. The tapestries reminded those sitting in the lords where their right to rule came from.

Originally the parliament had sought six tapestries, which would have also included depictions of William's landing, his entry to Dublin, the battle of Aughrim and the earl of Marlborough's victories at Cork and Kinsale. The project went over budget, and the parliament received just two. Nevertheless, the government proceeded to pay the full cost originally cited for all six, as well as awarding Bailie an annuity of £200.[37]

THE PARLIAMENTARY SYSTEM IN EIGHTEENTH CENTURY IRELAND

As Ireland's parliament met less frequently than the English parliament, it had not attained the same level of sophistication. Administration at Dublin Castle, managed by a lord lieutenant or Irish privy council, had been the traditional method of governing Ireland, and parliament had often been sidetracked. One of the main reasons for calling parliament had been to provide the king with financial aid, in the form of money bills. While there had been a pressing need for these bills in the seventeenth century, the monarchy had survived through extrajudicial—sometimes illegal—methods of taxation. Under Poyning's Law of 1495, the Irish parliament could not initiate bills; it could only amend those introduced into parliament by the lord lieutenant, which then had to be approved again by the English government (at privy council meetings in London) before passing into law. The act severely restricted parliamentary activities. However, the Irish parliament had developed a system whereby it would negotiate for a bill it sought in return for voting in favour of a money bill to the crown. In order to ensure that the government business in parliament was done effectively, the lord lieutenant used an undertaker to gain enough votes to pass money bills and ensure that no radical amendments were made to government bills. The historian Thomas Bartlett says that 'undertakers' were 'Irish politicians with influence who would undertake to get the king's business through the Irish House of Commons in return for a large measure of control of government patronage'.[38] They were granted power to disburse jobs to supporters in order to gain their votes.

MPs were not paid to sit in parliament, and they were expected to be gentlemen with their own income. As there had been no electoral reform of boroughs in the Irish parliament, a system had developed whereby some of the original parliamentary seats belonged to boroughs with few or no inhabitants. This meant these seats were controlled by the landowner. Some landowners owned several seats and they sold these parliamentary seats to the highest bidder. Being a member of parliament was desirable for Irish gentlemen, or even members of the bar, who sought power, a say in the running of the country and often a way of making money. Some of the finest MPs in both parliaments, including Henry Grattan and Edmund Burke, held 'rotten borough' (purchased) seats. Once a seat was purchased— and seats could be sold for as high as £30,000—many occupants set about re-couping their losses. They sold their votes in parliament, exercised their influence and assisted other interests for financial gain. While this seems hugely corrupt, it was the established method of getting business done in both the Irish and British parliaments in the eighteenth century.

ELECTIONS IN EIGHTEENTH-CENTURY DUBLIN

The most open and fair elections tended to take place in cities, where 'freemen' or tradesmen who belonged to guilds were allowed to vote in local elections. Elections like these were hotly contested and always lively, and show that ordinary citizens had a good grasp of the political system and how they could influence it with their votes. One of the liveliest Dublin elections was in 1749 when the Dublin barber-surgeon Charles Lucas ran for office.[39] He established his radical newspaper *The Censor* and, with popular support on the streets, he looked set to win. But Lucas was too radical for parliament, and frightened both the city council and Irish parliament. Days before the election took place he was accused of sedition for some of the claims he made in *The Censor*. He fled the country but was granted a royal pardon, returned in 1760 and was finally elected to parliament. Through parliament he assisted in reforming the corporation, and his statue now stands in City Hall.

While only a small minority of Dubliners voted in general elections (approximately three thousand at mid-century), the population of Dublin at large were protective of the rights of the parliament.[40] When rumours circulated in 1759 of an Act of Union being passed to combine the British and Irish parliaments (an Act of Union had been passed in 1707 between England and Scotland) riots broke out on the streets. MPs on their way to the parliament house were dragged out of their coaches and made to swear oaths that they would not support such an act. The mob invaded the parliament house, and, 'as a practical satire on the political imbecility of the peers, they placed an old woman on the throne in the House of Lords'.[41] The army was brought out to stop the rioters, a sign of the danger which this mob posed, and although they were warned not to fire on the crowd, rioters were cut down, with fifteen or sixteen killed. The next day MPs, shocked at what had occurred at College Green the previous day, passed a resolution against assaulting or insulting members of the house of parliament, and declared such actions a crime.[42] The Dublin populace was not deterred from protesting outside parliament, expressing its opinions and bringing pressure to bear on MPs. In 1768 an octiennial bill was passed which ensured that a general election would have to be called every eight years, rather than just once in the life of a monarch, and this allowed the population of a metropolis like Dublin to have more of a say in the election of the commons.

Just like today, candidates campaigned for votes, making speeches at rallies and visiting the electorate. So many people crowded into the hall of the printers guild on Fishamble Street to hear an election debate in 1782 that a bad accident occurred.[43] *Saunder's Newsletter* reported that as the crowds stood in the upstairs hall listening to the speeches, 'the floor gave way and they all went through except a few who were in the windows. A great number of people had their legs and arms broken and several received great contusions by the fall which was not less than 14 feet'.[44] While no one died, the press reported that many suffered severe injuries and *The Freeman's Journal* reported that over fifty people suffered fractures.[45] *Saunder's News-Letter* stated that 'Mr. Hartley and Alderman Warren, the candidates, received some bruises and Sir Edward Newenham had his collar bone broke'.[46] Election debates were held throughout the city, and these were entertaining spectacles. Many people showed up to hear the speeches. Although they could not vote, Catholics in the city had ready access to newspapers and pamphlets. Literate Catholics would certainly have read about such debates in the city newspapers, while electoral debates in guild halls, music halls and coffee houses would have allowed many of those who could not vote, including Catholics and women, to listen to the issues of the day.

THE 'PATRIOTS' AND LANDMARK LEGISLATION

By the second half of the eighteenth century a 'patriot' faction or party had come together in the Irish parliament that sought greater autonomy for Ireland from Britain. It had two main points of contention. The first related to trade, and the second to the constitution. The faction argued that the English government had hampered Irish commerce by using its powers to prohibit the export of Irish cattle in the 1660s, and later to prohibit the export of Irish wool and woollen produce in the 1690s. Many political agitators had argued against these laws. Jonathan Swift had famously remarked that we should 'burn everything English except their coal'. The second concern was that, because of Poyning's Law, the English government could intervene in the Irish parliament and pass further damaging laws. These patriots sought free trade and a legislature that was independent of English interference. During the American War of Independence (1776–83), an embargo was placed on British trade with America. This had serious repercussions in Ireland, as it shut down access to an important trading partner for Irish linen in particular. Linen was one of Ireland's biggest exports in the eighteenth century, and a large number of linen workers, from weavers, to bleachers, worked and resided in the Liberties. The embargo put thousands of Dublin workers out of work and put more jobs at risk. With no welfare state to protect them, many were forced to turn to charitable networks that were not sophisticated enough to support a large number for even short periods of unemployment.

In October 1779 the Irish House of Commons, supported by the Volunteers, an armed militia strongly linked with the patriots, and led by the duke of Leinster, presented the lord lieutenant with a petition for free trade to allow the Irish parliament to decide on her own trading partners, but the British government was not yet prepared to listen. On 15 November about 8,000 Dublin weavers armed with swords and pistols protested outside parliament. Their cry was 'Free trade! The rights of Ireland!' MPs were stopped and forced to take oaths that they would seek a free trade bill. The army was brought out to disperse them, but the lord mayor worried that fatalities would cause the situation to worsen, and several popular members of parliament managed to disperse the crowds. The force of popular opinion was felt and the next day the majority of the MPs voted in favour of a short money bill of only six months duration which would in turn place pressure on the government. Worried that this trade crisis would lead to open rebellion as it had done in America, the government capitulated and 'free trade' was passed through the Irish parliament.[47] The patriot movement had been stirred and would not stop there. On 19 April 1780 a Dublin MP, Henry Grattan, marked himself out as one of the leaders of the patriots when he addressed parliament calling for legislative independence to be passed. He asked the MPs 'are you … afraid to say that you are a free people? Are you—the greatest House of Commons that ever sat in Ireland, that want but this one Act to equal that English House of Commons that passed the Petition of Right—are you afraid to tell that British Parliament you are a free people?'[48] He concluded with the following: 'I wish for nothing but to breathe, in this our island, in common with my fellow-subjects, the air of liberty. I have no ambition, unless it be to break your chain'.[49] Speeches such as this marked Grattan out as the finest orator of his generation. It would take two more years to rally the majority of MPs behind legislative independence.

In 1778, worried about the defence of Ireland, the government allowed for the formation of volunteer regiments. The Volunteers were a popular movement, and 40,000 men joined various units across the country.[50] Many of these were led by patriot politicians who supported legislative independence. With such a large paramilitary backing, the patriots were emboldened. As late as February 1782 the parliament rejected Grattan's proposed bills for legislative independence, but, with pressure mounting from the Volunteers outside who were increasing their calls for a free Irish parliament, the bill was passed in April 1782.[51] Grattan made one of his finest speeches up to that point, declaiming that 'there is no body of men competent to make laws to bind this nation except the king, lords, and commons of Ireland, not any other parliament which hath any authority or power whatsoever, save only the parliament of Ireland'.[52] The news was declared at the door of parliament where people were waiting and 'a cry of joy and of exultation spread with electric rapidity through the entire city—its echo penetrated to the very interior of the House'.[53]

CATHOLIC RELIEF AND THE UNITED IRISHMEN

This constitutional revolution was followed up by a radical change in the social and economic position of Catholics. Catholics had not been excluded from all professions: they were permitted to work in the medical profession, as well as being merchants and traders. Although Catholics were in the minority within these occupations, they were vocal in calling for greater relief and equality. Catholic leaders had formed the Catholic Committee (a new lobbying group for Catholic rights), and pointed to the peace that had prevailed in the eighteenth century to show that Catholics could be trusted. In 1772 the prohibition on Catholic landowning was relaxed when they were given the right to hold fifty acres under a leasehold of sixty-one years. This may seem like meagre relief, but it was a start. In 1774 an oath of allegiance was formulated for Catholics which allowed them to show their loyalty to the Protestant King George without offending their own beliefs. In 1782 those Catholics who took the oath could open schools, purchase lands outright or hold leases for nine hundred and ninety-nine years. The act also released members of the Catholic clergy from the earlier restrictive acts. This marked a shift for Catholics and contemporaries recognised that it would go a long way to put them on an equal footing with Protestants. While there was undoubted good will towards Catholics, particularly on the part of Grattan and many of the patriots, the relief bills alarmed many other Protestants who saw it undermining their position. A new term was coined—'Protestant Ascendancy'—which was used repeatedly in parliament by Protestants fearful that Catholics were encroaching on their power. This term meant a Protestant parliament, voted for by a Protestant electorate who were loyal to a Protestant king. The term spread through the city and country and became a banner with which to terrify and rally Protestants. The Dublin Corporation issued loyal addresses to the king to uphold the Protestant Ascendancy of Ireland and were copied by many other cities reflecting 'endemic Protestant anxiety'.[54] One more relief act was passed before a landslide of Protestant opinion halted this progress. In 1793 Catholics were given a right to vote, although not to sit in parliament, on the same basis as Protestants (with a property qualification). They could also join guilds and municipal government which meant they could become freemen, and subsequently vote in city elections. But this was too much for some Protestants who feared that Catholics would undermine the state that they had created in the aftermath of the Williamite Wars.

If this Catholic relief was too much for some Protestants it was too little for others. In October 1791 a republican group calling themselves the Society of United Irishmen was formed in Belfast by a group of radical Presbyterians and radical Anglicans. A Dublin branch of the United Irishmen was formed in the Eagle Tavern in Eustace Street, several doors up from the Eustace Street Presbyterian congregation (now the Ark Children's museum) in Temple Bar.[55] Theobald Wolfe Tone, an Anglican lawyer from Dublin and an outspoken advocate of equal rights for Catholics, became the most famous leader of this organisation. He later summarised the aims of the society: 'To subvert the tyranny of our execrable government, to break the connection with England, the never-failing source of all our political evils and to assert the independence of our country'. He aimed to 'abolish all the past memories of dissensions', and to 'substitute the common name of Irishman in place of the denominations of Protestant, Catholic and Dissenter'. His noble aims were largely inspired by Thomas Paine's pamphlet *The Rights of Man*, as well as by the French revolution.[56] By the 1790s several hundred thousand men had joined the United Irishmen, and in May 1798 the country was plunged into an ill-fated rebellion.[57] Thanks to the work of informers, much of the leadership had been rounded up some days before the rebellion broke out and the risings across the country were uncoordinated, and lacked decisive leadership.[58] When Tone himself landed on the west coast of Ireland with a French fleet of 3,000 men in October 1798 it was too late. British troops had been poured into the country and were waiting for the French when they landed. The rebellion proved a disaster, not least because of the horrendous atrocities which were carried out in quashing it, and while disarming rebels and suspected rebels. While the rebellion's leadership was Protestant, many of the rank and file were Catholic, with a number of Presbyterians becoming involved in Ulster. Catholics were seen as the main participants in the rebellion and this whipped up a frenzy of anti-Catholic sectarianism. The rebellion was badly coordinated because of the arrest of its leaders, but 1798 was the closest that any Irish force would come to overthrowing the British government for the next 120 years. The republican aims of the United Irishmen were not forgotten, and the spectacular failure was celebrated by later Irish nationalists for the sheer scale of its ambitions.

The aftermath of the 1798 rebellion

If conservative Protestants were alarmed by the progress of Catholic relief, they were terrified by how near the United Irish rebellion had come to succeeding. The British government, at war with France, was equally terrified. The Glorious Revolution, only a hundred years earlier, had seen a French army land in Ireland with the Catholic King James II and they saw this as history repeating itself. Determined to deal with the Irish problem, William Pitt, the British Prime Minister, proposed an Act of Union between Britain and Ireland.[59] He felt that Ireland could be more effectively governed from London, and that the only way to make Ireland peaceful was through the introduction of full Catholic emancipation. Pitt, an astute politician, realised that 1798 had terrified many Irish moderates into conservatism and had whipped up fear of Catholics. He felt that Catholics would never be granted equality in a Protestant Irish parliament. In January 1799 the Act of Union was introduced into the Irish parliament and it was rejected by a narrow majority of 106 votes to 105. But this early union proposal had suggested that just one MP per county be returned to Westminster when the Irish House was dissolved.[60] This was hugely unpopular. The British government would not be so easily defeated, however, and another Act of Union was proposed in 1800. The city of Dublin came out against the bill arguing that it would lead to a decline in business and trade. The legal community also objected.

While opposition to the Act of Union was led by some of the greatest orators and political personalities of the day, including Henry Grattan (who had argued so effectively for legislative independence), John Ponsonby and John Foster, the anti-union faction was not as unified as the pro-unionists. Those in favour of the union also had more money to spend on publicity, newspapers, dinners, favours and pensions as well as simple vote buying. Patrick M. Geoghegan has shown that money flooded into Dublin for the government to spend on influencing votes, and this 'provided a means for government to keep its supporters happy'.[61] While we see this purchasing of votes as highly corrupt, this system had been used by the government throughout the history of the Irish parliament as a way of ensuring they got what they sought. Nevertheless, the money and patronage dispensed to pass the Act of Union was significant. Geoghegan notes that while 'patronage provided a legal way for government to reward supporters ... promises made [in 1800] were considerable, even by the standards of the day'.[62] In March 1800 the Act of Union was passed through the parliament, the same bill was passed through the British parliament in July, and the bill came into affect on 1 January 1801. Instead of 300 Irish MPs sitting in College Green, just 100 would now sit at Westminster with 32 Irish peers. Dublin was no longer a parliamentary capital and the focus of Irish politics moved across the water to London. Ironically, perhaps the biggest losers in the Act of Union were Catholics. William Pitt had used Catholic emancipation as a way of enticing Catholics to support the Act of Union. He discovered, too late, that George III would not budge on this issue, and he refused to sign any bill that granted full rights to Catholics. The king argued that it compromised his coronation oath which made him head of the Anglican faith. William Pitt, feeling that he had sold Catholics a lie, resigned. But all was not lost for Catholics, some of whom could still vote and buy land, two important routes to power.

BANK OF IRELAND

In the aftermath of the Union many proposals were put forward for the future of Pearce's gigantic and now empty building. It was not closed immediately. It had regularly been used to hold art exhibitions when parliament was not in session and this practice continued after 1801. The building was used as a barracks during Robert Emmet's rebellion in 1803. While the rebellion was short-lived, it was long enough for the regiment stationed in the Parliament House to damage the fabric of the premises. A fire broke out 'seriously injuring some columns in the south portico'.[63] Thomas Elrington suggested that the vacant building should be gifted to Trinity to be used as lecture halls and that a tunnel under College Green between the main building and campus could be dug to connect them. It was believed that if the college held the site it would allow easy access to the premises, and riots might occur in the halls.[64] This suggestion was disregarded when the Bank of Ireland (founded in 1783) took an interest in purchasing the building. They acquired it in 1803 for £40,000, the original cost of construction, but there were conditions to the sale. There was a real fear that the building would retain its connection with the old institution of parliament, and that it would become the focus of political protests or riots. The government stipulated in the articles of sale 'that the two chambers of parliament shall be effectually converted to such uses as shall preclude their being again used upon any contingency as public debating rooms'.[65] The bank invited proposals for the external and internal alteration and while many proposed the division of the chambers into offices thankfully this was not carried out. Francis Johnston won the contract and was appointed on 30 May 1803.[66] The chamber of the House of Commons was dramatically altered and the gallery was taken down. A fire in the chamber in 1792 had necessitated alterations so it was not in its original state anyway. The banking hall now inhabits the space where the House of Commons chamber once was and can be visited during banking hours. The chamber of the House of Lords was in its original condition, and thankfully the bank overrode the government stipulation and preserved it. It too can be visited and viewed by the public. The bank itself proposed bricking up the windows and creating porticos for statues. This was seen as a security measure, although Dublin wits suggested that the windows were bricked up to allow the building go into full mourning for parliament. Some other minor alterations were made to the entrance to the lords' chamber. In 1806 the bank occupied some of the site, but the redevelopment work was completed in 1808 and the building became fully occupied. Items from the building's parliamentary past are scattered throughout the city. Benches from the commons can be seen today at St Patrick's Hospital, the Royal Irish Academy and the City Assembly house. The commons' chandelier now hangs in Trinity College, and fitted bookcases from the library can be found in Trinity College and Leinster House.[67]

It is a sign of Dublin's loss of power and prestige in the aftermath of the Act of Union that the fight for Catholic emancipation did not centre on the capital, but on an election in County Clare. That said, Daniel O'Connell, the leader of the Catholic emancipation movement, recognised the importance of the capital. He was lord mayor of the city in 1841 and staged many meetings in Dublin when he later sought to repeal the Act of Union. During his repeal campaign he used the Parliament House, now the Bank of Ireland, to highlight the loss of an 'independent' parliament. When O'Connell was released from prison in 1844 (he was imprisoned for his role in the repeal campaign) he was paraded through the streets of Dublin on 'a triumphal chariot, consisting of three platforms, rising one above the other, gorgeous in purple velvet and gold fringe, and drawn by six splendid dapple greys' and followed by up to 20,000 men. This was a sure reminder to the government of his power and if they needed a reminder of his intentions to overturn the act of union they received a very clear one. The procession halted at College Green, outside the old parliament house where 'O'Connell removing his cap, pointed with his finger to the noble edifice', and stated that 'he hoped to re-animate with the soul of national life; and, turning slowly around, gazed silently into the faces of the people'. Michael McDonagh described the event as 'a dramatic episode—that silent gesture, eloquent of the national hopes and aspirations' was greeted by 'thunderous cheers'.[68]

Parliament did not return to College Green when independence was won in the 1920s. The bank were not prepared to give up their grand headquarters and so nationalists who viewed the building as symbolically important were denied the opportunity to see the parliamentary sun rise over College Green once more. While nationalists looked to the College Green building as the site of the passing of important legislation, such as the 'legislative independence' of Henry Grattan, they often neglected to mention that it was also where the Penal Laws were passed. As one of the most divisive sets of laws passed in Ireland, they were traditionally seen as a benchmark of oppression. The new parliament took up residence in Leinster House on Kildare Street and Merrion Square. The building, once the residence of the Duke of Leinster and subsequently owned by the Royal Dublin Society, is nestled between the National Museum and the National Library, allowing Ireland's modern parliament to take its place between two venerable cultural institutions.

5

Dublin City Hall

THE ROYAL EXCHANGE, now City Hall, was built by city merchants in the eighteenth century and is a reminder of the wealth of Dublin City at that period. The Georgian period was a golden era for Dublin, and this is evident in its remarkable architectural legacy. The story of City Hall is the story of the rapid expansion that came about in the eighteenth century as a result of this economic growth. The building of Dublin City Hall, originally as the Royal Exchange, and the Custom House illustrate this. The positions of the two buildings, one to the west of the city and one to the east, were determined by political wrangling. Two powerful groups in the city, the merchants and the property developers, tried to influence where the heart of the city would lie. Both groups had a lot at stake financially. By the late seventeenth century the medieval core of the city around Christ Church Cathedral and Dublin Castle had burst its seams, and significant building was taking place outside the old city walls. The core of the city was moving eastwards, away from the old medieval city in the west, towards College Green, Trinity College and St Stephen's Green in the east and south, and it would continue to do so.

PROPERTY DEVELOPERS IN EIGHTEENTH-CENTURY DUBLIN

Urban development in the seventeenth century was driven in large part by Dublin Corporation. To raise revenue and to develop the city for business, the corporation decided to lease out land not being used for 'pleasure or profit' for ninety-nine years at a time. As the largest landowner in the city it seemed like an obvious way for the corporation to generate income and to enhance the look of the city by imposing some regularity upon it.[1] Dublin Corporation's first initiative, and one that would set the standard for future development, was St Stephen's Green. The green was a commons on the south eastern edge of the city which was used by city dwellers to graze animals. In the 1660s the corporation divided up plots of land around a large central square which was to form a new city park and rented them out. The idea was that each person who leased a plot built a house on it; the corporation regulated their aesthetic qualities, and the building materials used. Instructions were detailed and specified the thickness of walls, the number of floors and where to source bricks. The corporation itself developed the garden. It spent as little as possible laying out the square, but managed to control the appearance and to increase its yearly rental income.[2] In 1756, when John Rocque published his map of Dublin, the area around St Stephen's green was even more built-up, showing the level of building that had occurred in the previous 40 years. By the opening of the nineteenth century, Merrion Square, Fitzwilliam Square and Baggot Street had developed to the east corner of the square, placing St Stephen's Green closer to the city core. Today the green is at the heart of the city, but the gardens were given an extensive facelift in the late nineteenth century, so they no longer reflect the original look of the square. It took some time for all of the houses to be built, but the square eventually became a fashionable place of residence.

St Stephen's Green set the standard for residential development in the eighteenth century. A small number of wealthy and influential property developers emerged in eighteenth-century Dublin who had considerable influence on the growth of the city. The development of the city escalated in the second half of the century, and the manner of this development took the form of squares and streets with regulated red-brick buildings. The uniformity and high standard of construction created an impressive Georgian core. As the leases were usually for nineth-nine years, the buildings were only to stand for this duration and yet, more than 200 years later, they are central to Dublin's domestic architectural heritage.

The Gardiner Family

Perhaps the most famous property developers of the eighteenth century were the Gardiner family. The Gardiners were wealthy, powerful and highly respected, with estates throughout the city and a seat in parliament. This dynasty—Luke Gardiner the elder, his son Charles Gardiner and and grandson Luke, Viscount Mountjoy—stamped their mark on the city through the layout of streets, estates and squares on their property. They also pushed the boundaries of the city to the north and east. Luke Gardiner the elder was a banker who acquired a large tract of land to the northeast of the city and began to develop it. Some of the streets the family developed include Gardiner Street, Rutland Square, Cavendish Row, Mountjoy Square and Sackville Street (later O'Connell Street) but there is a broad arc of land which was developed by the first generations of Gardiners which runs from O'Connell Street to Mountjoy Square and as far as the Royal Canal.[3]

The Gardiners were not the only developers of this kind. Francis Aungier built Aungier Street and Longford Street; Humphrey Jervis built Jervis Street, Mary Street and Capel Street; and the Moore family, earls of Drogheda, built Henry Street, Moore Street, Earl Street, Off Lane and Drogheda Street. The Fitzwilliam family were also heavily involved in late eighteenth and early nineteenth-century development, being responsible for Fitzwilliam Square, Baggot Street and Merrion Square, which became the most prestigious address in nineteenth century Dublin (the duke of Wellington, Oscar Wilde and Daniel O'Connell all resided on the square).[4] Today it is home to the National Gallery, the Natural History Museum, the Department of An Taoiseach and the Dáil. As well as these government organisations, the square is home to a number of cultural and heritage institutions including the Irish Georgian Society, the Irish Architectural Archive, the Irish Traditional Music Archive, 29 Merrion Square (where the domestic life of a Georgian house is recreated), the Royal Society of Antiquaries Ireland and the Central Catholic Library.[5] The Fitzwilliam and Gardiner estates were responsible for radically altering the residential landscape of eighteenth century Dublin and the families' legacies survive in the city today.

THE WIDE STREETS COMMISSION

As a result of poor planning, the seventeenth century city lacked many amenities such as bridges, roads and water supply, that would enable new growth. The medieval core remained a busy quarter for trade, and merchants' offices and warehouses were located around the old Custom House or in the Liberties, both in the west of the city.[6] This presented problems on the narrow medieval streets. The struggle to deal with traffic culminated in the creation of the Wide Streets Commission by an act of parliament in 1757. The commission was active in the city until 1851, and was responsible for many of the wide thoroughfares in the city centre. The commission was unique in Europe at this time. It was intended as a radical solution to the problem of city congestion, and was given powers to choose the location and design of the new streets, to purchase these areas and to carry out demolition and building. The commission did, however, have to consult with parliament on the re-development of any area that had not been legislated for, so its actions were watched.[7]

In its early years the main remit of the commission was to improve communications around the city, between the castle and the Viceregal Lodge in the Phoenix Park, and the parliament. It also sought to provide approaches to streets that would ease traffic at key city junctions. The commission's first project was Parliament Street, which was begun in 1762. It connected Dublin Castle directly to Essex Bridge. Parliament Street was considered a great success and a result submissions soon came from the inhabitants of Dame Street. In 1778 the street was widened and lengthened, creating one large axis that would reach from Trinity College to Christ Church Cathedral to make the parliament, the castle and the new Royal Exchange easily accessible. Soon afterwards Sackville Mall was widened and lengthened to reach the Liffey (present day O'Connell Street), Carlisle Bridge (present day O'Connell Bridge) was added, and Westmoreland Street and D'Olier Street were created, resulting in a second thoroughfare that stretched from the Rotunda (see chapter eight) to Trinity College Dublin. These streets were completed shortly after the Act of Union came into being. The commission imposed a uniform aesthetic on the city, improved communications in the city and continued to push the focus of development eastward.

THE ROYAL EXCHANGE

Property development was not the only thriving enterprise in eighteenth-century Dublin. Trade also flourished in the capital. One of the principal exports at this time was linen, and Dublin was the largest centre for exports of linen in the country throughout this period. Just like the property developers, the merchants were also thinking of shaping the city's topography for their own ends. The city corporation was not felt to be doing enough to encourage trade and to this end, the Committee of Merchants was formed in 1761 and unveiled its plans to erect an exchange building for the promotion of commerce in Dublin in an advertisement in the *Dublin Journal* of 23 June 1764, calling a meeting of anyone interested in erecting an exchange.[8] Such institutions could be found in most European capitals by the eighteenth century. Those were places where bills of exchange were traded, business conducted, shipping information advertised and where business meetings could be held. Prior to this the merchants had used rooms in the Tholsel on Winetavern Street, the equivalent of the medieval city hall, but it was small and was also used by the corporation and guilds. In *The case of the merchants of Dublin* (1768), the committee laid out its case, defending its right to control the erection of an exchange. Some members of the commercial community clearly felt frustrated with the city corporation. The pamphlet observed that 'the merchants of the city of Dublin having had long experiences of the utter inattention of corporate bodies to the interest of trade … formed themselves [together] in the year 1761'.[9] This was, perhaps a little unfair. In the opening decades of the eighteenth century the corporation had further developed the harbour, extending walls and erecting a ballast house. The corporation also believed that it was within its own remit to erect an exchange, and an argument broke out between the two groups as they scrambled to claim ownership over the new facility. In the end a compromise was reached. The body that was formed for the maintenance and preservation of the exchange, known as the Trustees of the Royal Exchange, was made up equally of members of the corporation and the Committee of Merchants. They petitioned parliament, and were granted land on Cork Hill, just in front of Dublin Castle.[10]

Despite the fact that the penal laws were still largely in effect, the membership of the Committee of Merchants was surprisingly open with Protestants, Dissenters and Catholics all taking an active part. The society had been formed with this liberal aim in mind, and accounts from 1768 stressed that it was 'composed indiscriminately of all merchants who were willing to join in defraying the necessary expense of such an institution'.[11] This was unusual for the period. The penal laws prohibited Catholics from becoming city freemen, joining guilds, participating in the corporation, taking office, sitting in parliament or voting. Catholics were also prohibited from certain professions including law. They were, however, allowed to become merchants, and this was an area in which many Catholic families thrived. The majority of the merchants in the city were probably Protestant or Dissenter at this time, and so they would not have been under pressure to include Catholics.[12] Nevertheless, the exclusion of Catholics from formal civic life, even though they made up a significant proportion of the city's traders, would have ensured the sympathy of some Protestants to their plight. It must have made trade and business relations awkward at times. Repeal of the penal laws affecting trade and civic membership would not come until 1793, but movements such as the Committee of Merchants encouraged and promoted tolerance as well as showing the benefits to be reaped from including Catholics.

Both the location and design of the exchange made a statement. When the building was first planned in 1767, the city merchants were doing well, and they sought a building separate from the Custom House to assert their importance within the capital. The site of the exchange, directly in front of the castle, took advantage of established routeways. Trade from the east tended to come into the city from Castle Street. The newly built Parliament Street provided a direct route from the Exchange to the Custom House. The building also sat at the top of Dame Street, a busy commercial district. What can seem odd

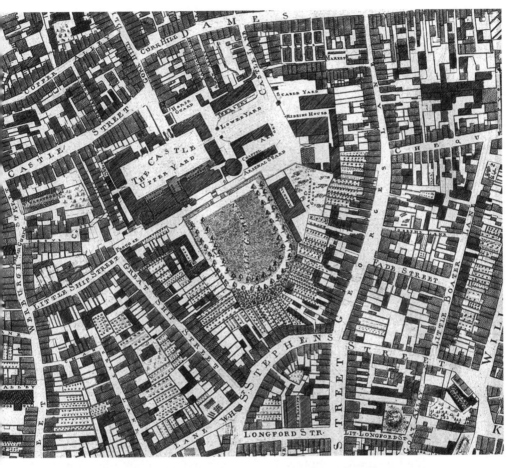

Bedford Square, where Dublin City Hall now stands, as featured on John Rocque's
map of Dublin 1756 (Dublin City Library and Archives)

to modern day observers is that both the front of the building, which
faces up Parliament Street, and the side of the building, which faces
north west up Castle Street, are both equally grand.[13] The volume of
traffic on Castle Street would have been far greater than it is today, and
it was intended that the building would be equal in its welcome to
national trade from outside Dublin and international trade docking at
the Custom House. Merchants were rarely elected to parliament, even
in a city such as Dublin, where trade was so important. Such a small
representation in parliament, and the belief that the corporation was

not doing enough to encourage trade, goes some way to explaining why the Committee of Merchants did not approach parliament for support in promoting the new exchange. Instead it went to the lord lieutenant and the castle for political backing. The Committee of Merchants lined up behind the government and supported the castle.

The Trustees of the Royal Exchange ran a competition to solicit designs for the building, which were then displayed in the Tholsel. The brief was simple: they needed a large hall, an assembly room and a large vault. Fifty-six architects submitted sixty-one designs. The competition attracted huge interest in England, where the bulk of the design entries—thirty-three—came from; twenty-three were submitted from Ireland. The winner of the competition was a relatively unknown architect, Thomas Cooley.[14] Second prize went to James Gandon, who lost out on this occasion but who would yet have an opportunity to significantly influence the city's architecture. If the exchange made a political statement and showed that the merchants supported the government at Dublin Castle, it was hoped that it would also make an economic statement. The building is neo-classical in style and has three formal facades (the fourth elevation backs on to the castle walls) made up entirely of white portland stone. Granite was usually used within the city, with Portland stone added to 'dress' the stone. Portland stone indicated not only wealth but good taste. The main entrance to the north has six Corinthian columns to indicate strength. The rotunda, which is forty-six feet high, is encased within a square ambulatory. The columns that uphold the central dome would have allowed some privacy for those who wandered around the interior to discuss business. There was a coffee shop upstairs for conducting business, where the newspapers of the day, complete with shipping and exchange rates, would have been on offer. The plasterwork was undertaken by Charles Thorpe who won the contract in 1777. Contemporaries seem to have been very impressed by the design and appearance of the building. One visitor to Dublin in 1775, Richard Twiss, became famous for his criticism of Ireland as a whole. Although the exchange was not complete when he visited the city, he praised it saying that it 'promises to become the greatest ornament of that city'.[15] In 1779 one visitor to the building described

Stereoscope of City Hall from Parliament Street *c.* 1860–1890
(National Library of Ireland)

the interior glowingly: 'The inside of this edifice possesses beauties
that cannot clearly be expressed by words, being a great curiosity to
those who have a taste for architecture'.[16]

The building took ten years to complete, and was funded by a
lottery scheme. Additional income from this lottery was used for
charitable purposes, and the society gave annual grants to the city's
philanthropic societies. Committee records tell us that in 1768 they
divided surplus funds from the lottery in the following manner: the
fund for rebuilding the Blue Coat School provided £1,000; the 'three
united hospitals', £1,500; the Lock Hospital and Magdalene Asylum,
£500; the Hibernian Marine School, £250; the Marine Nursery, £250;
the Meath Hospital, £100; and St Nicholas Hospital, £100. This was
a total of £3,700, a substantial sum. This left the exchange scheme
with a total of £9,282, showing that the lottery scheme was a huge
success.[17]

THE CUSTOM HOUSE

The construction of the building brought the merchants into direct
conflict with the property developers, pitting two important city
interests against each other. In 1707, a new Custom House was
opened, designed by the Irish architect Captain Thomas Burgh (also
the architect for the Royal Barracks and Dr Steeven's Hospital). It

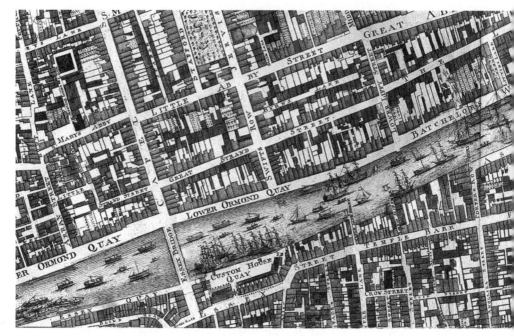

Old Custom House, as featured on John Rocque's map of 1756
(Dublin City Library and Archives)

was three stories high, 200 feet long and situated on the south of
the city at Essex Bridge, close to the old medieval core of the city.
While the Custom House was the largest and finest commercial
building in the city, Dublin's trade increased so much that by the
middle of the century the building was no longer fit for purpose. The
location of the Custom House meant that boats wishing to unload
their goods had to travel quite far up the Liffey and into the city to
reach it. With increased levels of trade by the mid-eighteenth century,
this led to major congestion on the river. This could be extremely
problematic when important goods were being delivered. Coal was a
vital commodity, particularly during winter, and city stocks were often
heavily depleted. There were frequent complaints in the city press
about the inability of coal ships to navigate the Liffey effectively to
unload their goods. Sometimes ships could be stuck on the river for
several weeks, which was hugely inconvenient and meant that market
prices were driven up while important commodities were inaccessible.

In 1773 the upper floor of the old Custom House was declared unsound and it was clear that a new custom house would have to be built.[18] Debate about the location quickly arose. Developers such as Gardiner (by then a member of the Wide Streets Commission) had been busy on the northside of the city which was considered, throughout this period, to be the more fashionable place to reside. The problem was that if you lived in the northeast, you had to travel west to one of the four city bridges to get to the southside of the city. Essex Bridge was the widest and busiest, and it stood beside the Custom House. Not only was the bridge congested, but the streets around the bridge were built up on both sides of the Liffey. It took a considerable amount of time to get across the city. Developers wanted a new bridge to the east, which would give tenants easy access to their estates. A new bridge downstream, however, would cut off access to the Custom House for ships. Through the Wide Streets Commission, it was proposed that a new Custom House be built to the east. While the city merchants would have been happy to have a new, larger building, they were very concerned about the location of that building. Most city merchants had warehouses and offices to the west around Burgh's custom house. Trade had been conducted in this area for centuries. City markets were located a five or ten minute stroll to the west of the existing custom house close to the old medieval city centre. Street names in the area recall these markets. Fishamble Street hosted a Fish market, the Cornmarket held a corn and bread market. The area around the Custom House would have been extremely busy with traffic from the unloaded vessels, merchants overseeing their new commodities. Many conducted their business out of doors, on the streets and in markets, and there were numerous small street traders. At the Custom House there would have been plenty of traders on the other end of the scale too: wholesale merchants overseeing their goods being loaded onto ships or being taken off ships. The Liberties were a ten minute stroll from the Custom House and weaving was a major industry in this area. Cloth could have been easily packed and loaded onto ships from this location.

The merchants were determined to resist a move of the Custom House farther east. The Committee of Merchants called a citywide meeting to object to the proposal. In 1774 merchants, brewers, weavers and manufacturers in the city signed petitions against a move, arguing that it would be too costly to their businesses. The reality, however, was that parliament held the power and wanted a new bridge to the east. This meant the Custom House would have to move. The argument was settled in 1780, after six long years of fighting, when John Beresford, first Commissioner of the Revenue, requested royal approval for the new bridge and Custom House to be built to on the north bank of the city. The government was so worried that the Custom House location would lead to unrest, that it conducted negotiations with the London-based architect of the building, James Gandon, in secret between 1779 and 1781.[19] While Gandon had lost the competition for the Royal Exchange in the 1760s, he had made influential friends over the following decade and had become a personal associate of Beresford, who was impressed with the architect. In the meantime Gandon had been responsible for designing the County Hall in Nottingham and a new design of London's Bedlam. His work in Dublin would make him a celebrated architect, however, and he would further add his mark to the city quays by designing the Four Courts.

The merchants were not yet prepared to give in, however, and a riot was instigated in July 1781 by Dublin traders who appeared at the construction site and tried to fill in the foundations. They failed on this occasion but were better prepared in September 1781, when they were led by James Napper Tandy (who went on to become a leading member of the United Irishmen). As late as 1781 various pamphlets condemned or defended the choice of site.[20] Nevertheless, the protest was too late; in August 1781 Beresford laid the foundation stone in secret. There was to be no going back, and Beresford was not afraid to make enemies of Dublin's merchants or the population at large. Beresford wrote to Gandon telling him not to worry about the protests, and to 'laugh at the extreme folly of people'.[21]

In today's streetscape the site of the old Custom House is occupied by the Clarence Hotel on Wellington Quay. The building became a barracks in the 1790s, when tensions were running high in Dublin. By the nineteenth century it had been abandoned and was torn down.

The new Custom House was completed and opened for business on 7 November 1791, when 20 vessels unpacked their goods at it. As the historian Christine Casey remarked, 'trophy buildings come no finer than this'.[22] The Custom House became one of the busiest parts of the city throughout the nineteenth century but city growth continued and the port of Dublin relocated beyond the Custom House and further east. Nevertheless, the building continued to dominate the landscape of the city. The Loop Line Bridge, today carrying the DART line, in front of the Custom House, carried countless travellers into the city and past the building every day, so although the building is not in the city centre, it is in a well-known part of the city. The traffic congestion faced by wealthy citizens who resided in these new residential areas, such as Gardiner Street, prompted city developers and other notables to call for a bridge to the east. This would have necessitated the removal of the Custom House to a site further down river. It could be argued that the merchants had the last laugh. The trade which surrounded the new building drove down prices in the area and meant that many wealthy citizens were pushed out by commerce and were forced to flee to the southside. This had been predicted by protesting tradesmen in 1774, who pointed out that 'all the hurry, crowd and annoyance which necessarily attend trade, will be brought to the doors of our nobility and gentry, and many of those elegant streets in which they now reside, will become the common passages for porters and cars, loaded with the necessaries of life, and all kinds of merchandise, to be diffused throughout the whole city. Wherever the seat of trade is fixed, to that neighbourhood the merchants, with all their train, will in time remove themselves'.[23]

THE ROYAL EXCHANGE IN THE NINETEENTH CENTURY

The Royal Exchange fell into decline in the first half of the nineteenth century, following the Act of Union. Trade had declined and, while there were many banks located on Dame Street close to the building, the opening of the General Post Office (see chapter eight) on Sackville (later O'Connell) Street pulled trade towards the northside of the river. It was still used on important occasions, however. A meeting

Troops outside City Hall in 1916 (National Library of Ireland)

to protest against the Act of Union was held there in 1800 at which Daniel O'Connell spoke. Unfortunately, its day-to-day business declined throughout the early nineteenth century and the building was never really used for its intended purpose.[24] In 1851 it was sold to Dublin Corporation, and on 30 September 1852 became Dublin City Hall. The corporation converted it into offices, dividing the gorgeous central hall with partitions so it could be more easily used for its new purpose. The coffee house upstairs became the corporation chamber, where councillors met and discussed official business. It was a centre of important activity once more. The building gained a far higher profile in its new incarnation as City Hall. Ulysses S. Grant, the first American president to visit Ireland, was formally greeted at City Hall in January 1879, on his tour of Britain and Ireland. At the reception, Grant joked that he would 'return one day and run against Barrington for Mayor and Brett for parliament. I warn these gentlemen that I am a troublesome candidate'.[25] Later, the funerals of Charles Stewart Parnell in 1891, and the Fenian Jeremiah O'Donovan Rossa in 1915, both departed for Glasnevin Cemetery from City Hall.

The Custom House managed to escape substantial damage during the Easter Rising of 1916 (surprising, considering its proximity to

Custom House on Fire, May 1922 (National Library of Ireland)

Liberty Hall, the headquarters of the Irish Citizen Army) but was embroiled in the later War of Independence. Just weeks before the truce that ended the war, the Dublin Brigade of the IRA attacked the building, and the Custom House was burned down and the interiors gutted. The image above shows the Custom House in flames following this fighting. The building was restored to its original splendour by the Office of Public Works (OPW) in the 1920s.

City Hall was also involved in the fight for Irish independence. The building was taken during the Easter Rising when members of the Irish Citizen Army fell back on the building from Dublin Castle (see chapter two). There are signs of the fighting on the exterior and in the central rotunda, such as bullet holes on some of columns, with a very visible hole between the legs of the statue of Charles Lucas. City Hall became an important building in the early days of the Free State. As the new government was reluctant to occupy the

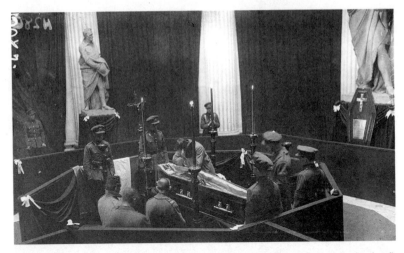

Michael Collins lying in state in City Hall, August 1922 (National Library of Ireland)

now empty offices in Dublin Castle because of its association with the British government, City Hall was used instead. When military barracks across the city were occupied by the new National Army, troops paraded past government officials in City Hall for inspection (the GPO would later become the central point for such displays of military strength). More sombre occasions in the history of the new state were also observed in City Hall. In 1922 the funerals of Arthur Griffith and Michael Collins, like those of Parnell and O'Donovan Rossa, also departed for Glasnevin Cemetery from City Hall. The picture above shows Collins' body lying in state.

CITY HALL AS IT STANDS TODAY

In 1998 Dublin Corporation restored the building to its original glory, and City Hall now looks as it would have when it was first opened. The city council still meet in the chambers upstairs, and in the basement vaults is a public exhibition entitled 'Dublin's City hall: the Story of the Capital'. Although the building is overlooked by many Dubliners, who tend not to visit City Hall even though entry is free, it has, however, become increasingly popular for civil wedding ceremonies. Four statues can be seen in the main rotunda today. The oldest statue is that of Charles Lucas, who created uproar in Dublin in the 1740s by challenging the city corporation and calling for its reform (see chapter four). As a controversial figure, it is perhaps not surprising that his statue was first placed 'in a niche in the west staircase'.[26] The sculptor responsible for the statue was Edward Smyth, a Dubliner.[27] Lucas's statue looks rather small when compared to the gigantic, eighteen-foot tall statue of Daniel O'Connell (which was originally located outside the building).[28] The relative size perhaps reflects the gargantuan stature of O'Connell in Irish history. He brought emancipation to Catholics, was the first Irish Catholic elected to the Westminster parliament, and he had the penal laws repealed. 'The Liberator' had a special relationship with the city, being the first Catholic lord mayor of Dublin since the Jacobite era. He also championed reforms of the corporation, which ensured that Catholic traders had greater access to positions on the city council. Thomas Drummond was under-secretary for Ireland between 1835 and 1840, and in this capacity he carried out a number of reforms, including of the police force, and assisted the introduction of the railway to Ireland.[29] He also invented a type of lantern that was used in lighthouses and could be seen up to sixty-eight miles away (his statue at City Hall has a lighthouse at its feet to mark its use in lighthouses all over Ireland). The final statue is that of Thomas Davis, the Young Irelander and founder of the newspaper *The Nation*. Davis and the Young Irelanders greatly advanced cultural or 'romantic' nationalism and inspired future generations of republicans. Davis wrote the popular nationalist ballad 'A nation once again'.[30]

While these four statues may attract the attention of any visitor to City Hall, you should take some time to look at the murals in the central rotunda which are just above the statues. There are twelve panels in all. The murals were suggested in 1913 by the head of the Dublin Metropolitan School of Art, James Ward, and were painted by students of the school. While four of the panels depict the four provinces of Ireland, eight more are of scenes of historical importance from Dublin's medieval past, including the landing of the Vikings, the battle of Clontarf, and St Patrick's baptism of the population of

Dublin.[31] If you look down to the mosaic floor (installed in 1898) you will see Dublin's coat of arms, which has been in use for over four hundred years. The image on the coat of arms is of three burning castles, with two women dressed in classical robes holding olive branches. The three castles are believed to have been ancient towers from the castle's defences. The fire does not represent any real or historical event but is supposed to symbolise the zeal of the citizens to protect the city. The city motto can be translated from the Latin as 'the obedience of the citizens produces a happy city', which could be read as a reminder from the authorities to the population that they should remain obedient.

Christine Casey has called the Royal Exchange the 'swan-song of the old-mercantile city' who 'had long resisted eastward expansion'.[32] The building entrenched the merchants even further in this part of the city, and was their attempt at keeping it the centre of trade. Ironically, it was the property developers who were responsible for influencing the decision to build a new custom house where trade would be conducted for another century, not the merchants who had formed a committee to encourage trade in the first place. The story behind the building of City Hall marks a turning point in the growth and development of the city. While the building now carries the functions of civic offices, in the past it was the commercial heart of the city, a building where important political meetings were held and where important guests to the city were greeted. It shows that a building does not need to continually house one institution to be at the centre of city life; civic life moves around some buildings. The architecture and interior of the building makes it one of the most aesthetically pleasing buildings in the city, and a gem to be treasured.

6

St James's Gate Brewery

A GUIDE TO DUBLIN published in 1947 warned tourists that, as Guinness was the most popular alcoholic drink in the city, they would not find much variety in Dublin pubs. 'Draught beers and ales are not much drunk, Guinness being the popular beverage of the masses. "Mild and Bitter" are words never heard in a Dublin pub'.[1] Guinness is still the most popular alcoholic beverage in Ireland. It has been brewed in Dublin for over 250 years and is consumed around the world but its brand remains synonymous with Ireland. As such, St James's Gate is a must-see attraction for many people who visit the city. It is a credit to Guinness's ability to market itself that so many make the trip to this industrial complex. The Guinness Storehouse has become one of the most popular tourist attractions in Dublin. The exhibition takes visitors through the history of the Guinness family, how the company was built up, and how Guinness is brewed and marketed. The tour concludes in their bar where visitors receive a complimentary pint, said to be the best Guinness you will drink in your life, while enjoying a 360 degree panorama of the city. While the tour has proven a spectacular hit with tourists, the brewery is much more than a tourist trap. The site tells us a great deal about the industrial history of the city, as well as about the thousands of men and women who worked at St James's Gate. The Guinness family invested heavily in the city where they founded their empire in the nineteenth century and their philanthropic projects such as the Iveagh Trust transformed social housing in Dublin. By looking at a history of Guinness, we also learn about the relationship between Dubliners and drink, an oft bemoaned partnership.

St James's Gate is the largest, and one of the few, industrial complexes located in the heart of Dublin. For many Dubliners the St James's Gate Brewery represents Irish excellence; Guinness is a product we perfected and exported all over the world, and it is now inextricably linked with Ireland, and more specifically Dublin. The growth of the plant charts the rise and expansion of one of Ireland's most important industrial exports, beer, and one of Ireland's most famous exports, Guinness. During the nineteenth century the brewery was the largest in the world. The sheer scale of production at the brewery ensured that Guinness outstripped any other alcoholic beverage being produced in Ireland. Much of the Guinness produced at St James's Gate was exported, but Guinness dominated the home market as well. In addition to having the largest share of the Dublin-based market, by the mid-nineteenth century more than half of all beer consumed outside Dublin was Guinness.[2] The home-grown market and international demand for Guinness positioned brewing as the second most important industry in Ireland after farming.[3] Brewing was the capital's most important industry throughout the nineteenth and into the twentieth century. The brewery was pioneering not just in terms of its size and the scale of its output, but in terms of its engineering prowess, brewing techniques and the philanthropy with which it was associated, not to mention the company's first rate care for its workers. While the brewery is an important source of revenue, a tourist attraction and even a point of pride, it has, on occasion, also had a turbulent relationship with the population.

ARTHUR GUINNESS

The creator of this famous drink has been so well marketed as to ensure that anyone familiar with it will know of him: Arthur Guinness. A strong family connection at the helm of the company has ensured that Arthur, and the St James's Gate brewery, are so well-connected with the beverage that even many who don't drink Guinness know the man who first brewed the stout as well as the date the brewery opened in 1759; both are incorporated into the insignia of the drink and stamped on most of their glasses, pumps, bottles and cans.

The story of this Irish industrial giant begins fairly modestly. Arthur Guinness himself was a brewer from County Kildare. Sources that touch on Arthur's life, especially his early life, are thin enough on the ground and there is a lot of uncertainty surrounding the actual time and place he first brewed the black stuff. Strangely, the foundation of the Guinness empire can be traced back to the Anglican Church. Folklore has it that the money used to set up Arthur Guinness's first brewery came from the pockets of a bishop, Dr Arthur Price. Arthur Guinness's father, Richard Guinness, worked as a steward on Dr Price's estate in Celbridge. Family legend also suggests that Arthur was named after the clergyman.

It was not uncommon for favoured servants to be left bequests by employers in their wills. When he died Arthur Price left £100, a fairly substantial windfall, to his steward's son. It is assumed that this money was used to found the brewery. Richard Guinness had business interests in addition to his stewarding job, and so it is possible that Richard had laid out portions for each of his four sons and that Arthur used family money to first establish himself as a brewer.[4] Arthur was, however, literally born into brewing. His mother, Elizabeth Read, gave birth to him in 1725 in a malt house in Celbridge that his father had been leasing from Dr Price.[5] Richard was busy and was interested in expanding his interests wherever and whenever possible. The malt house became known as the Mucky Duck Inn, and, while the original building does not stand, there is still a pub on the site which is celebrated as the birthplace of the man, and also claims to be the original spot where the stout was first brewed.

Unfortunately Arthur's mother died while he was young. When Richard remarried, he built up his brewing connections by marrying Elizabeth Clare, the owner of the White Hart Inn. Inn keepers and estate owners had brewed their own beer and ales from the middle ages. By the eighteenth century, the family connection with an inn would have allowed Arthur to become very familiar with the brewing process. Richard would, as a middle-class father, have had his four sons apprenticed to a trade. Unfortunately we can only speculate whether or not his father chose to have him apprenticed to a brewer. Arthur's two younger brothers were apprenticed as a goldsmith and a merchant respectively, while his elder brother also worked in the brewing industry.[6] In 1753 Dr Price, Richard's employer, died and left his bequest of £100 to Arthur. By 1755 Arthur had moved from Celbridge to Leixlip and had leased a brewery with his brother. From here they supplied the large Castletown estate with beer.[7] The brewery was so successful that by 1759 Arthur had moved out on his own and set up a brewery in Dublin. He was just thirty-four when he made the move. He settled at No. 1 Thomas Street, just a few minutes' walk from his brewery.

On Arthur's move to Dublin in 1759, he purchased the lease of the Espinasse brewery in St James's Gate.[8] The location was perfect. St James's parish and the Liberties were densely populated and provided both a workforce and a customer base. There were fifty-two licensed premises on St James's Street alone by the middle of the eighteenth century. There were probably many more selling alcohol illegally or out of carts. The site was close to the city bridges, which allowed for easy access in and out of the city. Traffic was a major problem in eighteenth-century Dublin, and this was an important consideration. St James's Gate was one of the medieval gates into the city and so was a well-established city road.[9] Perhaps most importantly, the site was close to the city reservoir, providing easy access to a source of clean water. The suitability of the location is attested to by the fact that five breweries had established themselves around this area when Arthur Guinness took over his site. Many more would follow, and by the nineteenth century and well into the twentieth, this area was the centre of brewing in Dublin.[10]

ALCOHOL CONSUMPTION IN MEDIEVAL AND EARLY MODERN DUBLIN

In the reign of James I, Barnaby Rich stated that 'there is no merchandise so vendible' in Dublin as alcohol. He added that 'the whole profit of the town stands upon alehouses and the selling of ale ... There are whole streets of taverns, and it is a rare thing to find a house in Dublin without a tavern, as to find a tavern without a strumpet'.[11] The large number of drinking establishments in the capital had been commented upon for centuries. Most people would have drunk a weak beer instead of water as most water supplies, particularly those within cities, were contaminated. Beer acted as a substitute, and was drunk by everyone, including children. By the 1660s the number of taverns in the city was believed to be 1,180.[12] By 1667 Dublin Corporation counted 1,500 taverns in the city.[13] This is a staggering figure considering that the population was about 40,000 in 1680, but most of these were probably very small businesses.[14] In some streets more than half of the buildings were used to serve alcohol. At one point in the seventeenth century the crypt in Christ Church Cathedral was even used as a tavern. The cathedral was attempting to raise some money by renting out space, including the crypt, for various commercial enterprises. This part of the city was densely populated with taverns, particularly along Winetavern Street, which had been a busy drinking spot since the medieval period. This area was also synonymous with civic government throughout the medieval period and into the eighteenth century, as the Tholsel (the city and guild hall) and many of the guild premises were to be found on Winetavern Street or the adjoining Skinner's Alley, and the law courts were within the Christ Church precinct.[15] As the population expanded rapidly in the eighteenth century, so too did the number of places to buy alcohol. By 1750, when the population of the city was 80,000, there were 879 licensed taverns or pubs in Dublin and 930 licensed breweries across the country.[16] Thomas Street was still a busy drinking spot in 1798, when fifty-two of the 190 buildings on the street were licensed to sell alcohol.[17]

Many traders sold their alcohol illegally, either from carts or from their homes to neighbours, so the numbers of those actually selling drink was probably far higher. Dublin might seem to have been excessive in its drinking habits, but it may not have been. When compared with London in the same period, Dublin emerges favourably. The consumption of gin by the working class in London startled the British government, which investigated and limited the amount of gin consumed. A petition to Westminster in 1751 claimed that 9,323 children died as a result of parental neglect brought on by excessive consumption of gin.[18] The artist William Hogarth was moved by this trend to draw attention to the problem in a series of engravings. In 'Gin Lane' he points to the horrors of gin consumption, which included parental neglect of children and a decline in industry. He was not advocating temperance, however, and his second engraving in the set, 'Beer Street', depicted a prosperous community where the population looks more healthy and happy and the children are safe. Beer was seen as a healthier alcoholic drink for the lower classes to consume. The population of London was 675,000 in 1750, and per annum it was believed that 11,200,000 gallons of spirits (primarily gin), 2 million barrels of ale and 30,000 tons of wine were consumed each year by the population. There were 207 inns, 447 taverns, 5,875 'beer houses' and 8,659 'brandy shops', as well as a large number of street vendors and illegal traders.[19] While Londoners might have outdrunk Dubliners in the eighteenth century, Dublin would surpass the British capital in the nineteenth century in consumption of alcohol.

ARTHUR GUINNESS AND ST JAMES'S GATE

Dublin was a prime location to open a brewery in the eighteenth century and ensured a large customer base on its doorstep. It was to Dublin that Arthur looked to expand his empire. The lease that he purchased in James's Street on New Years Eve in 1759 shows that his new site was a modest establishment. It covered four acres, and included some brewing equipment, stables and a hay loft from the previous resident (unfortunately there are no images of this early brewery to show us what it looked like). The lease was acquired for just £45 for a period of 9,000 years (a rather long period even by the standards of the day).[20] While it was a modest start, most breweries were small-scale enterprises and Arthur had a good background in brewing, and had made a success of the Kildare brewery which he had run with his brother. From this modest four-acre site, the business expanded to become the largest brewery in the world.[21] Although the Mucky Duck pub and Arthur Price's estate (both in Celbridge) claim that the first pint of Guinness was brewed on their premises, this is highly unlikely. The famous porter was not brewed at St James's Gate until 1778.[22] Up to this point ale was produced at the brewery. Porter was a popular drink in London in the early 1720s. The porters of Covent Garden drank this style of beer in such quantities that

Engraving depicting a Guinness drinker from the London publication
The Gentleman's Magazine in 1794 (Guinness Archives, Guinness Storehouse,
St James's Gate, Dublin 8)

they lent their name to it. The drink became very popular in Ireland
in the 1760s and imports into Ireland increased dramatically at the
expense of home-produced beers. Arthur developed a Dublin porter
to compete with the imported drink. It was an inspired move, and
the Guinness porter became so popular that by 1799 he decided

to concentrate all of his production on this product.[23] It was being exported to Britain by the end of the eighteenth century. In 1794 an engraving (not an advertisement) in the *Gentleman's Magazine*, a London-based magazine, which depicts a man drinking in an ale-house, clearly shows the Guinness brand stamped on one of the kegs in the background. The porter was known in London, and would soon become an important product in the British market as well as the Irish.

GUINNESS DYNASTY

The Guinness empire was not built in one generation, however. It would take several generations of family members, active in the business, to build up the brewery. Arthur was lucky to have had so many enterprising descendants who were prepared to work within the brewery to assist its expansion and success. Within two years of coming to Dublin, he had met and become engaged to Olivia Whitmore. The couple were married on 17 June 1761.[24] Olivia's dowry was £1,000, which proves that she came from a wealthy family. She was also well-connected within Dublin, which would have been a further draw for Arthur. Her uncle was James Grattan, the recorder of Dublin Corporation, and her cousin was Henry Grattan, the celebrated parliamentarian whose statue now stands on College Green (see chapter four). Famed for his oratorical skills, he is depicted addressing the parliament house across the road (now the Bank of Ireland). Grattan was a patriot, and one of the leading voices within the Irish parliament calling for greater parliamentary freedom from Britain and the ability to legislate without interference. Arthur Guinness is said to have supported him in his belief that Catholics should be given greater relief from the penal laws. As a leading Protestant businessman in Dublin, this stance made him quite liberal and progressive.[25]

Olivia and Arthur had a large brood of children: six sons and four daughters. In a period of high infant mortality, it is believed that Olivia became pregnant 21 times in order to produce a family this large.[26] Arthur's first-born was a daughter, Elizabeth, who married Frederick Darley, Lord Mayor of Dublin in 1801. His next was Hosea, who entered the Church of Ireland. His third child, Arthur, was born in 1768 and was destined to take over the family legacy. Arthur Guinness (junior) ran the brewery until his death in 1855 but he trained his youngest son from an early age to take over from him. His eldest son, Benjamin Lee, was educated for a profession in the church, while his second son was uninterested in learning his father's trade. Before taking over the complete running of the business, Benjamin had made a name for himself in business and within civic and national politics. Benjamin Lee was elected Lord Mayor of Dublin in 1851 and was a Conservative MP for Cork city from 1865 until his death in 1868. His sons Arthur Edward and Edward Cecil Lee are the most celebrated nineteenth-century Guinness family members. They shaped the city not only through their industry, but through the money they spent on property, architecture and philanthropy.

THE GUINNESS FAMILY'S PHILANTHROPIC ACTIVITIES

Benjamin Lee Guinness invested heavily in developing the brewery, expanding the site and improving its equipment. This allowed the brewery to increase its production to meet greater demand in the nineteenth century. The Guinness family had a strong social conscience and the family donated money to existing charities, and helped to found new philanthropic schemes. One of his most important philanthropic legacies was the £150,000 that Benjamin Lee invested in the renovation of St Patrick's Cathedral. He was personally involved in this renovation, and oversaw some dramatic changes to the church.[27] The work carried out on the cathedral has become quite controversial, however, as Benjamin Lee insisted on all final decisions. Much of this work was not restorative and dramatically altered the fabric of the building. He outlined the conditions under which his donation was made, primarily that he would direct the renovations and the overall aesthetic of the church, writing that 'I should be glad to assist the dean and chapter in part (if not all) of those necessary repairs if they are pleased to entrust to me unrestrictedly and without any interference such parts of this sacred and time honoured building as may be necessary for the purpose'.

80 St Stephin's Green
24th April 1860.

To the Honble & very Reverend
The Dean & Chapter of St Patrick's,
Dublin,

Gentlemen,

The dilapidated State of your Venerable Cathedral, has long been a Subject of general regret and must have been peculiarly so felt by those who have been or who now are officially connected with it — The Southern Wall of the Choir with its buttresses & demi-arches are known to be in an unsafe state while a considerable portion of the Southern Transept and the entire South Wall of the Nave with its Pillars & its Arches are evidently tottering to their fall — The great damp of the Cathedral is also very objectionable and can be remedied only by the excavation of the entire building excepting the Chancel. The Nave and South Transept with their several Isles are destitute of their original groined

Benjamin Lee Guinness's letter to St Patrick's Cathedral stating that he would like control over the restoration of the cathedral (St Patrick's Cathedral)

Nevertheless, the building was in major need of repair, and this money saved the cathedral and restored it to its glory. The population of Dublin had changed in the eighteenth and nineteenth centuries from being primarily Anglican to being overwhelmingly Catholic. While St Patrick's Cathedral was one of the premier places for Dublin Anglicans to worship, a dwindling congregation and the generally poor condition of the Liberties neighbourhood in which the Cathedral was located, meant the cathedral badly needed attention and, most importantly, money. Benjamin Lee was created a baronet in 1867 and died the following year. While Benjamin Lee left the brewery to his two sons, Arthur Edward and Edward Cecil, Arthur Edward had little interest in the running of the business and sold his interest in the firm to his brother in 1874. Edward Cecil continued his father's philanthropic activities, carrying out the remainder of his father's plans for St Patrick's Cathedral and helping to reconstruct Marsh's Library (see chapter three).[28]

Edward Cecil Guinness's greatest social legacy within Dublin is probably the wonderful red-brick Iveagh Trust buildings. These buildings are located adjacent to Christ Church Cathedral and within the vicinity of the family's beloved St Patrick's Cathedral. It is well worth taking the time to walk around the perimeter of these buildings or appreciate them from a bench in St Patrick's Close. The grey brick (largely limestone exterior) of the cathedral is in remarkable contrast to the startling red brick of the Iveagh Trust buildings. In 1890 Edward Cecil announced his plan to donate £250,000 towards social housing. This money would be invested in a trust, later to be named the Iveagh Trust after the family's recently acquired noble title, and was to be spent providing sanitary affordable housing for the working poor in Dublin and London; £200,000 was earmarked for London, with £50,000 for Dublin (the trust later split to deal with each city separately). The scheme was pioneering, although something similar had been attempted by the Dublin Artisan Dwelling Company (of which Arthur Edward Guinness was the chairman) in the 1870s in Rialto.[29] By the time the trust had completed its work in Dublin, it had spent more than £250,000 and had transformed one of the most notorious slum districts in Dublin, which has been described as 'a

maze of alleys, courts and lanes, centuries deep in filth'.[30] The Liberties
had been populated by city artisans, weavers and linen bleachers for
much of the eighteenth and early nineteenth century. This was quite
a poor part of the city, and poverty was exacerbated by the fact that
the cloth industry was very susceptible to fluctuations in the market
and the depressed nature of weaving in Dublin by the mid-nineteenth
century. A warren of tenements existed in and around St Patrick's
Cathedral and along Bride Street. While legislation had been passed
in 1868 and 1875 to enable the corporation to pull down slum and
tenement buildings, Dublin Corporation could not afford to replace
these buildings and reinvigorate the area.

The Iveagh Trust buildings are spread over Thomas Court, Kevin
Street and Bull Alley. A warren of tenements were located in this
district of the city. The land had to be acquired through an act of
parliament. The decrepit houses were demolished, with the aim that
those who were moved out would be moved back in once the new
buildings were completed. The plan was to build large blocks, which
would allow a large number to be housed within the new buildings.
The design was for eight four-storey buildings, with enough space
for 250 working-class families in what were called 'tenements' at the
time but were more like apartments. There were two classifications
of apartments within the dwellings that varied in size; self-contained
apartments, and associated dwellings which had a laundry and toilet
area shared by three or four families.[31] The complex would also
include public baths, a working man's hostel, and a play centre for
children. The buildings were to be functional but also aesthetically
pleasing, and they are an important architectural addition to the city.
The architectural historian Christine Casey says that 'stylistically the
most interesting in the group is the Iveagh Baths of 1905 ... which
combines elements from Arts and Crafts, Art Nouveau and Edwardian
Classicism'.[32] St Patrick's Park was established by an act of parliament
in 1897 and allowed for the clearing away of slums on Bride Street
and the creation of a 2.5 acre park between the Iveagh Trust buildings
and the cathedral.[33] Once completed in 1915, the complex served
as a fully-functioning community with apartments that were very
impressive by the standards of the day. The trust had completely
re-invigorated the ancient slum area into a sanitary, efficient and

aesthetically pleasing city district. The buildings were not rent-free and those who took up residence paid rent to the trust. This varied from apartment to apartment. The trust is still going strong to this day and is celebrated for a number of contributions it made to working class Dublin life. One of the three-bedroomed flats has been preserved as a museum and can be visited by the public. The flat belonged to Nellie Molloy who moved in as a child in 1915. When she died in 2002, the Iveagh Trust purchased the contents of her apartment. The furniture and artwork dated from the early to mid-twentieth century. They have maintained the apartment as a 'living space frozen in time', and have captured a remarkable slice of twentieth-century working-class Dublin.[34]

By the late-nineteenth century the Guinness brewery was becoming more and more concerned with the conditions in which its workers lived, as well as with their health and diet. In order to improve these they adopted a number of initiatives. Workers were encouraged to partake in sports through company clubs. There was an on-site medical officer, who carried out health inspections on those interviewing for work at the brewery and who took care of sick employees. In 1900 the medical officer carried out an inspection of all employee residences and found many of them wanting. In order to increase the standards of habitation, bonuses were given as incentives to raise the standard of poor homes, and some people were encouraged to move.[35] Subsidies were provided for clothing, and a food shop was set up at the brewery which provided the essentials at a reduced cost. The brewery even established cooking and nutrition classes for Guinness wives.[36] All of these measures were revolutionary for the time and set a new standard in employer-employee relations. They also made Guinness one of the most desirable employers in Dublin.

THE GUINNESS FAMILY IN THE NINETEENTH AND TWENTIETH CENTURIES

The Guinness family owned extensive private property and residences. Edward Cecil Lee purchased Farmleigh house and estate (which contained seventy-eight acres) in 1874. The property is located beside

Phoenix Park. From here he entertained in lavish style. This property is now owned by the Irish government which uses it as a residence for visiting foreign dignitaries and for government functions. Edward also purchased 80 St Stephen's Green and renovated it extensively. The resulting property, Iveagh House (now the headquarters of the Department of Foreign Affairs), has been described as 'the most opulent city residence of the period'. They also held extensive estates and properties in England.[37] The Guinness family knew how to live according to their status as Ireland's greatest industrial tycoons. Edward Cecil was honoured for the work he had undertaken on behalf of the working-class poor in London and Dublin. He was created a baronet in 1885, a baron in 1891, a viscount in 1904 and the first Lord Iveagh in 1919.

Edward Cecil married his second cousin, Adelaide, in 1873. Their son, Rupert, took the title of Lord Iveagh, as well as becoming chairman of the company, on his father's death in October 1927. Rupert was not as hands-on in the running of the company. He was a unionist MP for two English constituencies between 1908 and 1927, and spent much of his time farming on his estate in Surrey.[38] When Rupert died in 1967 he was succeeded by his son Benjamin, who oversaw the rationalisation of the company in the 1980s. Rupert's nephew, Bryan Guinness, was vice-chairman of the company during this period, and was the last member of the family to be involved with the company at any managerial level.[39] The Guinness family today is, for the most part, resident in England and has no operational connection with the firm.

THE EXPANSION OF THE JAMES'S GATE BREWERY

The nineteenth century was a golden age for the family and the brewery, and it was during this period that the company expanded from its four-acre site to become the industrial giant it is today. Kevin Kearns has described the purchase of the lease at James's Gate as 'the most important date in the history of Irish brewing'.[40] With Ireland's weak industrial output, particularly when compared with the rest of Europe in this period, brewing, and Guinness in particular, were extremely important to the Irish economy. By the late nineteenth century Guinness was being consumed worldwide. Production was not limited to Dublin, however, and Guinness breweries were established all over the world.

Trade had boomed in Ireland during the Napoleonic wars (1803–15), as Ireland exported agricultural goods to feed the British army. Irish produce, such as salted beef and butter, also ensured strong trade links with the West Indies. This traditional Irish trade link was important for Guinness and allowed it to expand and diversify. In 1801 'West Indies porter' was brewed. The recipe was slightly different, being brewed with extra hops as a preservative, to ensure that it survived the long distance. By 1827 it was being shipped to the Gold Coast, and other new markets were emerging for the brewery. During the Napoleonic wars, output grew quickly, doubling in just one year between 1801 and 1802.[41] By 1810 Guinness was the largest brewery in Dublin.[42] After the Napoleonic wars there was a decline in all exports from the brewery. This was also the case with many other Irish agricultural goods and products, as Britain was free once more to trade with whomever they liked. There were signs of a return to growth and an expansion of the brewery by the 1830s, however, as the Irish economy began to recover.

By 1833 St James's Gate production had grown steadily and the brewery outstripped the largest Irish brewery, Cork's Beamish & Crawford.[43] Cork was traditionally a large exporter of agricultural goods such as beef and butter and an export trade in beer had grown on the back of this. There were twenty-five wholesale breweries in Cork in the 1770s, but the landscape changed when William Beamish and William Crawford established their brewery in 1791. It was known as the Cork Porter Brewery, as Beamish and Crawford also set out to take advantage of the new market for porter.[44]

By the early nineteenth century Beamish & Crawford, as the company had become known, was exporting its porter to England and the Caribbean. The fall off in demand after the Napoleonic wars allowed Guinness to eventually out-produce them. The majority of Beamish & Crawford's customers were based in Cork and Munster, and Guinness had a larger customer base on its doorstep which also helped it to grow.[45] Beamish is still brewed in Cork city today but has a far smaller share of the Irish market and its main customers remain its Cork locals. The profits Beamish & Crawford was making in its early days shows how lucrative brewing could be. In their first trading year (1792–93) net turnover was £38,966. It increased to £151,098 in 1801. Later in the decade sales were £190,000 per annum.[46]

Guinness was like a juggernaut from the 1830s. In 1845 production of Guinness increased by 20 per cent. By 1846 the company produced more than 100,000 barrels, increasing to 200,000 by 1860.[47] This helped to drive other industries in the capital, including bottling. While profits were reinvested back into the brewery at a steady pace throughout the nineteenth century, much of this late nineteenth-century expansion came about through funds raised when the company was floated on the stock exchange in 1886. The brewery was valued at £800,000 in 1869 but at its stock exchange launch just fifteen years later that had increased to £5 million. Twenty years later the firm was valued at £7 million, confirming the brewery's status as one of the most important industrial entities on the island. Dividends for the company's shares were only less than 15 per cent and could climb as high as 20 and even 25 per cent.[48] By 1914 the St James's Gate brewery was the largest in the world, and production continued to grow.

In 1873 the company acquired a large site across the street from the original brewery stretching to the Liffey. This coincided with a restructuring of the company, which took place between 1870 and 1880. New mechanised processes were introduced. Most of the earliest buildings at St James's Gate date from this period. The oldest building at St James's Gate was not actually built by the Guinness brewery: this is the 1805 windmill, which had been erected by Roe's distillery (the distiller involved in renovating Christ Church Cathedral), which had held the site before an earlier Guinness expansion. There are also some early-nineteenth century brick vat houses. A brewhouse was added in 1875, designed by the company Ross & Baily, and construction on a hopstore that still stands on the site was begun in 1879. The Robert Street Malt Store, which visitors to the brewery pass on their way into the storehouse, was added between 1885 and 1886. Tunnels were added to connect the north and south of the brewery.

THE BUNG FRANKENSTEIN;
Or, the Collar of Gold.

The profits of Messrs. A. Guinness, Son & Co. in the year 1895 (the year before the label was issued) were £717,259. In the year 1908 the profits had increased to £1,247,627.

[Extract from Messrs. Guinness's agreement to traders using label :—   "4th December, 1896.
"3.—That I will not bottle or sell in bottle, or supply in bottle, the Extra Stout, Porter, or other Brown Beer of any other Brewer or Manufacturer while you continue to supply me with your said Trade Mark Labels."]

'Guinness as a king' from *The Lepracaun: Cartoon Monthly*, 1908
(Dublin City Library and Archives)

One of them, the bolted steel tunnel, was built by Harland and Wolff, in conjunction with the Art-Deco power house.[49]

This expansion and entry to the stock market allowed production to increase even further. A landmark in production on the site came

Guinness's Toucan advertisement. Guinness branding is recognised throughout the world. (Guinness Archives, Guinness Storehouse, St. James's Gate, Dublin 8)

in 1881, when more than a million barrels were brewed. Most other Dublin city breweries at this time were producing 100,000 barrels, so production at Guinness exceeded the eight other city breweries combined.[50] There was a workforce of 2,650 at St James's Gate, making Guinness a very significant city employer. The very success of Guinness made it difficult for other breweries to survive, and, slowly but surely other smaller breweries shut down. The economic historian Mary Daly has commented that 'the impression is thus of a successful giant, Guinness's success threatened the very existence of competitors'.[51] This was noted and commented on by contemporaries, some of whom saw Guinness as a bullying figure with too great a monopoly in the Irish market. The image on p. 151 is taken from the *Lepracaun* magazine in 1908. It depicts the giant Guinness, pushing other breweries around and putting them out of business, and points to their net profits for the year of £1,247,627. It also points to the stranglehold that Guinness had over pubs, grocers and even the Vintners Association.

ALCOHOL CONSUMPTION IN NINETEENTH AND TWENTIETH CENTURY DUBLIN

It could be argued that in the nineteenth century Dubliners came into their own as drinkers. Charitable institutions, social reformers and government organisations had begun to recognise that Dublin had a serious drinking problem. Beer and porter were the most widely consumed drinks in the city. From the eighteenth century there had been a recognisable class distinction in the drinking habits of Dubliners; the upper classes drank champagne, claret and wine, the middle class drank port, while the lower class drank beer, ale and porter. This was not peculiar to the city. One historian has commented on these class preferences when it came to drinking: beer 'was the cheapest and most widely consumed alcohol in town and country. Its competitors, cider, wine, imported spirits (rum, brandy and Geneva) and home-made grain, were all rather more exclusive beverages'.[52] The working class continued to consume beer and porter more than any other class well into the twentieth century. Porter, and Guinness in particular, was seen as a working man's drink. This is something that Guinness captured in their advertising images, ads and slogans. Guinness is said to 'give strength' to the working man because it has a high quantity of iron. Many advertisements show the strength of

Maurice McGonigal, *Dockers*, 1933–34 (Dublin City Gallery The Hugh Lane, reproduced with permission of Ciarán MacGonigal)

tradesmen and labourers as a result of their consumption of Guinness.

The Dublin-based writer Flann O'Brien satirised this in his novel *At Swim-Two-Birds*, which was first published in 1939.[53] A small group of men, described as 'plain upstanding labouring' men, are sitting in a pub and begin to discuss 'poets of the people'.[54] One of them suggests a poet called 'Jem Casey', and he recites one of his poems, which is called 'The workman's friend':

When money's tight and is hard to get
And your horse has also ran,
When all you have is a heap of debt
A pint of plain is your only man ...

When food is scarce and your larder bare.
And no rashers grease your pan,
When hunger grows as your meals are rare –
A pint of plain is your only man.[55]

The poem hit on a number of common themes surrounding drinking in Dublin but also the sad reality of life for many working men. Poverty was rife in the city, and men escaped this hardship by drinking. Alcohol could be procured even when men had no money. It was illegal in the first half of the twentieth century to give credit in pubs, but many publicans did so anyway. Pubs remained an important social sphere for men. A central part of this was pub chat. Many believed the art of conversation was brought to a higher level within a pub, obviously when drink had been consumed. For some workers within the city, a pint of porter would replace a meal. One publican stated that 'for dockers, drink was their main diet. Dockers lived on that. They lived for pints. It was food—they used to call it liquid food'.[56] The nature of the dockers' manual work meant they had to replenish with fluid, and so they drank in pubs throughout the day, not just in the evening. Many dockers were paid in pubs, which encouraged them to drink much of their wages in pubs too. Another publican stated that dockers 'were the toughest men in all Dublin ... they had a tremendous capacity for drink. They'd drink pints all day. Their whole life seemed to revolve around Guinness'.[57] The idea that dockers drank all their wages and lived for their next pint of Guinness is, however, something of an exaggeration.

Regardless of beer consumption by dockers, we know from reports and investigations of the time that Dublin had a drinking problem. From the nineteenth century onwards alcohol abuse was recognised as one of the biggest social problems of the day. Arrests for drunkenness in Dublin between 1871 and 1901 far exceeded London, Belfast,

Liverpool, Birmingham or Sheffield. Dublin also had the highest rate of arrests per head of population on the island. In a period between 1871 and 1918, Belfast surpassed Dublin in arrests for drunkenness only once, in 1911.[58] Drinking was rampant across all social classes in Ireland but the working class seemed to come off worst, with drinking repeatedly being associated with poor health, increased poverty, and problems within the home. The lengths some went to for alcohol were shown during the Great Whiskey Fire of 1875. A malt house and warehouse in the Liberties went on fire, releasing whiskey from its barrels and send it flowing down Ardee Street like a stream. When news got out, men and women came streaming into the street to drink the free alcohol. It was reported that men and women had to be dragged off the street by fire-fighters.[59] The blaze was stemmed, and the crowd brought under control, by loading horse manure on to the alcohol on the street.[60]

A temperance movement sprang up in the 1820s led by Fr Theobald Mathew (his statue stands on O'Connell Street today), but the movement faded away in the second half of the century, in the wake of both the Famine and the death of the charismatic priest. Parliament and city authorities tried to intervene in the problem in the second half of the century. In 1877 a select committee of the House of Lords was formed to investigate the problem of drinking in Dublin. The chief health officer for Dublin, Charles Cameron, subsequently produced a report entitled *How the Poor Live*. After investigating the conditions of working class homes in Dublin, Cameron's sympathies on the issue of drinking ultimately lay with the working man: 'The workman is blamed for visiting the public house but it is to him what the club is to the rich man. If he spends a reasonable proportion of his earnings in the public house is he to be more condemned than the prosperous shopkeeper or professional man who drinks expensive wines at the club or the restaurant?'[61] Drink was considered as a form of relief for the working man. The middle and upper classed indulged in it, so why should the working man not? While alcohol consumption was connected with poverty, poor housing conditions, domestic abuse and other social problems amongst the working classes, it was endemic across all social classes making it difficult to eradicate in just one. J.V. O'Brien points out that working-class alcohol consumption became a stick that the middle class used to punish the working class with. 'It suited the moral properties of the middle classes to defer generally to the notion that the condition of the poor was due to a state of "voluntary" poverty induced by profligate habits and, most of all, drink. People are poor because they waste their money, intoned otherwise sympathetic clerics ... And, declared others, they drink Guinness as a food'.[62] This propagated the convenient notion that the working classes of Dublin were poor because they were drunk. Excessive drinking in Dublin (and throughout Ireland as a whole) could not be stamped out, and was a continuous source of problems. Social commentators constantly linked it with the problems of the poor and the social ills of Ireland. In the twenty-first century high alcohol consumption remains a major social and cultural problem in Ireland, and one that the government and society continue to struggle with.

GUINNESS IN TWENTIETH CENTURY IRELAND

The first half of the twentieth century proved to be a more turbulent time for the Guinness family and Dublin. The family had located almost permanently to Britain by the early twentieth century, with Rupert, soon to inherit the family title and chairmanship of the company, serving as a unionist MP in England. His politics stood in stark contrast to the majority of the population of Ireland who were voting for increased Irish autonomy at this time. The Home Rule party was the largest political grouping on the island, and was the antithesis of unionism. With the outbreak of the 1916 Rising the Guinness family and company, like many Irish industrialists, were firmly against the republicans. The South Dublin Union (now St James's Hospital) was one of the principal sites held by the rebels and was very close to the brewery. Some of the workers were committed nationalists, and left work to join the rebels at their city barricades. The company responded by firing any Guinness employee thought to be involved in the rising.[63] The Robert Street Malt House was occupied by the King Edward Horse Regiment during the rising. Two of the brewery night staff were killed during the rising, having mistakenly been thought to be rebels.

While the number of rebels fighting in 1916 was small in comparison to the British army that fought them, the rebels initially had the upper hand. They knew the streets and could station themselves strategically. One Volunteer unit caused much trouble for the British by stationing itself at Grattan Bridge and disrupting the British army's ability to manoeuvre from the south to the north of the city. It also provided cover for additional rebels, who were arriving in the city up the quays. One British officer hit upon an ingenious idea to break the blockade: by commandeering boilers from the Guinness brewery and using them as covers on army trucks. Drilling holes into the boilers allowed soldiers to shoot but be protected from snipers shooting at them.[64] The vehicles became quite an attraction in the city but also reminded people of Guinness's connection with the British army.

Many within Dublin seemed uncertain of what to think of the rising while it was taking place, but in the aftermath many came out in support of the rebels. This support for the republican cause grew steadily in the years after 1916. The brewery, however, continued to support the British government's occupation of Ireland. Accommodation and meals were given to British soldiers in the brewery, and various regiments were stationed at St James's Gate. This failure to support the republicans must have led to a difficult relationship with the new Irish Free State, which came into being in 1922. One major bone of contention for Taoiseach (prime minister) Éamon de Valera, who came to power in 1932, was the payment of land annuities. In the late nineteenth and early-twentieth century, the British government had provided mortgages for small rural land holders, which allowed them to purchase the land they lived on. These mortgages had a long life and were still being repaid to Britain. De Valera objected to this for a number of reasons, and believed that the Irish economy would be best served if the money was kept in Ireland so refused to send the money to Britain. This resulted in an economic war between the two countries with Britain placing large tariffs on Irish agricultural and industrial goods. Britain was Ireland's largest trading partner, and exports to Britain made up the bulk of all Irish exports, so this was very damaging for a company such as Guinness who exported to Britain.

With a depressed Irish economy and unfavourable export conditions, the brewery decided to move its headquarters to London in 1932, while maintaining production in Dublin. In 1937 it consolidated this move by opening the Park Royal brewery in London, after which Guinness was produced there for the British market. Guinness was still produced in Dublin but primarily for the domestic market. The fact that the company headquarters were in London, and taxation was paid to the British government, prompted some commentators in Ireland to question the 'Irishness' of the drink. This did not stop sales, however, and Guinness continued to be the most popular beer in Ireland throughout the twentieth century.

Following a number of mergers between Guinness and Grand Metropolitan in 1997, Guinness is managed by Diageo, which produces a vast array of alcoholic beverages including Baileys, Bushmills and Smirnoff. Diageo's Irish headquarters is at St James's Gate, but its European headquarters remain at London, at Park Royal. Despite this, the Park Royal brewery ceased production of Guinness in 2005, and St James's Gate is once again the largest producer of the 'black stuff'. The location of Guinness production created controversy in 2007, when Diageo threatened to move production from St James's gate to a proposed plant in Kildare. Dubliners were outraged at the proposals, and these plans were shelved. Regardless of where the headquarters are, Diageo has continued to promote the connection between Arthur Guinness, the St James's Gate brewery and the drink itself. On 22 September 2009 they launched 'Arthur's Day' to celebrate Arthur Guinness and his drink. This celebration was marketed worldwide but particularly in Dublin with concerts featuring international acts taking place across the city and in the brewery itself. This celebration was hugely successful, but was criticised as a marketing ploy to sell more beer. In response, Diageo, who support a responsible-drinking campaign, cancelled Arthur's Day in 2014 and announced they would replace it with a music festival. The St James's Gate visitor centre is the most visited tourist attraction in the city centre. One of the highlights of the tour, apart from the pint of Guinness at the end, is the Gravity Bar, with its panoramic view of the city skyline. It is one of the best viewing points in the city.

7

Kilmainham Gaol

KILMAINHAM GAOL operated as a prison for more than 130 years and is remarkable for the number of prominent Irish men and women who were imprisoned within its walls. Indeed, the prison is a who's-who of venerable Irish nationalists. Nearly every significant nationalist or republican leader active while the prison was open, with the exception of Edward Fitzgerald (held in Newgate) Theobald Wolfe Tone (taken directly to Dublin Castle) Daniel O'Connell (held in Richmond Jail for three months) and Michael Collins (who evaded arrest), was held within the prison. The most celebrated prisoners associated with the jail are the leaders of the Easter Rising of 1916, who were held there before being executed in the prison yard. Stories that emerged from the prison of their final farewells to loved ones ensured that the prison became firmly entrenched in republican memory. These stories were evoked throughout the War of Independence, the Civil War and even during the more recent 'Troubles' in Northern Ireland. Because of this political connection, the prison has been described by some as the 'Irish Bastille'.[1]

As the county jail, all Dubliners would have been familiar with the prison and Kilmainham, perhaps more than any other building, would have represented the justice system. This was particularly true during public executions when Dubliners flocked to the prison to see famous and infamous prisoners executed. The prison can also tell us much about what life was like for ordinary, and sometimes not so ordinary, Dubliners in the eighteenth, nineteenth and early twentieth centuries. Dubliners found themselves incarcerated in the jail as a result of crimes they committed, political beliefs they held and often because of the poverty they were born into. There are the four square

The main entrance to Kilmainham Gaol (National Library of Ireland)

gaps still visible above the door of the prison that were used for the erection of temporary gallows. Timber was inserted into these holes to hang the bodies of those who had been executed. The sight of these dead criminals was intended to warn the public that those who erred would be punished to the full extent of the law. The corpses of many of the 143 people who were executed at Kilmainham would have been hung over the main door. The prison would have been a fearful place for most Dubliners.

PRISONS IN DUBLIN

The location of Kilmainham, now a city-centre suburb, is a reminder of how much the city has grown since the eighteenth century. Early images of the jail show it surrounded by a rural expanse, which contrasts heavily with its current location within a built-up residential and commercial area. When Kilmainham was opened in 1796, it acted as the county jail, replacing an earlier county penitentiary. There are some claims that there was a prison in the area as early as 1210, when the crusading order, the Knights of Jerusalem, had a manor house at Kilmainham that included a prison.[2] Newgate Gaol had acted as the city jail from as early as 1485. It had originally stood on the southside of the city, adjacent to Christ Church Cathedral, but in 1773 the foundation for a 'new' Newgate on the northside of the city, in the parish of St Michans, was laid.[3] In the seventeenth and eighteenth centuries there was also a debtors' prison, or marshalsea, which was known to Dubliners as 'the Black Dog', near Dublin Castle. While this might suggest that prisoners were segregated based on their crimes, this was not the case. The jailer at the marshalsea was interviewed in 1783 and stated that 'his jail is rather at present a reception for debtors than criminals, but he receives both'.[4] In 1780 a prison on Green Street was built which became known as Mountjoy Prison. By 1794 the Marshalsea was abandoned. Mountjoy took in its prisoners and become the principal prison for Dublin city.[5]

Prisons had very bad reputations in the eighteenth century and prisoners were of very little concern to society. During a crop failure and famine in 1740, the *Freeman's Journal* reported that four people in Newgate Gaol had died from starvation, having eaten the tongues from their own heads.[6] Criminals were incarcerated and forgotten about, especially in times of national crisis, when their plight was pushed far down the list of those in need. The structures themselves were reported throughout the eighteenth century as being in appalling conditions. In 1783 Sir Jeremiah Fitzpatrick undertook an inspection of the Marshalsea and described it as badly located, poorly ventilated and without proper toilets. The bulk of prisoners had no access to a doctor or apothecary. Fitzpatrick said the jail was 'in a most unwholesome situation in New-hall Market, surrounded with every exaltation necessary to promote putrefaction; it has neither yard nor necessary, except in the cellar, to which none have access except those on the first floor. The prison is four stories high, wainscoted; and in a most ruinous condition'. He was worried about the health of some of the prisoners and stated that, when he visited there were 'five venereal female patients [who would normally be treated at the Lock Hospital], and eight labouring under an inveterate itch in one room'.[7] Disease spread quickly in overcrowded prisons, so access to a doctor was important.

The conditions in which these people languished tells us much about the mentality of the time. Prisons were intended to incarcerate criminals and protect society from them, not to reform or rehabilitate. During the medieval and early modern period it was widely believed that people could be born evil. It was also believed that crime and immoral behaviour could contaminate and affect the minds of others, so it followed that criminals should be hidden away where they could not impinge upon decent members of society. Poverty, with little opportunity for the poor to better their situation, and utter neglect by parents and guardians were often seen to be at the root of these problems, particularly for young offenders, but these were seldom cited as a cause for a life of crime. To add to this burden, the prison system in the seventeenth and eighteenth centuries was riddled with problems. Jailers were poorly paid and saw prisons as a source of income so prisoners were forced to pay for their bed and board. This meant if you entered jail as a debtor, it was very difficult to leave. If a prisoner was wealthy, however, he could afford to rent better rooms and have food brought to him. He could also request that his family join him. Those who were not wealthy were forced to beg at the prison windows for food and money. The old Kilmainham Gaol was fitted with three grilles that faced on to Kilmainham Road, which allowed the inmates to beg.

THE CONSTRUCTION OF 'NEW' KILMAINHAM GAOL

In 1787 construction began on a new Kilmainham Gaol, to replace the old building. The new prison was opened in 1796, and it was believed that it would go a long way to rectifying the problems of its predecessor. Prison reformers had convinced governments to pay jailers proper salaries to stop jails being run for profit but reforms went further. John Howard an English preacher, was the leading figure in this reform movement.[8] He travelled to prisons all over the British Isles and Europe, and even visited 'old' Kilmainham prison where he found the inmates drunk at 11 o'clock in the morning. Two laws passed in Ireland under Howard's influence were especially important in improving conditions in prisons. In 1763 an act was passed to establish a prison inspectorate, and in 1778 a law was put in place to have surgeons and apothecaries visit jails to treat those suffering from illness.[9] This law benefited many prisons in the long term too, as prison reformers were often surgeons and apothecaries who visited and wrote about the horrendous conditions they observed.

Howard emphasised the importance of separating the prisoners. With overcrowding being a common problem in jails, it was believed that prisons could be schools of crime. Rather than having one large room where all prisoners were held together, they would be kept separately in individual cells. It was believed that this would give them time to contemplate their crimes and would stop repeat offenders from corrupting first offenders. This was taken into consideration when the new jail was designed. The west wing of the prison, which still stands today, dates to the opening of the prison. Designed by Sir John Traille, the prison originally consisted of two rectangular blocks—the east and west wings—linked by a jailers' quarters.[10] It was very difficult to uphold the one prisoner, one cell rule, however, and overcrowding was a problem from the start. The historian Pat Cooke wrote that 'virtually from the day it opened, right up to the 1860s, overcrowding was to remain a problem at Kilmainham'.[11] The separation of prisoners was very difficult to implement as the county could not afford to build prisons large enough to house all these inmates. Overcrowding became a huge problem during the Famine, and when republican rebellions broke out.

An accidental fire broke out in the prison in 1817, causing a lot of damage to the west wing. When it was rebuilt, the wing was expanded and improved, with added 'day rooms' for the inmates. In these rooms, the prisoners could carry out work, giving them a break from their cells.[12] This work varied from breaking stone in the yards for men or picking oakum from rope, to laundry work or making shirts for women.[13] The original eighteenth-century east wing was demolished in the 1840s to make way for a new building, which is still standing today.[14] It was designed by John McGurdy who was also responsible for an extension to the lavish Shelbourne Hotel in Dublin.[15] This new wing was influenced by the principles of the social reformer Jeremy Bentham. He believed that reform of one's mind started with outward reform, and he was so influenced by this idea that he designed what many believed to be the perfect prison, known as the Panopticon. If all inmates believed that they were being watched at all times, then they would behave well at all times. The horse-shoe shape of the east wing allowed prison guards to view all of the cells while standing at any point in the central hall. Carpets were placed along the floor to act as walkways, so that prison guards could walk without being heard and could view prisoners through spy holes in the doors. The large windows in the central hall of this wing were supposed to encourage prisoners to think of God and heaven.

CRIME IN DUBLIN

The most common reason for people to be incarcerated in Kilmainham Gaol was theft. Dublin was one of the poorest cities in the British empire for much of the prison's history, and many of those incarcerated within Kilmainham's walls had stolen to survive. In a society where many households employed servants and where security was unsophisticated, theft was difficult to prove. Heavy sentences for stealing were imposed because it was believed that they would act as a deterrent to criminals. The theft of £5, or goods to that value, could lead to the death penalty, and in the eighteenth century it often did. Just one example among countless is that of James Casady, who was executed on 27 January 1725 at Kilmainham for highway robbery, including items such as plates and dishes. He protested his innocence in his speech from the gallows: 'I do not know any of these prosecutors, and on the dying words of one who expects salvation I know nothing of the matter that I am charged with'. He added that 'as for what money I had by me, it was very honestly got, and I designed it for my son. But having an extravagant wife, was the reason I always carried the said money always with me'.[16] Long before modern detective work, which began to emerge slowly in the nineteenth century, it was easier to sentence people for crimes they did not commit.

By the late eighteenth century transportation was imposed as a sentence for theft more often than execution, and this trend continued over the course of the nineteenth century.[17] Nevertheless, the sentences can look severe by modern day standards. For example, Peter McCormack was sentenced to six months in solitary confinement in Kilmainham in July 1816 for stealing blankets. In 1853 Thomas Smith served five months' hard labour for stealing money from the chapel poor box in Dalkey.[18] You could also be imprisoned for simply not being able to pay your debts. Ann Kearns entered the prison 1 May 1819 for debts of £41. She died in the prison on 3 January 1828 as she was unable to pay her debts to gain her release.[19]

For the first 60 years of the jail's existence, it would have been home not only to adults, but to children as well. The youngest child recorded in the books is seven-year-old Mathew Gaynor who was sentenced in 1872 to 14 days in Kilmainham, followed by five years in Glencree Reformatory in Wicklow, for setting fire to a hay load. Eight-year-old Alicia Kelly was sentenced to five months' hard labour for stealing a cloak in 1839. Punishment was not restricted to incarceration and hard labour. In 1857 the fourteen year-old James Doyle and Daniel Byrne were sent to Kilmainham for seven days and given twenty lashes. After 1859 children were sent to reformatories. Boys were sent to St Kevin's in Glencree, County Wicklow, while the reformatory in Drumcondra, in County Dublin, took in girls.[20] By the turn of the twentieth century there were about 1,300 Dublin children per annum in these 'reformatories' or industrial schools scattered across the country. There were seven within Dublin city and county including the most notorious, the Artane Industrial School, which was run by the Christian Brothers and which held about 800 boys. Children could spend up to ten years in these institutions.[21]

Kilmainham was also a holding prison for those awaiting transportation to Australia, and this is another reason cited for the overcrowding at Kilmainham Gaol. Prisoners were moved by boat to Cork before sailing on to Australia. The journey to Australia took three months and a study of the jail archive has shown that more than 4,000 people were transported from Kilmainham Gaol to Australia. Many chose to stay on after they had served their terms. Historian Niamh O'Sullivan says that 'people were frequently sentenced to transportation for trivial offences. Shortly after the Great Famine, a group of six boys, all aged either 11 or 12, were held in Kilmainham after being sentenced to seven years' transportation for stealing shorts'.[22]

CRIME AND POVERTY IN DUBLIN

From a modern perspective it is easy to see that a major contributing factor to crime in Dublin was poverty. The capital was exceptionally poor, particularly when compared with industrial cities of Britain. Many Dublin workers were seasonal labourers, who struggled to gain employment for long periods. The economic historian Mary Daly says that three factors led to high unemployment in Dublin: a failure in rural Ireland to develop and diversify products for sale and export, a failure to build up a manufacturing base in cities to supply rural Ireland with the goods being produced, and stagnation in the urban economy. This led to high unemployment and 'Dublin failed to provide adequate employment, either for the indigenous Dublin population or for even a small proportion of the surplus population of rural Ireland'.[23]

The Irish Poor Law was introduced in 1838. It provided for the establishment of poor law unions throughout the country. These would take over the relief of poverty, which was usually distributed by parishes. These 'unions' or workhouses held an infirmary and a dispensary, and provided 'outdoor' relief in the way of meals for those who did not live in them, while taking in the homeless and destitute to work within their walls. There were two in Dublin city centre: the South Dublin Union and the North Dublin Union. The South Dublin

Union was very close to Kilmainham Gaol, just off James's Street (St James's Hospital currently stands on the old site of the South Dublin Union). Life expectancy for children was actually worsened by their admittance to these institutions, which were supposed to help them survive. A report into the conditions in Dublin's workhouses in 1841 found that from May 1840 to May 1841, 63 per cent of all children admitted to the North Dublin Union had died in the workhouse.[24] The report stirred up a very negative reaction in the Dublin press, and Daniel O'Connell, who was serving as lord mayor of Dublin at the time, was petitioned to intervene. Those responsible for running the workhouse blamed the nature and terms of the act itself rather than their own management. Another investigation in 1904 into the running of the North Dublin Union revealed that 327 babies out of 1,000 died in the union, an appalling figure, yet half of what it had been in 1840.[25] The improvement was probably less to do with better care and more to do with better information on sanitation and hygiene; part of the problem was that 'there were no nurses in the workhouse with special experience in the management and care of children'.[26]

There were also disagreements over how a workhouse should be run. Governors were worried about making the workhouses too comfortable, in which case people might prefer to go there instead of working. As a result conditions were made especially harsh. All inmates had to work for their bed and board, and none were provided with pay which would have helped them to work their way out of difficult situations. Simply put, poverty was their trap. Workhouse inmates got up at 5.45 a.m., had breakfast at 6.30–7.00 a.m., work began at 7.00 a.m. and continued until 6.00 p.m., with a one-hour break in the middle of the day. Everyone was expected to retire at 8.00 p.m. Children worked the same hours as adults, with three hours at school before returning to work. Work varied from stone-breaking and picking oakum for men, while women washed laundry, just like in prison.[27] Prisoners were separated by sex and age which broke up family units.

Both the workhouses and the city jails experienced a huge increase in the number of inmates during the Famine. The Famine is now often accepted as having taken place between 1845 and 1852, but the effects of the potato blight were felt for years after. While the immediate effect of the Famine was felt by the rural population, it quickly had a knock-on-effect in the cities as they depended upon the countryside for food. Not only did food prices rise, but migration to towns and cities meant that charities and institutions set up to help the poor, had larger numbers of people relying on them. Between 1841 and 1851 the population of Dublin rose by 11 per cent. In St Michan's Parish, where the North Dublin Union was, the population increased by 12 per cent.[28] The South Dublin Union likely saw a similar increase. In 1844–45, 19 per cent of those admitted into the North Dublin Union workhouse had come from outside Dublin city and county; 34 per cent were from the city and county; and the origin of the remainder was recorded as 'not stated'.[29]

The prison boards feared that people were so desperate during the Famine that they were committing crimes in order to gain entrance to prisons, where they were guaranteed a bed and some food. Food rations were reduced to the bare minimum to counter this. While there is some anecdotal evidence to suggest some sought imprisonment, this increase in numbers is likely down to the fact that, as one prison inspector stated, 'men will steal food rather than die'.[30] In Kilmainham up to five people were crammed into a prison cell during the Famine and some prisoners were kept in the halls.[31] The prison had fewer than 200 cells throughout the Famine yet it managed to hold an extraordinary number of inmates. In 1847 it held 2,500 prisoners, 4,655 in 1848 and 6,888 in 1849. In 1850 prison records show that at one time the prison held up to 9,502 people, the greatest number it would ever hold.[32]

POLITICAL PRISONERS IN KILMAINHAM

Almost since the year of its opening, Kilmainham had been used to house political prisoners and Irish republicans. The first political prisoner held there was Henry Joy McCracken, one of the founders of the United Irishmen. He was incarcerated in the prison on 11 October 1796. He was released and took part in the failed rebellion

(L–r) A soldier, Thomas Francis Meagher, William Smith O'Brien and Patrick
O'Donoghue at Kilmainham Gaol (Kilmainham Gaol Museum)

of 1798. Thomas Addis Emmet was imprisoned at Kilmainham for
his part in the rebellion and was kept there until 1802, when he
was allowed go into exile in America, where he lived until his death.
Thomas Addis was a brother of Robert Emmet, who spearheaded
another unsuccessful United Irish rebellion in 1803. He too was

imprisoned in the jail, along with many of his co-conspirators. Emmet's death mask is held at Kilmainham. Michael Dwyer was held there for his involvement in Emmet's rebellion, and was then transported to Australia. William Smith O'Brien and Thomas Francis Meagher were held in Kilmainham after the failed Young Ireland rebellion of 1848, which was also inspired by events in France. One of the earliest photographs taken in Ireland was taken in one of the prison yards, and shows Thomas Francis Meagher, William Smith O'Brien and Patrick O'Donoghue. The picture was so popular that it was retaken, this time with actors posing.[33] In the aftermath of the failed Fenian rising of 1867, Kilmainham became the main detention centre for political prisoners, and regular prisoners were moved from there. James Stephen, founder of the Irish Republican Brotherhood, had escaped from Richmond Prison in 1865, and this had alarmed the government. One of the reasons for keeping such prisoners in Kilmainham was because the government felt it was 'the most secure prison in the kingdom'.[34]

Charles Stewart Parnell and leading members of the Land League were imprisoned in Kilmainham for their radical political and social ideas rather than their militant nationalism. As head of the Land League, Parnell was spearheading a campaign to give land ownership to those who actually worked and resided on the land. Small tenants in post-Famine Ireland had little security on their landholdings and if they fell behind on their rent they faced eviction. This was a prospect that many, particularly in the west of Ireland, were faced with. The Land League, established in Mayo in the 1870s by Michael Davitt, encouraged the community as a whole to put pressure on landlords by boycotting them and any tenant who took up a farm after a family had been evicted. Parnell had famously said:

> When a man takes a farm from which another has been evicted, you must show him on the roadside when you meet him, you must show him in the streets of the town, you must show him at the shop-counter, you must show him in the fair and at the market-place, and even in the house of worship, by leaving him severely alone, by putting him into a sort of moral Coventry, by isolating him from the rest of his kind as if he were a leper.[35]

The west of Ireland seemed like a tinderbox, and the government believed that Parnell held the match. On 13 October 1881 Parnell was arrested at Morrison's hotel on Dawson Street, Dublin, and was imprisoned in Kilmainham Gaol along with many of his supporters.[36] During his six-month incarceration Parnell's female supporters sent him numerous green gifts including smoking caps, tea cosies and even hosiery. Green was the well-established colour of nationalism, but many did not know that the superstitious Parnell despised the colour. One close supporter even sent a green eiderdown quilt with Parnell's monogram in gold to the prison. William O'Brien described it as 'a present worthy of a king', but added that, while 'he must have sent a sweet and gracious acknowledgement ... the gorgeous quilt never rested on his bed. It was hidden away carefully underneath a press, where I am afraid, the mice soon tarnished its glory'.[37]

Incarceration in a prison was quite a change in circumstances for many of the Land Leaguers who spent the winter of 1881–82 within Kilmainham's walls. One of the luxuries they allowed themselves was to have their food brought to them from an outside restaurant. They continued this until the prison governor pointed out that the government had no need to outlaw the Land League as their food bills alone would quickly bankrupt the association and put an end to it.[38] Parnell ordered everyone to eat the prison food instead, leading the way himself when it came to the changeover. William O'Brien describes how they dealt with this:

> The prison fare included twice a week a lump of inferior beef per man, and Parnell conceived the project of pooling all our lumps of beef together in a common pot, from which, with the aid of broken bread and of the vegetables fished out of the prison soup of the previous day's dietary, he concocted a famous dish of Irish stew ... we grimaced more [over the stew] than over the unadorned prison food, which was to the cook a source of never-failing joy and pride.[39]

Parnell was released on parole on 10 April 1882 following an agreement with Prime Minister William Gladstone, which became known as the Kilmainham Treaty. Under the terms of the treaty Parnell would work to pacify militants, and arrears that tenants had amassed during the land war would be cancelled. Ireland would not remain peaceful for long, however. On 6 May 1882, just four days after the Kilmainham Treaty was announced and the Land Leaguers released, the new chief secretary for Ireland, Lord Frederick Cavendish, and his under-secretary, Thomas Henry Burke, arrived in Ireland. Within hours they were stabbed to death in the Phoenix Park. The murders shocked public opinion in Britain and Ireland, including Parnell, who denounced it immediately. A group calling themselves the 'Invincibles' wrote to Dublin newspapers claiming the assassination was their work.

Twenty-six men were arrested for membership of the Invincibles and brought to Kilmainham Gaol. Some became informers and gave details of who the society were and what they sought. They were bound by a secret oath to overthrow British government in Ireland by any means. Five members of the group were publicly executed outside Kilmainham Gaol for the murders of Cavendish and Burke between May and June 1883. The trial was followed with great interest in Ireland and Britain. Many were intrigued by the executions. The first man to be executed, Joe Brady, stated on the platform before his execution that he was not guilty of the crime and that the evidence submitted against him had been imparted by paid informers.[40] Others admitted their guilt but the reliance on informers cast a doubt over the executions for some.

Kilmainham Gaol and the 1916 Rising

The 1916 Rising (see chapter eight) is inextricably linked with Kilmainham Gaol, more so than any other event. While the prison had ceased to function as a jail in February 1910, it was used as a barracks during the First World War. In the aftermath of the rising the authorities arrested 3,430 men and 79 women for taking part. Those arrested for taking part in the rebellion, many incorrectly, were sent to the military prison at Arbour Hill and Richmond Barracks, with Kilmainham Gaol being reopened to take extra prisoners. Many of the prisoners were wrongly arrested. Within a fortnight, 1,424 were released and only 579 were detained for a lengthy period.[41] More than seventy women were kept at Kilmainham. The conditions in the prison were appalling. Court-martials were held in late April and perhaps as many as ninety-six men were sentenced to death. Those deemed to be the leaders were scheduled to be executed first, and were moved from Richmond Barracks, where they had been held for the court-martials, to Kilmainham where the executions were to be carried out.

The first leaders to be executed were shot in the stone breakers yard of the prison on 3 May 1916. They were Thomas Clarke, Thomas MacDonagh and Patrick Pearse. The next day the Irish Parliamentary Party leader, John Redmond, made a speech in the House of Commons warning the British government that 'if any more executions take place in Ireland, the position will become impossible for any constitutional party or leader'.[42] Redmond could not understand the need for a large number of executions. But that day they stepped up the action by executing Edward Daly, Willie Pearse,[43] Michael O'Hanrahan and Joseph Plunkett. These were followed by John MacBride on 5 May, Seán Heuston, Michael Mallin, Éamonn Ceannt and Con Colbert on 8 May, and finally James Connolly and Seán MacDiarmada on 12 May. Thomas Kent was executed in Cork Detention Barracks on 9 May. In an open letter published in the *London Daily News*, George Bernard Shaw warned that 'to slaughter a man in this position without making him a martyr and a hero' was impossible.[44] It was too late for the British to turn the tide at that point. They had created martyrs, and Irish nationalists would use them effectively.

Stories that emerged from the jails, and of the rising itself, swayed many people's opinions towards supporting it after the fact. Families were allowed into the prison to see their loved ones before their executions, and they emerged with stories of the last hours of these men's lives. Kathleen Clarke was allowed to visit her husband, and she remembered later that the prison presented 'a scene of doom and decay. It had been abandoned as a prison for many years. A damp smell pervaded the place, and the only light was candles in jam jars'. Kathleen was pregnant when she said goodbye to her husband but never revealed this to him as she would did not want to add to his burden. They were married in 1901 and had three children together.

Kathleen made two trips to Kilmainham: her brother, Edward Daly, was also executed for his part in the rising, and the day before his execution she went to say goodbye. Kathleen was a formidable woman, who continued her family's fight. She set up the National Aid fund which provided money to the families of those who were executed and imprisoned as a result of the 1916 Rising. She went on to become the first female lord mayor of Dublin, serving from 1939 to 1940.[45]

Michael O'Hanrahan's family were told that they had come to see him 'before his deportation to England'.[46] They were devastated to hear of his execution. Stories like this leaked out and impressed upon the public the tragedies that these families were dealing with in the aftermath of the rising. On the night before his execution, Michael Mallin, like the other leaders of the rising, was moved from Richmond Barracks to Kilmainham, where he would face execution. Mallin lived in Kilmainham with his wife and children and he passed by the house en route. When passing he eagerly sought to catch a glimpse of his wife and children but to no avail. In his last letter to his wife, he wrote that 'the only one of my household that I could cast my longing eyes on was poor Prinnie the dog. She looked so faithful there at the door'.[47] Brought so close to his own front door, Mallin must have been devastated to miss the opportunity to see his wife from the window one last time. One of the most touching stories was that of Joseph Plunkett and Grace Gifford. The two had been engaged when the rising broke out, and had originally planned to marry on Easter Sunday. They were given special permission to marry just hours before his execution. This humble ceremony took place on 3 May by candlelight in the Catholic chapel in the prison. Grace found herself incarcerated in the prison later that year, and again during the Civil War. A cartoonist by profession, Grace left a very visible reminder of her time in the prison, painting the 'Kilmainham Madonna' on her cell wall in the east wing. It can be viewed by visitors to the jail today.[48] Kilmainham has become an important place for the public to pay homage to their memories.

KILMAINHAM GAOL, THE WAR OF INDEPENDENCE AND THE CIVIL WAR

Kilmainham was to play a pivotal role in the War of Independence too. At the end of 1916 the jail was under the control of the General Prisons Board but in 1920 it was handed over to the British army. It was used to detain members suspected of IRA involvement, and it tended to be the most important and highest-ranking who were held in the jail. Interrogation tended to take place in Dublin Castle, however. The senoir IRA organiser Ernie O'Malley was arrested in late 1920, interviewed and beaten in Dublin Castle, and was then detained at Kilmainham Gaol. He was not told where he was going and he described his stay as follows: 'I was in a gaol, which one, I did not know. Cold thick shadows and ugly walls, my boot crashed off the flags … A soldier walked in front of me with a Webley in his hand, down a gloomy passage. He opened the iron door of a cell, the door clanged. The gas came through a weak jet which spluttered and gasped, lighting up slightly, now dimming the outlines of the bare walls; shadows jumped up, fell and climbed again. I sat on a few dirty, brown army blankets in a corner'.[49] If the jail had been dark, gloomy and uninviting in 1916, it had not improved by 1920. Once inside, many of these IRA men were worried that other prisoners were plants, sent there to gather intelligence, so they had to observe the utmost caution.[50] In February 1921 O'Malley, along with Simon Donnelly and Frank Teeling, managed to escape, three of only a small number of people to do so in the jail's history.

A truce came into effect on 11 July 1921, and the Anglo-Irish treaty that established the Irish Free State was signed on 6 December 1921. O'Sullivan says that 'two very different approaches to the document developed, and the divisions widened even further, until the two sides could barely speak to each other … For some it was the best they could have hoped for at that time; for others, it fell short of the republic that had been declared on Easter Monday in 1916'.[51] The first prisoners to be executed during the civil war that followed were executed in Kilmainham Goal. Those were Peter Cassidy, James Fisher, John Gaffney and Richard Twohig on 17 November 1922.

They were shot in the yard next to the stone breaker's yard. It was believed they were executed first so that Erskine Childers would not be the first prisoner to be executed—his death would have caused a huge outcry. He was executed a week later, on 24 November, at Beggars Bush Barracks.

Five hundred women were incarcerated in the jail between February and September 1923 for their part in the fight against the treaty.[52] Some undertook a hunger strike in the prison when their letters and parcels were withheld by the Free State government. The strike started on Friday 23 May 1923 and ninety-six women, including W.B. Yeats's former muse Maud Gonne, took part. Within a week the governor had given in and restored their letters and parcels. However, three of the women decided they would continue the strike in order to gain full release. On 12 April they were joined by two other hunger strikers. One of these new hunger strikers was Mary MacSwiney, sister of Terence MacSwiney who had been elected lord mayor of Cork during the War of Independence and who had died while on hunger strike. On 25 April Annie O'Neil and Nellie Ryan had to be taken from the prison to hospital after 35 days of fasting, and the strike ended.[53] May Malone undertook her own hunger strike on 23 June 1923 which lasted until 1 July 1923. One of the poems that she wrote, called 'The Return' is still visible on a cell wall in the west wing.[54]

Conditions in the prison during the Civil War were horrendous. This was reflected on by two sisters who were inmates at the time: 'We learned afterwards that some of these cells had housed patriots down the ages and that the 1916 men occupied them for some days before their execution. However having no knowledge of this at the time … [we were] more likely … thinking of the rats and mice that might be running over us and our mattresses during the night but even these visitors did not trouble us and we never saw one of their kind during our time'.[55] By March 1923 the west wing, which had long since been declared unsafe, was brought back into use. Sanitation was very poor, and the wing smelled very bad as a result. The prisoners were given disinfectant to clean their cells, but this did little to remove the smell. Some women removed the glass from the windows to try and relieve the smell, but when it became cold the prison authorities refused to

East wing of Kilmainham, before restoration, 1953 (National Library of Ireland)

replace the glass.[56] Poor sanitation led to ill-health for many women, and while there was a prison doctor, outside doctors and family doctors were not allowed into the prison. There were two doctors among the female prisoners, Dr Elenora Fleury and Dr Elsie Murphy, and they did their best to administer to the women, although they had few resources.[57]

THE CLOSURE OF KILMAINHAM

The last prisoners left the jail in March 1924, and in 1929, because the building was falling into disrepair, it reverted to the ownership of Dublin County Council. There was interest in the building, however. The National Graves Association (NGA) wanted to erect a commemorative plaque to those nationalist leaders executed there.

View of Kilmainham Gaol east wing from prison yard

In 1932 Seán Fitzpatrick, the chairman of the NGA, requested that the prison be open to visitors who were in the city for the Eucharistic Congress. When he was turned down, he wrote to the minister for local government, Seán T. O'Kelly, suggesting a meeting with the NGA to discuss suitable commemorative markings for the prison. The suggestion was passed on to the commissioner of public works with the backing of Taoiseach Éamon de Valera, and the building was surveyed to assess its suitability as a national monument. Some objected to this, including the minister for education, Tomás Derrig, who had been a prisoner in the jail during the Civil War. Fianna Fáil was descended from those republicans who had not supported the treaty, and many of their sitting TDs and ministers had been incarcerated in Kilmainham and other prisons over the course of the War of Independence and Civil War. It is unsurprising that the plans to restore the jail touched a nerve in government circles. Nevertheless, on 4 December 1936 the government finally decided to acquire the building from the county council.[58] Seán Fitzpatrick managed to get the press behind the project in the 1930s, to help ensure that the idea was not forgotten or shelved.

In 1938 the building was bought for the very low sum of £100.[59] But plans for its development stalled again. The outbreak of the Second World War meant that the government had other priorities. In the meantime, the building began to fall into further decay. The image on p. 178 of the east wing shows the condition of the prison before the restoration. While the east wing was remarkably well preserved, weeds, plants and even trees had grown up inside parts of the jail. The fabric of the building was in a precarious state in many places. The idea of saving the jail and preserving it as a museum was resurrected in the 1950s, and in August 1953, the government unveiled its plans to make the jail a national monument. In 1954 there was a change of government, however, and the new Fine Gael-led coalition lumped the development of Aer Lingus, the preservation of Kilmainham Gaol and the building of the Bray Road into a list of projects that could be sacrificed to save money. One Fine Gael TD said in the Dáil that 'we believe that all these schemes were nonsense and should not have been introduced by Fianna Fáil. I often wonder how Deputy de Valera allowed this party to introduce them.[60] The shelving of these projects proved to be short-sighted.

Government inaction prompted a Dublin engineer, Lorcan Leonard, to step in and rouse local support to restore the building. A provisional restoration committee was formed in 1959, which produced a proposal for the renovation of the jail. The plan was approved at a government meeting on 26 February 1960 and the restoration work was undertaken by a large team of volunteers. It is perhaps disappointing that the government failed to develop the plan, but, as Rory O'Dwyer points out, the restoration of Kilmainham was a grass-roots movement promoted by a very determined leader: 'Seán Fitzpatrick ... deserves credit for his vision of developing the gaol as a national monument and for his perseverance with that aspiration. His endeavour, and that of other little-known men and women who came to share his vision ... represents a unique and inspiring instance of active citizenship and passionate volunteerism towards a patriotic cause'.[61]

Thankfully Kilmainham was preserved, despite successive governments failing to support schemes to re-open it. Today it stands as a reminder of the sacrifices that many men and women made for Ireland; their freedom and often their lives. It is also a landmark building that can connect us with the ideals of these leaders. The exhibition and guides at Kilmainham do an excellent job in evoking the personalities of the dead nationalists and republicans who were incarcerated within its walls, and particularly those leaders of the 1916 Rising who drew their last breath there. Nevertheless, these leaders are linked with many buildings and sites throughout Ireland. Some of the most fascinating stories that Kilmainham has to offer are those stories of Dublin's ordinary prisoners, including men, women and children sent to Kilmainham because of poverty. It is an extraordinary link to our social history.

8

The General Post Office (GPO)

THE GENERAL POST OFFICE opened on Sackville Street (now O'Connell Street) in 1818. In the nineteenth century the post office was the very symbol of a modern state. The design was 'large and sober' and was intended to convey the progress and scientific developments of the nineteenth century. Like the extensive network of railways that were being rolled out across the country, the post office was a reminder that a modern age of speedy and efficient communication was at hand. The development of the telegraph and the telephone system reinforced the importance of the post office and its connection with modernity, the progress of science and the extension of the British Empire, of which Ireland was an important part. While the GPO was a symbol of modernity in the nineteenth century, it became a very potent republican image in the twentieth century. As the headquarters of the 1916 Rising, the building seemed to encapsulate all of the ideals and dreams the rebellion's leaders had fought for. Most of the building was destroyed in a fire that engulfed Sackville Street during the rising. It remained a shell from 1916 until 1924 when the new Free State released funds to rebuild it. It was not completed until 1929. The building is largely a reconstruction of the original, as after the rising only the front façade of the building and its Doric columns and rooftop sculptures remained.[1] But the building was venerated because it seemed to symbolise the sacrifice that the men and women of 1916 had made. The symbolic importance of the building to the republican movement was recognised even before the rebellion was over. James Connolly, leader of the Irish Citizen Army and overall commander of Dublin's rebel forces during the Easter Rising, wrote in his last communique from the GPO that 'the enemy feels that in this building is to be found the heart and inspiration of our great movement'.[2]

SACKVILLE STREET

Sackville Street, renamed O'Connell Street in 1924, came about due to the amalgamation of two streets. The houses on the original eighteenth-century street would have attracted some of Dublin's richest citizens. The northside remained the more fashionable part of the city throughout the eighteenth century. When the Custom House opened on the North Quays in 1791, more commerce and business gravitated to the northside of the city as banks, insurance businesses and merchants began to move from the southside closer to the Custom House. The Royal Exchange and later, the Commercial Buildings on Dame Street, had been the home of the post office throughout the eighteenth century. After the Act of Union the post office re-located to the northside following the building of the Custom House.

The postal system in Ireland dated back to the Tudor conquest. Communication was central to colonisation and to implementing authority. It was essential that Dublin Castle had regular news reports of the state of counties throughout Ireland, and that the lord lieutenant could report back to London quickly. Horses were used to carry post back to Dublin, and the capital became the centre of a postal system that relied on passenger ships travelling from Dublin to Britain. By the eighteenth century mail coaches took advantage of the regular coach services that connected towns and cities throughout Ireland to quickly and efficiently deliver post. During the nineteenth century, railways connected towns and cities throughout Ireland, meaning post could be delivered more quickly and cheaply. The post office developed the range of services it offered throughout the nineteenth and twentieth centuries which made it a significant government office. As well as providing a telegraph service and later telephone service, it undertook banking services.[3] The post office was a necessary public service for many people in nineteenth-century Ireland.

The General Post Office on Sackville Street was to become the headquarters and hub of all of these services. As late as 1814 a plot on

General Post Office, *Dublin Penny Journal* (Dublin City Library and Archives)

Sackville Street, adjacent to Nelson's Pillar, remained vacant. As it lay close to the Custom House and to Carlisle Bridge (which connected the busiest southside and northside districts), it was perfect for the new city post office. The purchase of the site and building came to more than £50,000. It was designed by Francis Johnston, who along with William Wilkins had designed Nelson's Pillar in the centre of Sackville Street. The building, started in 1814, was finished by 1818, and was 225 feet wide, and 50 feet high. It was imposing, and had an expensive Portland Stone facade. A large pediment stood on six massive ionic pillars that jutted out into Sackville Street. Statues of Hibernia, Mercury and Fidelity, along with the royal coat of arms, crowned the pediment. Up until this point the street had been dominated by residential or office buildings which created a uniform vista. The addition of the post office would have dramatically altered the streetscape. The building was greeted warmly by Dubliners, and the *Dublin Penny Journal* described it in 1834 as 'one of the finest structures of the kind in Europe'.[4] They were more critical of the interiors of the building, stating that 'there is no object worthy of the notice of the tourist in the interior'.[5]

GP.O. AND NELSON PILLAR DUBLIN.

2278

Nelson's Pillar postcard (Dublin City Library and Archives)

Even aside from the GPO, Sackville Street was an important part of the social and economic life in the city. The eighteenth-century Rotunda ballrooms were later joined by dance halls, theatres (the Pillar Theatre in 1913) and cinemas (the Savoy in 1929 and the Carlton in 1937). The Gresham Hotel, founded in 1817 at 21 and 22 Upper O'Connell Street, was one of the premier hotels in the city from its foundation. The street was also filled with important financial service offices such as the Colonial Insurance Company, the Standard Life assurance, the Royal Bank and the Hibernian Bank. Clerys, one of the largest department stores in the city, provided a focus for shopping on the street. The store was established in 1853 as McSwiney, Delaney & Co., but in 1883 it was taken over by M.J. Clery and is still open today. Clerys' clock was a meeting point for generations of Dubliners. As the focal point for Dublin trams, the street remained easy to get to and from. This helped to ensure that it retained its importance.

NELSON'S PILLAR

The most iconic—and yet controversial—monument on Sackville Street was Nelson's Pillar which was designed by William Wilkins and Francis Johnston. The foundation stone of the monument was laid in 1809. When the monument was unveiled it consisted of a doric column 111 feet high topped with a statue of Admiral Horatio Nelson by Thomas Kirk (the statue was a tribute to a victory: Nelson defeated the French and Spanish navies at the battle of Trafalgar, but was injured during the battle and subsequently died of his wounds).[6] When it was completed in 1811 it gave the street 'a dramatic and monumental focus'.[7] The monument was paid for by a public fund headed by prominent citizens seeking to commemorate Nelson's great victories, which had brought peace to Britain and Ireland as well as renewing access to European trade routes that had been blocked by the war. The column contained 164 steps, which could be climbed to reach a viewing point with 'a panoramic view of the city, bounded by the bay to the east, the Wicklow mountains to the south, and, on a clear day, by the Mourne mountains to the north'.[8] Entrance was 10d, later reduced to 6d, with the money collected put to charitable purposes. While the stunning views made the pillar a popular tourist attraction, in the 1940s the publisher and author G. Ivan Morris wrote that the pillar was used by courting couples for privacy: 'this noble monument has become a resort for young couples, who invariably grow tired of the long climb to the top and like to rest themselves on the steps on the way up. Who can blame them if, in the darkness, they exchange a kiss or two?'[9]

While the pillar might have symbolised peace and prosperity to some of the city inhabitants, to others it was a symbol of British repression. The early-nineteenth century journalist Watty Cox saw it as a reminder of the Act of Union. He said the statue was a reminder that 'our independence has been wrested from us, not by the arms of France but by the gold of England. The statue of Nelson records the glory of a mistress and the transformation of our senate into a discount office'.[10] Criticism by nationalists continued throughout the nineteenth century, and, by the foundation of the Free State, there were calls to remove it. Nationalists may have seen Nelson as an imperial figure surveying the Free State, but objections to the pillar were made for other reasons too. In 1922 the *Irish Builder* outlined reasons why the statue should be removed: 'The Pillar is most unsuitably placed, a great obstruction to traffic, and forms an objectionable barrier, severing the north from the south side of the city, with very ill results for the trade and commerce and the residential amenities of Dublin'.[11] In a period when cars and vans were increasingly being employed on the street, the monument obstructed traffic.[12]

THE BACKGROUND TO THE 1916 EASTER RISING

The most dramatic event in the street's history, and a seminal event in the history of the GPO, was the Easter Rising of 1916. With the growth of Irish nationalism in the nineteenth century, Sackville Street became an important political thoroughfare. As the widest street in the city, it was used for demonstrations. Historian Clair Wills says that 'the urban landscape in Dublin had become intensely politicised', and Sackville Street became a focal point for that politicisation.[13] It also became home to statues and monuments of significant nationalist leaders. The figures that were chosen by Dublin Corporation, such as Daniel O'Connell (see parliament chapter) and Charles Stewart Parnell, had often clashed with the British state. Parnell and O'Connell had both been imprisoned by the government and were viewed as radicals by many. These statues were erected at the same time as statues of the British royal family and imperial figures. These conflicting ideologies of loyalism and nationalism co-existed uneasily in Dublin's urban landscape, and highlighted the political divisions in Irish society. By the late nineteenth century Dublin Corporation was a strongly nationalist body and its 'concerted attempts to commemorate figures drawn from the sphere of Irish nationalist politics began to gather pace'.[14] While many public statues had been erected in the seventeenth and eighteenth centuries of Stuart and Hanoverian monarchs, by the nineteenth century public figures and politicians were becoming popular choices for commemoration.

The 'O'Connell Monument Committee' was formed in 1862 and a fund was opened to raise subscriptions to commemorate Daniel O'Connell, 'the Liberator'. The statue was to be erected at the bottom of Sackville Street, placing him in a more prominent position than Admiral Nelson. Around the same time a competition was launched to build a new bridge, which would be as broad as Sackville Street, and so the O'Connell Statue would be the centre of a vista that stretched from Sackville Street, across Carlisle Bridge and down Westmoreland Street.[15] The foundation stone to O'Connell's huge monument was laid with great ceremony two days after the centenary of O'Connell's birth in August 1875. The monument itself was not completed until 1882. When it was finished thousands of people flocked to the city centre to see it.[16] The corporation voted later in the century to have Sackville Street renamed, but this was too much for some of the residents of the street, who objected, and the decision was overturned. While commonly referred to as O'Connell Street, it was not officially renamed until 1924.

The next nationalist statue erected on the street was to Sir John Gray, a former owner of the *Freeman's Journal*. This was followed by statues to William Smith O'Brien (who had been sentenced to death for treason for his part in the 1848 rebellion) and Fr Theobald Mathew of the temperance movement. The foundation stone for Parnell's monument was laid on 8 October 1899, although it was not unveiled until 1911. Of course, these nationalist statues were not the only ones to be erected within the capital. Statues of Queen Victoria and Prince Albert were unveiled on the lawns of the Royal Dublin Society (Victoria's statue was removed but Albert's is still there). It is significant that these statues of royalty were not in the busy thoroughfare of Sackville Street.[17] While investigating the naming of public spaces and the erection of public monuments, Yvonne Whelan has shown that 'the geographical positions' of these nationalist monuments as well as 'the choreography of the unveiling ceremonies … are indicative of a broader change in the politics of power in late nineteenth-century Dublin'.[18] Loyalism seemed to be losing out to nationalism, at least on the capital's streets.

THE PRELUDE TO THE 1916 RISING

The opening decade of the twentieth century seemed to promise much for the Home Rule movement led by John Redmond. The party held the balance of power in parliament after the 1910 election and formed a government with the Liberal party, which agreed to introduce a Home Rule Bill. The bill was introduced into the House of Commons in April 1912, and while it passed in the lower house, it had a more difficult time in the House of Lords. In August 1911, however, a bill had been passed that removed the House of Lords' veto and modified it to a two-year delay (from when it was passed in the commons). Irish nationalists knew that the bill would have to pass into law some time in 1914 providing a form of self-government for Ireland.[19] The parliamentary successes of the nationalists panicked unionists into action. Unionists wanted to maintain the Act of Union and ensure that Ireland did not move away from Great Britain. They also believed that their economic interests were best served within the union. Ulster unionists in particular argued that the other three Irish provinces were economically backward, and that Protestants (the bulk of unionist supporters were Protestant) would lose political and social rights within a politically autonomous parliament. In fact the 'distinctiveness of Ulster unionism … came inevitably at the expense of southern unionists' which meant that unionism was increasingly associated with Ulster, with unionists in the other three provinces left behind.[20]

The Unionist Party, under the Dublin-born lawyer (and MP for Trinity College) Edward Carson, began to mobilise against Home Rule. The Ulster Volunteer Force was formed in early 1913. This was a private army that vowed to defend Ireland from what was seen to be the threat of Home Rule. In April 1914 they imported 25,000 rifles and 5 million rounds of ammunition.[21] In November 1913 nationalists responded to this unionist mobilisation with the formation of the Irish Volunteers. The idea for the body did not come from militant nationalists but from Eoin MacNeill, a professor of medieval history and key a member of the Gaelic League (a movement to restore the Irish language).[22] While the body may have been established by a mild-mannered academic, militant republicans were soon attracted to the organisation. The Irish Republican Brotherhood (IRB), or Fenians (a secret society who argued the only way for Ireland to gain independence was through violent means) quickly infiltrated key positions in the organisation, and planned to use the movement for their own ends. While the IRB operated in secret, John Redmond also moved to take control of the new movment. Unbeknownst to him, the IRB secretly held key senior positions, and were hostile to the Redmondite takeover

The ranks of the Volunteers swelled in 1914, and by April of that year they had a membership of 27,000 men, which increased dramatically to 190,000 by September. By the outbreak of the Great War, 250,000 men across the island were in a paramilitary organisation—one in five of the male population.[23] While a civil war over the issue of Home Rule looked imminent, the Irish Volunteers split over whether or not members could enlist in the British army during the First World War. On 20 September 1914, while addressing a large number of Irish Volunteers at Woodenbridge in Wicklow, Redmond urged the Volunteers to enlist. He had made the commitment for the Volunteers to enlist in the British army without consulting the Volunteer executive council, and on 24 September, when he met with MacNeill and members of the council they were displeased at his actions. MacNeill expelled the Redmondites from the council, but most of the Volunteers decided to follow Redmond's lead and reconstituted themselves as the Irish National Volunteers. Only 9,700 Irish Volunteers stayed behind (out of a membership of 156,750).[24] The outbreak of war had greatly reduced their ranks.

There was a core within the Volunteer leadership who saw the outbreak of the war as an opportunity. The old Fenian dictum that 'England's difficulty is Ireland's opportunity' was resurrected, and it was decided that a rebellion should be planned to take place before the war ended. When the Fenian Jeremiah O'Donovan Rossa died in June 1915, his funeral in Glasnevin Cemetery acted as a display of strength for militant activists. One of the speakers at the graveside was Patrick Pearse, who stated his enthusiasm for an armed insurrection. He famously said that 'they have left us our Fenian dead, and while Ireland holds these graves, Ireland unfree shall never be at peace'.[25]

The Irish Volunteers were not the only radical nationalist organisation active in Ireland on the eve of the rebellion. Cumann na mBan, or the Women's League, was a female alternative to the Volunteers (women were not allowed join the Volunteers). The Irish Citizen Army (ICA) was formed during the Dublin 'lockout' of 1913. James Connolly, the leader of the ICA, was a socialist, and believed that for socialism to become a reality in Ireland, Ireland would have to be independent. With this in mind he made independence as a primary goal.

PLANNING THE REBELLION

Part of the difficulty with shedding light on the planning stages of the 1916 Rising is its secretive nature. Few documents remain so we do not definitively know what the plans and intentions were. The executions of the leaders added to this problem. The historian Fearghal McGarry has pointed out that we cannot even be sure if 'the organisers believed they were likely to be successful or whether they acted in the knowledge that there was a little prospect of victory'.[26] The oldest leader was Tom Clarke, an IRB man who had been imprisoned in England for taking part in a dynamite campaign in 1883. Along with Seán MacDiarmaida, Clarke 'provided the inspiration' for armed insurrection before the war was over.[27] They felt that a rebellion in war time would take the British by surprise. They also planned to take advantage of the war with Germany to gain German military aid. Clarke and MacDiarmada were the driving forces behind the insurrection, and the military council that planned it in secret was formed in May 1915, and consisted of Joseph Plunkett, Éamonn Ceannt and Patrick Pearse. James Connolly was brought on board in January 1916 as there was a worry that he might start a rising himself otherwise. Clarke and MacDiarmada joined the council in September 1915, and Thomas MacDonagh in April 1916.[28]

The basic plan was that the Irish Volunteers, in conjunction with the ICA and Cumman na mBan (acting as medical aid, and dispatch service among other duties) would rise across the country on Easter Sunday 1916. It was believed that up to 15,000 men would partake in the rising. They were to seize strategic and prominent buildings in their local areas, and wait for a British attack. In order to keep the rebellion secret to the last minute, each of the groups would be asked to drill on Easter Sunday, and only on that morning would they be told of the plan for the rebellion. A shipment of weapons from Germany was expected to arrive in the south-west to arm the Volunteers in the south, the west, and the midlands. The plan was for an Ireland-wide rebellion, so why did fighting break out in Dublin only, focusing on key buildings such as the GPO?

THE RISING

Eoin MacNeill remained the head of the Irish Volunteers throughout this period, but he believed that the Volunteers should only be used to defend Home Rule. He was completely unaware of the plans for an armed insurrection. The military council produced a forged document suggesting that the Volunteers were to be suppressed, thus gaining MacNeill's support. When he discovered the truth on Good Friday, 21 April 1916, he tried to prevent the rebellion by placing a notice in the Sunday newspapers that all Volunteer drills for Easter Sunday were to be cancelled. Michael O'Rahilly—a prominent Volunteer leader known as 'The O'Rahilly'—and others travelled around Ireland contacting local leaders and calling off the planned movements. While his visits to local leaders and the countermanding orders might have encouraged leaders to stay put, there were other reasons why they did not rise. Local leaders in Cork and Belfast had been left out of the planning from the start, and when an attempt was made to contact leaders in Cork on Sunday they refused to join the rebellion, arguing it was the madness of hotheads in Dublin.[29]

By Saturday morning a British vessel at sea had intercepted the arms ship *Aud*, which was then scuttled by its crew. Convinced that the rebellion had been prevented by the loss of the weapons, the British made no immediate moves to increase security over the Easter Weekend. Worried that the government was close to uncovering the rebellion, members of the executive council met at Liberty Hall (located on the site of the modern Liberty Hall, on Beresford Place and Eden Quay[30]) on Sunday 23 April, and debated their next move.

It was decided that if they did not act, their preparations would be in vain so they decided to go ahead with their plans at noon on Easter Monday. The rebel proclamation, declaring independence from Britain and outlining the aims of the rebels, was printed in secret in Liberty Hall. Connolly had detained the printer, Christopher Brady, and the two compositors, Michael Molloy and Liam O'Brien, so that if they were discovered by the authorities in the process of printing the proclamation, they could use the defence that they had been forced to print it.[31] Connolly wanted 2,500 copies but just 1,000 could be printed. The Wharfedale printer they worked on was in poor condition and they did not have enough type to print the document. As a result, the composers had to be inventive with the type they had to hand, and used a mixture of letters and typefaces throughout the document. These mistakes have become an integral mark of the document and today they are signs of authenticity.[32]

On Easter Monday, the turnout was far lower than expected. Once the Volunteers occupied their garrisons and assessed their situation, they must have known their chances were bleak. Over the course of the week, perhaps 1,600 men and women took part in the rising. It is estimated that 1,000 Volunteers showed up on Easter Monday, and that the number had increased to 1,300 by the end of the week. Almost two-thirds of the Irish Citizen Army showed up, about 219 men and women.[33] The low numbers worked against the rising from the start. Many rebels argued that their movements were chaotic, because they did not have enough men on the ground. At noon, rebel units moved to seize the GPO, the Four Courts, Boland's Mill and Jacob's biscuit factory, the South Dublin Union, St Stephen's Green and Dublin Castle, amongst others. From there they set about turning their buildings into garrisons and contacting outlying posts to let them know their position and situation.

One of the first positions to be taken up was the GPO which had been earmarked as the headquarters for the new republic. The iconic building had been in operation as a communications hub for nearly a century at this point. It had recently undergone a very expensive restoration, and had reopened just six weeks before the rebellion. While the GPO might seem an odd choice for a headquarters, in

1916 a post office was the equivalent of a modern-day TV studio. It gave the rebels access to communication networks: telegraph lines and telephones. Defensively it made sense too, as the building was made of thick Portland stone, which would have offered resistance to an attack.[34] The large number of leaders who were stationed at the GPO gives us some idea of how important the building was for the rising. Five of the leaders who had signed the proclamation were stationed at the GPO, including Pearse (the 'president' of the new republic), Clarke, Connolly (the commander of the rebel forces in Dublin), Plunkett and MacDiarmada. So too were approximately 400 men and women, more than a quarter of the available forces. Before occupying the GPO, Pearse stood at the front door and read aloud the proclamation. Few passers by on Sackville Street seemed to care about what was happening. The public were used to seeing the Volunteers drilling, so the march to the GPO would not have seemed unusual.

While some of the staff were at first reluctant to give up the post office to the insurgent forces, the building was taken with little trouble. One British solider objected but was tied up and placed inside a phone box in the central hall. Desmond Ryan, who worked as Pearse's secretary, described the taking of the building: 'Pearse and his brother appear and survey the scene calmly within … Vessels are filled with water everywhere. Cooking is carried on where the GPO staff left off. The great door leading into Princes Street is eventually covered with a rough barricade'.[35] Access to food and water was a primary concern, as the leadership was unsure how long they would be stationed at each garrison. The most coveted position was the roof, which provided a great vantage point from which to see advancing British forces. A phone line connected the roof and the ground floor so they could be kept abreast of any approaching troops. The roof also provided a panoramic view of the city, and the Liffey, Trinity College and Liberty Hall could all be seen from that point. It was also a difficult post, however. Once up on the roof it was difficult to get relief. Snipers on the roof slept there and were often bored. The parapet didn't provide great cover, and, when British snipers were stationed on other Sackville Street rooves later in the week, they had a clear view of anything that moved on the GPO's roof.[36]

By Monday afternoon the news had spread that a rising had broken out. Rebels had been repelled from Dublin Castle but were holding firm in the other garrisons. Despite their small numbers they had success-fully taken their target buildings. The government soon sent troops to investigate what was happening in the GPO. This was ill-conceived, consisting as it did of mounted troops coming down Sackville Street towards the GPO. Inside the building the Volunteers were well pro-tected by barricades against the windows, and they were in a prime spot for shooting down the horses and soldiers. They opened fire. One horse was killed during the engagement and the horse's body remained outside the building for the rest of the rising. Over the next few days, those inside the building could smell the rotting carcus. One of the Volunteers inside the building described the attack: 'A young officer dashes in cheering, a smile on his flushed features. Later he is hurried by, the lower part of his face severely injured with a bomb explosion, his hands, chin and neck streaming blood. He is ordered at the revolver's point—for he grows obstinate—when his wounds are dressed and shock subsides to hospital. Blood is new to us and we only learn later that he has recovered. Inside organisation proceeds'.[37] Many of the rebels were young and inexperienced but optimistic and excited that they were part of the rising. Many, like the injured soldier in this story, would not have wanted to leave so early in the fighting.

Occupied buildings attracted a lot of attention from Dubliners. Martial law was soon imposed, and as newspapers were not in circulation, official news was limited and rumours were rife. People were eager for information on what was happening. Some Dubliners travelled into the city centre to see what was happening. Alfred Fannin, a business owner who lived in the city suburbs, went as far as Stephen's Green on Wednesday 26 to see for himself what was happening. He described the scene in a letter to his brother who was serving in the Great War at the front: 'I went down Leeson Street, there was no horse or motor traffic. The two private hospitals had white flags with a red cross up. People stood at street corners and at the windows ... Over at the railings and gate opposite Leeson St a line of carts formed a sort of barricade but I saw from the corner no sign of life in the Green ... A few people stood along close to the railings, curiosity sightseers'.[38] St Stephen's Green was a military outpost held by Countess Markievicz at the Royal College of Surgeons and it saw action later in the week when British snipers were placed on the rooves of hotels in the area. Despite this, Fannin tells us that Dubliners felt safe enough to wander on to the streets in search of news and to see what was happening first hand. Given this picture, it is easy to understand how citizens, desperate for news and for essentials such as bread, were injured or killed while travelling around the city during the week. In fact, more civilians were killed during the rising then British and Irish fighters together.

Attracted by the department stores and the absence of the police, who had been withdrawn from the streets, looters sensed an opportunity. They seem to have been particularly active on Sackville Street. There were stories of one looter taking golf clubs from Lawrence's Sporting Goods, but stopping to try them by driving a golf ball up the street. Another Volunteer reported that he had seen a piano being taken from a department store and driven away on a truck.[39] The wife of the postmaster general was staying at the Hibernian Hotel and reported that 'the mob were chiefly women and children, with a sprinkling of men'. Most of the goods being looted seem to have been luxury items. Children were reported to have stolen sweets and fireworks, while women took fur coats and silk gowns. Necessities were stolen too. The post master general's wife described women working together to steal groceries. One woman went in to throw fruit and tins out the windows to other women who caught them in their skirts.[40] All this activity led to what Clair Wills has called a 'carnival atmosphere' on Sackville Street towards the beginning of the week.[41]

On Tuesday the insurgents broadcast their first message from O'Connell Street, using a wireless transmitter. It announced that Dublin had been captured and that a republic had been established. The message was picked up by ships and relayed to the United States.[42] A printing press was set up not far from the GPO, and an official publication called *Irish War News* was printed, along with communiqués that were circulated to garrisons.[43] These messages were important, as they lifted the morale of those fighting in other garrisons and reminded them that they were not alone. They were a way for the provisional government to communicate directly with the population at large to get their message out. The tone was initially optimistic. The first issue of *Irish War News* set out the purpose of the struggle. It stated that 'the valour, self-sacrifice and discipline of Irish men and women are about to win for our country a glorious place among the nations'.[44] The text of the newspaper shows that the leaders of the rising were aware that, whether successful or not, they were making history. They also remind us of the power of print. Pearse and Connolly had been determined that once in the GPO, regular updates about their aims and progress would be issued to the public. In the original plans for the rebellion, the leadership had sought to take Independent House, the home of the *Irish Independent*. Because of the reduced numbers of Volunteers, this had to be revised. Once the GPO was secured on Monday, Pearse raised the idea again, but was advised against it. Joseph Stanley, a well-known city printer who was stationed in the GPO, was tasked with establishing a print works. He organised five other printers to take over a works on Halston Street, close to the GPO, and from there they began to print Pearse and Connolly's text.[45]

By Wednesday the Volunteers had taken the lower half of Sackville Street and the corner of Eden Quay right up to North Earl Street.[46] Once the area was secured, they were given tasks such as scavenging for food and securing type for composing text from the outlying newspaper offices. On Tuesday British troops were moved into the city, and by Wednesday morning they were pouring into the city centre. One of the greatest rebel successes occurred on Wednesday. Two members of the Volunteers were stationed in a house at a junction by Mount Street Bridge in Ballsbridge. British troops from the Sherwood Foresters who were landing at Kingstown (modern Dún Laoghaire) marched into town and up Mount Street, which made the bridge a strategically important entry point into the city. From their vantage point, the rebels managed to mow down large numbers of troops. The British insisted on employing military tactics learned on the Western Front in the city. Once the shooting began, the Sherwood Foresters were ordered to drop to the ground and crawl over the bridge: under no circumstances were they to turn back. From a window the

Volunteer snipers could pick them off. As a result they inflicted over 230 injuries and fatalities.[47]

On Wednesday morning the *Helga*, a British gunboat, moved up the Liffey and caused severe damage to Liberty Hall, although the building was, to all intents and purposes, empty. The rebels would finally see some action after 'two days of relative inactivity' as the 'GPO took on a siege atmosphere'.[48] It was not until Thursday afternoon that the GPO and Sackville Street came under direct fire. Connolly left the GPO to direct the taking of outposts, but he was shot in the leg. He received medical attention and remained active on the ground floor giving commands. On Thursday evening the worst of the bombardment came. The fire was aimed at the GPO, but many buildings on Lower Sackville Street were also destroyed by this shelling and subsequent fires, which soon spread to the GPO and the lower half of the street. The Sackville Street area was devastated by the fires that followed the bombardment. The shelling in this part of the city was so bad on Thursday night that the garrison 'could do little more than prepare for the end'.[49]

Heavy bombardment from British artillery brought into Dublin by rail from Athlone had caused fires all over the building. Seán McLoughlin, appointed a lieutenant by Connolly on Thursday, described the view from the GPO roof: 'In front was a roaring sea of flame, leaping to the sky, with the crackle of musketry and canon-pealing the accompaniment. Behind was another terrific blaze from the Linen Hall Barracks, which had also gone up. It was apparent now we were doomed. Now stories of landing Germans would not be believed. It was a handful of daring men facing the wrath of a mighty empire, with the odds on the Empire'.[50] Pearse addressed the Volunteers and gave them a rousing speech to prepare them for a final assault on the building. Pearse and Connolly both produced communiqués which were circulated to other garrisons. By Friday morning the GPO was surrounded by snipers and British troops. There were snipers on the roofs of the Gresham and Wynn's Hotel, as well as the Rotunda and Amiens Street station.[51] Despite the danger from these snipers, messengers continued to leave the GPO. In his communiqué Pearse praised the spirit of the Volunteers and the ICA,

Sackville Street in the aftermath of the 1916 Rising (National Library of Ireland)

stating that 'if they do not win this fight, they will at least have deserved to win it'.[52] Connolly wrote 'we are hemmed in, because the enemy feels that in this building is to be found the heart and inspiration of our great movement'.[53] It was expected that the Volunteers in the GPO would have one last military engagement. The building was evacuated because of the extensive damage to the roof rather than because of an assault by the British army. Many Volunteers were dismayed when the evacuation order came, because they wanted to fight on.

The O'Rahilly was also stationed in the GPO. Although he had tried to stop the rebellion from going ahead once it was clear that fighting was inevitable he committed himself to the rebellion, famously remarking that as he had helped to wind the clock, he had come to hear it strike. He left the GPO on Friday to try and clear the way for an evacuation. McLoughlin was familiar with Sackville Street, and he knew that it would be impossible to gain additional posts. He left the GPO and tried to make contact with O'Rahilly on Moore Street, but the city centre was surrounded and O'Rahilly had been shot dead. With the roof of the GPO about to collapse, evacuation was necessary. This was going to be an incredibly difficult task: the building was surrounded by British troops. A meeting of the leadership was held on Friday evening. Connolly, the commander of the Dublin forces, was too badly injured to organise a withdrawal. MacDiarmada proposed that McLoughlin take over, and this was seconded by Connolly. The decision was made to retreat nearby to Moore Street. One Volunteer described how 'Pearse stood at the exit sword in hand. Every so often he dropped the sword as the signal for two more men to leave and make the short dash across Henry Street. We all got over safely into Moore Lane'.[54] Headquarters were established in one of the houses on Moore Lane. By the next morning they had burrowed through the buildings as far as Sackville Lane (now O'Rahilly Lane). On Saturday morning, after a meeting of the leadership, it was decided that a surrender should be negotiated. Elizabeth O'Farrell, a Cumann na mBan nurse, was sent to the British with news that Pearse sought to negotiate a surrender. She returned with a message that the British would accept nothing less than an unconditional surrender, an offer that Pearse accepted. O'Farrell was asked to travel from garrison to garrison to deliver Pearse's order to surrender.

The legacy of the Rising

The importance of the events that had taken place within the GPO was clear immediately. Fannin wrote that 'there has been nothing like this in a generation'.[55] This was something that the leaders too were aware of and had pointed to in the text of the proclamation. The proclamation stated that 'in every generation the Irish people have asserted their right to national freedom and sovereignty: six times during the past three hundred years they have asserted it in arms'. This would be their contribution to the history of Irish struggles: they revived the separatist tradition. Public opinion moved in favour of the rebels in the weeks and months after the rebellion. With martial law declared the British army began arresting suspects. These arrests were out of proportion to the numbers who had risen. Although 1,600 men and women took part in the rising, 3,430 men and 79 women were arrested. Of these 1,836 men and women were interned without trial.[56] Numerous people arrested had played no part in the rising or its planning. Arthur Griffith, leader of Sinn Féin, was arrested because the rising had been incorrectly dubbed the 'Sinn Féin rebellion' by the authorities almost as soon as it had broken out. His party would later be reconstituted as a democratic vehicle by republicans.

Those deemed the worst offenders were court-martialled, and, while over 90 were sentenced to death, most had their sentences commuted; ultimately, only 16 were executed in the aftermath of the rising (see chapter seven). Nevertheless, the round-ups, internments and martial law imposed on the population had a tremendous impact:the British response to the rising was seen as heavy handed. The stories that emerged of British brutality during the rising exacerbated this. Politicians, most famously John Redmond's deputy, John Dillon, came out against the British response. The celebrated playwright and author George Bernard Shaw wrote in the London *Daily News* on 10 May 1916 that 'my own view is that the men who were shot in cold blood, after their capture or surrender, were prisoners of war, and that it was, therefore, entirely incorrect to slaughter them'. He added 'I remain an Irishman and am bound to contradict any implication that I can regard as a traitor any Irishman taken in a fight for Irish Independence against the British government, which was a fair fight in everything except the enormous odds my countrymen had to face'.[57] After their executions, the leaders became public martyrs.

By 1917, when those interned after the rising were released, republicans began to regroup. New members joined their ranks. They rejected Home Rule as not going far enough. On 21 January 1919 the War of Independence began, with the first shots of a guerrilla campaign being fired in Tipperary. On the same day, other republicans, elected to parliament in 1918 but who had refused to take their seats at Westminster, sat in the Mansion House on Dawson Street, proclaiming the gathering to be a sitting of a new Irish republican parliament called the Dáil. Thousands died on both sides of the subsequent conflict as the violence escalated and peaked in the first half of 1921. A ceasefire was called in July 1921, and, after talks with the British government, the Irish Free State, a 26 county state, came into being. The treaty was accepted by a majority in the Dáil. When put to the country the majority of the population voted in favour of it. Nevertheless, some rejected it, saying that it was not the full embodiment of the 1916 proclamation; it was not a republic. Between June 1922 and April 1923 a bloody and vicious civil war was fought in Ireland. The new Free State government defeated those republicans who fought against the treaty. The bitterness that the Civil War created would be felt in Irish politics for decades to come. Each side rallied to associate themselves with the dead heroes of 1916 and to create a connection with their aims and beliefs.

THE GPO IN THE FREE STATE

In the aftermath of the Civil War, the new government sought to disassociate itself from British rule. The leaders of the 1916 Rising and the GPO became central to this. Sackville Street was officially renamed O'Connell Street in 1924. The GPO was rebuilt between 1924 and 1929. Train stations around the country were given the names of dead heroes from the 1916 Rising. Streets were renamed after important nationalist figures. Loyalist and imperial statues were gradually removed. One of the monuments most complained about was Nelson's Pillar. Many felt that a figure so strongly connected with British imperialism should not be represented on the capital's main street. Seán Lemass, who served as Taoiseach from 1959 to 1966 and who fought in the GPO during the 1916 Rising, believed that the statue was an embarrassment to the state. Some defended the statue on the grounds of aesthetic or historical value, but in March 1966 Nelson's Pillar was destroyed in an explosion carried out by persons unknown (presumably the IRA). *The Irish Times* reported on 3 March 1966 that 'the top of Nelson's Pillar, in O'Connell Street, Dublin was blown off by a tremendous explosion at 1.32 o'clock this morning and the Nelson statue and tons of rubble poured down into the roadway'.[58] It was a miracle that no one was injured. A dance was just about to end at the Metropole Ballroom, and crowds were heading home after their evening socialising. Before the debate could open again about the pillar, the army was sent in to destroy the stump. On 11 March they blew it up. £43,000 worth of public liability damage was claimed from the broken windows and damage done in the ensuing blast, but Nelson and the long shadow he had cast over O'Connell Street was gone.

For all the controversy that surrounded it, when the pillar was gone it created a vacuum on O'Connell Street. In the 1990s the government unveiled plans for a new monument that would occupy the space Nelson's Pillar had once occupied, called the 'Monument of light' or more commonly known as the Spire. The monument, originally intended to to commemorate the millennium in 2000, was also intended to be politically impartial and modern. The stainless-steel needle, designed by Ian Ritchie, was erected in 2003.[59] It is six times higher than the nearby GPO. The Spire has attracted much praise and criticism. Dublin wits have come up with a number of nicknames for the structure including: the stiletto in the ghetto, the nail in the Pale, and the pin in the bin (the statue of James Joyce on North Earl Street which is visible from O'Connell Street has also been dubbed 'the prick with the stick').

The continued importance of the GPO and O'Connell Street to Irish nationalism was highlighted during the fiftieth anniversary commemorations of the 1916 Rising, key components of which focused on O'Connell Street. The 'Garden of Remembrance' was opened in Dublin's Parnell Square in memory of those who died fighting for Irish freedom. It created a stretch of streetscape celebrating Irish nationalism, both democratic and militant, that runs from North Frederick Street to O'Connell Bridge. O'Connell Street itself was used for military parades at Easter. The GPO was a focal point of these parades, with politicians and VIPs seated outside the building. The link between past and present leaders would not have been lost on contemporaries who watched the parade. During the Northern Ireland 'Troubles', parades were considered to be antagonistic to unionists, and the practice was done away with.

Nevertheless, the street retained its historical and political significance. In May 1974 bombs were planted in Dublin and Monaghan to object to southern support for the IRA campaign in Northern Ireland. Although the loyalist Ulster Volunteer Force (UVF) eventually claimed responsibility for the bombs, allegations have persisted to the present that members of the British security forces

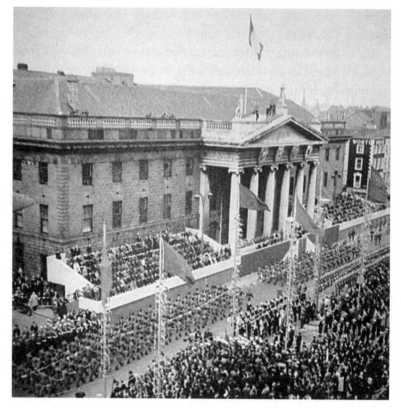

Military parade outside GPO in 1966 (*Cuimhneachán 1916–1966*)

were involved in the attacks.[60] The Dublin bombs were planted just off O'Connell Street on Talbot Street and at Parnell Square. Thirty-three civilians were killed and more than 200 were wounded. The attacks brought the Troubles to the Republic. Most people in the Republic had not experienced such atrocities at first hand. The attack was also a stark reminder of the symbolic importance of the GPO and O'Connell Street.

Nearly one hundred years after the 1916 Rising the GPO has retained its significance in the history of the state. Although the fabric of the original building was largely destroyed during the rising, and the building was remodelled during the reconstruction, the GPO retains its importance. Many people believe it is central to our understanding of what happened during the struggle for independence. In the aftermath of a civil war that had divided counties, communities and families, Irish people needed founding fathers for the new state that would unite the country. They found these men in the GPO, and the building went on to play a central part in the myths and symbolism of the new Irish state. It is remarkable that after two centuries of rebellion, civil war, explosions, protests and parades the GPO still operates as a post office. As the centenary of the 1916 Rising approaches, a number of proposals have been made for the building. It was mooted as a home for the Abbey Theatre and, at the time of writing, there are plans to put an exhibition specifically dedicated to the 1916 Rising in the building. The GPO has been a central part of the lives of Dubliners for generations as they undertake their business. There is a neat continuity in the building remaining a post office. When visitors enter the noisy building they are greeted by Dubliners hurrying to get their business done.

9

The Abbey Theatre

THE ABBEY THEATRE on Abbey Street is the most famous theatre in Ireland. It is considered by many to be the cradle of modern Irish drama, and is one of the country's most important cultural institutions. The theatre was established by one of Ireland's Nobel laureates, William Butler Yeats, who, along with Lady Augusta Gregory, used it to develop and encourage a distinct Irish literary and dramatic scene. Its foundation can be seen as part of a wider movement in late-nineteenth century Ireland that has become known as the 'Gaelic Revival'. While the growth of political nationalism can be traced to the first half of the nineteenth century, it was only later that forms of cultural nationalism developed. In this period nationalist groups throughout Europe argued that a 'nation' was not simply a state ruled by a political body; rather, it was a community of people who had a culture, language and possibly even a religion in common. Cultural activists in Ireland began to examine all aspects of Gaelic culture to prove that an Irish 'nation' existed. The Irish language, which had been in steady decline since the eighteenth century, began to attract the attention of cultural nationalists. Cultural nationalists also began to collect folk stories and to revive traditional Irish pastimes and craft techniques from the west of Ireland. There was a strong belief that the western seaboard had preserved this culture, being less anglicised than anywhere else on the island. Many Gaelic revivalists believed in the purity of such rural life. One commentator said that 'rural Ireland is real Ireland'.[1] Literature and plays became an important way of bringing these folk stories and traditions to life, particularly for Dubliners. In the early years of the Abbey, its stage became a place

Theatre Royal (National Library of Ireland)

where Irish culture could be showcased and promoted. The theatre did not just further Irish literature and the Gaelic Revival however; plays staged there could challenge many social and political views as well. The plays presented at the Abbey, and the writers involved in the theatre, shaped social and cultural discussions in modern Ireland. These debates often centred on questions such as: who were the Irish? What was their identity? Should Ireland be rural or urban? What was Ireland's place within the world?

IRISH THEATRE BEFORE THE FOUNDATION OF THE ABBEY

The first Irish theatre was opened *circa* 1635 on Werburgh Street, close to Dublin Castle, where it catered for the tastes of the Irish nobility and government officials who resided in Dublin. Although this might seem surprisingly late, before this plays would have been performed in the homes of the nobility and in large halls. The new theatre on Werburgh Street was the first purpose-built centre for drama in Ireland. It was followed by the opening of the Royal Theatre on Smock Alley in 1662. A building on the site still operates as Smock Alley Theatre, and while the site has not been in continuous use as a theatre since 1662, it claims to be the oldest theatre in Dublin. It was here that Oliver Goldsmith's *She Stoops to Conquer* was first performed. In 1734 another theatre opened on Aungier Street while the first theatre outside of Dublin was opened in Cork city in 1736 under the name the Theatre Royal. In 1829 the Adelphi Theatre was opened on Pearse Street. It was demolished and re-opened under the name of Queen's Theatre in 1844. The 2,000 seat Gaiety Theatre was opened in 1871 and the Star of Erin music hall (now the Olympia Theatre) in 1878. Theatre licences were limited by royal patents after the Act of Union, meaning that theatres could not be established without an act of parliament. This meant that purpose-built 'theatres' were difficult to found. However, dance halls and concert rooms, such as the Antient Concert Rooms on Great Brunswick Street, could be rented out for the purpose of staging drama.

Although the founders of what would become the Abbey Theatre, Yeats and Gregory, believed that Ireland was without a truly 'Irish' theatrical culture, there were five theatres in Dublin when the Abbey opened its doors: the Theatre Royal (pictured p. 207), the Gaiety, the Empire, the Queen's and the Rotunda. They all produced Irish plays and staged the works of Irish playwrights albeit to varying degrees. There was a strong appetite for English plays, however, and the majority of plays produced in Dublin at the time were English. This is especially true of works at the Gaiety and the Theatre Royal.[2] The Queen's Theatre, on the other hand, stood out in terms of the number of plays it produced that had Irish 'themes', written by Irish playwrights. The Queen's presented Irish plays for 15 weeks of the year, and these plays were well received.[3] Dublin had a store of literary and dramatic writers. Oscar Wilde, George Moore and George Bernard Shaw were all near-contemporaries of the founders of the Irish Literary Theatre. Shaw and Wilde had made their careers outside Ireland, however, and their plays had dealt with many British themes rather than exclusively Irish topics. Indeed their works have been described as 'portraying the English to themselves'.[4] If Wilde and Shaw had left Ireland to make a name for themselves elsewhere, however, others, like Hubert O'Grady, had stayed.

As Irish nationalism became a stronger political force in the nineteenth century, it impacted on all aspects of Irish life, including art, literature and theatre. A strongly nationalistic theatre emerged to satisfy a demand for plays with Irish themes. Hubert O'Grady founded the Irish National Company in 1885. It produced political plays and historical dramas that struck a chord with a growing nationalist audience. O'Grady's own plays include *Eviction* (1879), *Emigration* (1880), and *The Famine* (1886). The names of these plays alone imply strongly political themes. A common character in his plays was the villainous informer for the English authorities, who ultimately came to a bad end.[5] Irish rebellions in the previous eighty years had failed in part or wholly due to information provided by such informants. Audiences would boo when they came on stage, and cheered when they met their end.

W.J. Whitbread followed a similar model when he began writing plays. He took over the running of the Queen's Theatre and encouraged the continued production of Irish plays.[6] His play *Shoulder to Shoulder* was produced in 1886, and his follow-up, *The Nationalist*, in 1891. Again, both dealt heavily with political themes from Irish history that resonated with a nationalist audience. By the 1790s he was writing plays that dealt specifically with the 1798 rebellion, including *Lord Edward* (1894), *Theobald Wolfe Tone* (1898), *The Insurgent Chief* and *The Ulster Hero* (1902).[7] The production of *Wolfe Tone* in 1898 coincided with the centenary of the Unitied Irishmen's rebellion and was very successful. Word spread so quickly about the play that, by its second night, 'the crowds pushing their way into the Queen's' to see the play 'were so big that they threatened to block the fire station across the street and the police insisted that the doors be opened early'.[8] One critic wrote that 'This is the sort of play that will ultimately put a new spirit into Ireland'.[9]

These theatres also created touring companies. Plays opened in the Dublin theatre and after a short run set out across the country, to Belfast and Cork and perhaps Waterford and Limerick. Some would go abroad and take in Glasgow and Bristol, sometimes also Manchester and London, or even to New York and Sydney.[10] Touring allowed Dublin theatre companies to influence audiences far beyond their immediate constituency. According to Christopher Morash, these tours 'sent out ripples around the country, helping to decentralise the Irish theatrical world'.[11] They were also important for building up the reputations of emerging playwrights as well as generating revenue. This was something that the Abbey would take advantage of, as tours were an important means of fund-raising.

W.B.YEATS AND AUGUSTA GREGORY FORM A THEATRE COMPANY

In the summer of 1898, Gregory vacationed in Duras in France. By this time she had been widowed six years. Her husband had, however, introduced her to a literary circle and she had produced some political pamphlets and prose. By the 1890s she had developed a growing interest in the collection of Irish folklore. The stories she collected inspired her later plays. Her folklore collecting was important in its own right, and laid the foundation for many later folklore collectors. During her holiday in France her neighbour Edward Martyn, an Irish nationalist and playwright, often visited her. He had the young playwright and poet W.B. Yeats staying with him. During one of their evening discussions Martyn mentioned that he was experiencing difficulty having two plays with an Irish setting, *The Heather Field* and *Maeve*, staged in Ireland. Gregory expressed disappointment that there was no Irish theatre to stage the plays, and Yeats said that it 'had always been a dream of his' to found one, 'but he had late thought it an impossible one, for it could not at first pay its way, and there was no money to be found for such a thing in Ireland'.[12] Gregory suggested he write to political and literary figures asking for a contribution so that they could hire a theatre and stage *The Heather Field* and Yeats's *Countess Cathleen*.[13] They proposed to have a series of 'Celtic and Irish plays' produced in Dublin each spring. These would be 'written with a high ambition' and would help 'to build up a Celtic and Irish school of dramatic literature'.[14] Morash says that the founders of what would become the Abbey created a theatre 'by imagining an empty space where in fact there was a crowded room'.[15] They ignored what the Queen's and other Dublin theatres were producing. They also disregarded the contemporary work of playwrights active in Dublin. This new theatre would be literary rather then political or commercial. They stated that they were 'confident of the support of all Irish people, who are weary of misrepresentation, in carrying out work that is outside all the political questions that divide us'.[16] The statement ignored the contemporary Irish theatrical scene. In doing so, however, Yeats and Gregory managed to create an atmosphere from which a modern body of Irish dramatic works could emerge. These works broke with the tradition of many nineteenth-century writers, particularly those who focused exclusively on political themes. This new body would be known as the Irish Literary Theatre. The founders' successfully solicited the support of many people, who promised money and their attendance.

The first performance was on 8 May 1899 in the Antient Concert Rooms on Great Brunswick Street. Yeats's *Countess Cathleen* and Martyn's *Heather Field* were performed. George Moore assisted them in finding actors, who were brought over from England. The Irish Literary Theatre proved controversial at an early stage, when a member of the public complained that *Countess Cathleen* was 'libel on the people of Ireland' and against the teaching of Catholic Church. The play was submitted to Catholic clergymen who found no problem with it.[17] This would not be the last time that the contents of the plays chosen by the directors would upset Dublin audiences. Over the next three years, Irish literary plays were produced and staged in hired venues. The plays of Yeats, Moore, Martyn, Douglas Hyde and Alice Milligan were chosen for these seasonal performances. Although these plays were set in Ireland, and more often than not had Irish mythological themes, they were performed by English actors. In its fourth year the theatre company became more ambitious, deciding to employ Irish actors who could be trained by the society. Two brothers associated with the Queen's Theatre, Frank and William Fay were brought on board. Gregory remarked of them that 'William had a genius for comedy, Frank's ambitions were for the production of verse'.[18] In 1891 they had formed the Ormonde Dramatic Company, and, along with other Irish actors they performed at various halls throughout Dublin.[19] This was the beginning of a native school of acting. The brothers could not, however, support themselves through these productions and both men had to work full time to pursue their first passion of acting in the evening. William worked as a scene painter at the Gaiety. He made his first appearance in a comic role at the Queen's Theatre in 1901. He did not limit himself to acting, however, and in 1901 he produced the first Irish-language play to be staged in Dublin, Fr Patrick Dinneen's *An tobair draoidheachta*.[20] In 1902 the Fays' drama company produced George Russell's *Deirdre*. During this production Russell introduced the brothers to Yeats, who gave them permission to produce his play *Kathleen Ní Houlihan*. Both plays were staged in Clarendon Street Hall, with the actors rehearsing every evening after work. Yeats was hugely impressed with their production, and commitment, and said that 'they did what amateurs seldom do, worked desperately'.[21]

In the following year the Irish Literary Theatre re-formed as the National Theatre Society. The Fay brothers became central to this new movement, and to the foundation and development of the Abbey Theatre. The brothers were young, talented, and had ideas. William went on to become the first manager of the Abbey. Furthermore, as the Fay brothers were so keen to develop a school of drama, they influenced all actors who were hired for Abbey productions. They trained these actors and are credited with developing the Abbey 'style' of acting. In May 1903 the National Theatre Society brought the Fays' production outside Dublin for the first time, to London. As most of the actors worked full time Gregory admitted that 'it was hard for the actors to get away'. Their tour of London lasted just one weekend: 'They left Dublin on Friday night, arrived in London on the Saturday morning, played in the afternoon, and again in the evening at Queen's Gate Hall, and were back at work in Dublin on Monday morning'.[22] Although brief, the tour was a huge success. Yeats said 'I never saw a more enthusiastic audience ... I think them better then we could have hoped'.[23] Even more significantly, the tour led to substantial patronage. The plays were attended by Annie Horniman, a wealthy English heiress. She was impressed with Yeats and his scheme to found a national theatre, donated money to acquire a premises, and assisted towards the early running costs.

THE MECHANICS' INSTITUTE, ABBEY STREET

Finding a suitable home for the theatre was difficult at first but Yeats came across the Mechanics Institute Theatre on Abbey Street. Abbey Street was known originally as Ship's Buildings. Timber yards, glasshouses and warehouses would have been found in this part of the city during the eighteenth century. It was widened in the 1780s when the Wide Streets Commission was developing the area. Abbey Street became an integral part of the city centre in the early nineteenth century. Although there were three non-conforming churches on the street in the 1840s, the buildings on the street tended to be occupied by business premises, shops and pubs.[24] Today's Abbey Theatre is not the original theatre that the National Theatre Company occupied. Sadly, that theatre was destroyed by fire in 1951. The Abbey does, however, occupy the theatre's original site on the corner of Marlborough Street and Lower Abbey Street. This location needed a good deal of work to convert it into a theatre but it was an appropriate size and in a fantastic city centre location. The total cost of renovation and extensions set Horniman back £1,300.[25] The original Mechanics Theatre was expanded next door, into the site of the old city morgue. The entrance to the theatre actually ran through the old morgue, which was a source of much entertainment for Dublin wits. The theatre was far smaller than the Gaiety or the Queen's but this meant that it would be easier to fill. The stalls held 178 seats, while the pit contained 198. Sarah Purser created two peacock-coloured stained-glass windows for the foyer. W.B. Yeats's brother, Jack, provided portraits of William and Frank Fay. and Annie Horniman, which were hung in the foyer. Neo-Celtic copper decorations adorned the walls, presenting an immediate visual link between the theatre and the Gaelic Revival.

As well as providing the funding for the theatre, Horniman made provision to hire a manager. The position was given to Willliam Fay, who not only acted as manger but also as a producer and even an actor. He brought his brother on board to act and assist in training new actors. William was paid £70 per annum as manager, a position that allowed him to focus full time on his main passion. Nevertheless, Gregory complained that 'even large sums of money would have been poor payment not only for William Fay's genius and his brother's beautiful speaking of verse, but for their devotion to the aim and work of the theatre, its practical and artistic side'. She added that the Fay brothers more 'than almost any others had laid the foundation of the Irish theatre'.[26]

THE EARLY ABBEY THEATRE

The Abbey Theatre opened on Tuesday 27 December 1904. Stall tickets were 3 shillings and balcony seats were 2 shillings.[27] Four plays were staged: Lady Gregory's *Spreading the News*, Yeats's and Gregory's *Kathleen Ní Houlihan*, Yeats's *On Bailie's Strand* and JM Synge's *In the Shadow of the Glen*. *Kathleen Ní Houlihan* would have satisfied nationalist audiences. The one-act play, set around the 1798 rebellion, depicts a young man on the eve of his marriage who is called to fight for Ireland. Equally, Gregory's plays would have proved popular with many nationalist theatre-goers. Her plays were steeped in Irish folklore and dealt with strongly nationalistic themes. She proved to be a hugely popular playwright with the Abbey's audience, and, between 1904 and 1912, 19 of her plays, and seven of her translations, were staged in the theatre.[28] Synge soon made an impact on both domestic and international drama. His emergence as a playwright on the Abbey stage showed that the theatre could nurture young Irish talent. This play was chosen for the opening night, indicating that the Abbey Theatre directors would not shy away from controversy. There had been complaints about *Shadow of the Glen* when it was performed in Molesworth Hall in 1903. The first three-act play to be produced in the theatre was Synge's *The Well of the Saints* in 1905. The play, based on a French story, can be described as a 'sombre comedy' and was well received.[29] The Abbey toured the play around Britain to good reviews, and there was even a German-language production.

In 1907 the Queen's Theatre shut for extensive renovations. It remained closed until 1909, and the Abbey succeeded in attracting some of its audience.[30] During the renovations, the Queen's Theatre licence to run as a dramatic theatre ran out. When it re-opened in 1909 their main productions were music concerts. New managers took over who seemed to have little appetite for producing Irish political and historical drama, with the result that the Abbey became increasingly recognised as the home of Irish drama.[31]

The theatre struggled financially in its first few years, and without Horniman's assistance it would have failed very early on. Gregory admitted that 'building up an audience is a slow business', especially 'when there is anything unusual in the methods or the work'.[32] The general public were unsure about the form and content of some of the plays staged. As often happened with the emergence of modernist movements, people were initially bewildered. One contemporary felt that 'Yeats could be sorted out by a good lesson in how to write a play'.[33] Morash says that many were 'baffled by the deliberate obscurity of this first wave of Irish modernist theatre'. Nevertheless, there was an audience for the plays. A steadily growing interest in Gaelic culture had led to a small, but significant, number of people learning the Irish language, and reading Irish folklore and history. Abbey plays, particularly Gregory's, influenced as they were by mythology, provided a live enactment of the stories that this new audience was consuming. Some of these plays, which can be described as 'peasant plays', suggested that the real Ireland was not to be found in the city but in the west of Ireland, where communities were untouched by British influence. Historian Diarmaid Ferriter has calculated that twice as many 'peasant plays' were being produced in urban areas then 'poetic plays' in the early decades of the twentieth century.[34] These plays proved popular with Dublin audiences.

The increasingly nationalist direction of the theatre was beginning to worry Horniman, however. When the theatre failed to shut for the death of King Edward VII on 6 May 1910 she pulled her funding. To survive, the theatre became a limited company, the National Theatre Society Limited, and was floated on the stock exchange, with shares priced at £1 each. The theatre evolved in these years from an amateur venture into a professional dramatic institution. By 1910 the actors were being paid a regular salary. By 1911 the theatre was paying its playwrights.[35] By 1910 Abbey productions were touring throughout Britain on an annual basis.

THE PLAYBOY OF THE WESTERN WORLD

Some of the Abbey's earliest productions challenged and shocked nationalist audiences. When Synge's *Playboy of the Western World* opened, on 26 January 1907, the Abbey was thrown into the centre of a major controversy that sparked month-long riots from Dublin audiences, who refused to accept the play's damning portrayal of rural Irish life. The play was set in Mayo, and tells the fate of a young man, Christy Mahon, who ran away from home claiming to have killed his father. When he arrives in a public house in a nearby village, the locals hail him a hero, while the barmaid Pegeen Mike falls for him. Pegeen was played by Molly Allgood, who was romantically linked with Synge and went on to star in a number of films in the 1930s. On the opening night there were cheers after the first act, prompting Gregory to telegram to Yeats in Scotland: 'Play great success'. After the second act, however, Gregory could see that 'the audience were a little puzzled' and 'a little shocked at the language'. The third act went badly and before the end 'there was some hissing'. Along with their unhappiness about the portrayal of Irish peasants, the audience were particularly upset at the use of the word 'shift', or underskirt, and the depiction of women in the play. A second telegram was sent to Yeats: 'Audience broke up in disorders at the word shift'.[36] There were more organised and louder protesters on the second night of the production and on the third night 50 policemen struggled to contain the riots. Several arrests were made and fines were issued. The riots became national and then international news, drawing significant attention to the Abbey.

The riots did not deter the directors, and the play continued on its run. Yeats said he would not allow Synge's work to be censored by the mob. During one production, with the actors struggling to perform their lines because of the loud objections from the crowd, Yeats interrupted the proceedings to tell the audience that they should be thoroughly ashamed and that they had 'rocked the cradle of genius'. Yeats later wrote that Synge was hated 'because he gave his country what it needed'.[37] Synge was attempting to hold a mirror to Irish peasant society to show that Irish society was not the great civilisation many nationalists claimed. This made him distinctive in

Original Abbey Theatre building which was destroyed by fire on 17 July 1951.

pre-revolutionary Ireland. He embraced Ireland and Irish themes but he was critical too of a tendency to romantice the Irish peasantry. Diarmaid Ferriter has said that 'the reaction to the play revealed huge ironies', as Dublin audiences assaulted actors to show that 'we are not a violent people'.[38]

The Fay brothers did not last long after the *Playboy* riots. Fay had anticipated that the play would not be well-received, but his objections to the play were ignored. There were further artistic differences, however. William wanted to produce populist plays that would draw a crowd, and he was unashamed about admitting it. He said that the best audience in a theatre was a working-class one. Yeats and Gregory disagreed. 'Having been informed that the theatre had to operate as a venue for intellectual drama, however unpopular it proved, both Fays promptly resigned from the Abbey and left the country'.[39] This was a huge loss to the Abbey, but Gregory and Yeats would not be swayed from their attempts to promote literature and the arts over what they deemed to be popular theatre.

THE ABBEY THEATRE FROM THE EASTER RISING TO THE CIVIL WAR

The period from the 1916 Rising to the end of the Civil War was a difficult time for the Abbey. While some of the Abbey actors and workers took part in the rising, Gregory and Yeats were appalled by the bloodshed, which was brought right to their door: Abbey Street was devastated by fighting during the 1916 Rising. They remained sympathetic to the nationalist cause, but Yeats began to review some of his opinions. He feared that some of his more overtly nationalistic poems and plays, such as *Kathleen Ni Houlihan*, which was due to be staged during Easter week 1916, had sent young men to their deaths. He remained wary of political violence from this point on, and felt that nationalism did not have to take such a militant form. The War of Independence also had a big impact on the running of the theatre. Performances were affected by the curfew that was imposed. Theatre-goers were well aware of the danger to be found on Dublin streets from British and Repulican fighting, particularly at night. As the audience shrank, the theatre had to face up to its precarious financial situation. Permanent players had their wages reduced by two-thirds, and fund-raising became more important than ever before.[40] Yeats was increasingly absent from Ireland, and Gregory provided the main direction for the company.[41] As well as reading new plays and helping to choose what would be staged, she was also left with the responsibility of fund-raising to keep the theatre going.

THE ABBEY THEATRE AND THE IRISH FREE STATE

Equally, the foundation of the Irish Free State affected the theatre. The Anglo-Irish Treaty that established the Free State was signed in December 1921, and as early as April 1922 the Abbey dramatist and

Abbey Street in ruins after the 1916 Rising (National Library of Ireland)

producer Lennox Robinson claimed that the intention had always been 'to hand the Abbey Theatre over to the Irish government'.[42] The government were unsure of what to do with this offer. The Free State was poor, under-resourced and unsure of its own capabilities. The new government was wary of being tasked with managing a theatre. In 1923 Yeats won the Nobel Prize for poetry. The state began to realise the importance of recognising and supporting Irish literature and the arts. It took two years for a reasonable deal to be worked out, with President W.T. Cosgrave offering financial assistance. In August 1925 this assistance materialised with a revenue grant from the Department of Finance of £850.[43]

A crucial debate that emerged in the Free State related to the nature of Irish society and culture. Literature, and drama in particular, would be an important platform for these debates and a measure of what audiences, and the general public, wanted. T.C. Murray's *Aftermath* was the first play to be produced in independent Ireland, opening at the Abbey in January 1922. The play focused on the efforts of a matchmaker to marry her son. Rural themes, such as those touched on in the play, would continue to be popular on Irish stages well into the twentieth century. While many of the early plays staged between the 1920s and the 1950s focused on such rural themes, they also highlighted the disappointments of many with a new state that many artists deemed restrictive. The first government in this new state, headed by Cumann na nGaedheal, acknowledged the importance of the Catholic Church and promoted their teachings. In 1929 the Censorship of Publications Act came into law. Although the act did not directly affect the stage, it established a censorship board and censors, along with senior church figures, who kept a keen eye on the plays being produced on Irish stages.[44]

The rapid growth of cinema (especially 'talkies') meant that theatre audiences were shrinking and would continue to do so. The cinema also affected the type of shows the theatre offered. The Gaiety and the Theatre Royal began to offer more musicals and variety acts in order to draw in audiences. Guest appearances by Hollywood stars such as Charlie Chaplin were used to draw crowds.[45] Despite this new threat, drama held its own as an important source of entertainment. New theatres emerged and drama groups flourished around Ireland. The Abbey opened its second stage, the Peacock, in 1926, and in 1928 a new theatre, the Gate, opened in Dublin. In 1930 the Gate moved to the Rotunda buildings at the end of O'Connell Street; there had been a concert hall and ballroom in the Rotunda Hospital since its opening in the eighteenth century. While the Gate developed a strong reputation for staging international plays and the works of nineteenth-century Irish writers, these were quite unlike the Abbey's productions. In vying for its own share of the theatre going-audience, the Gate challenged the Abbey. One of the Gate's most remarkable legacies must be the resurrection of Oscar Wilde in Ireland. Wilde's reputation had been destroyed after a trial in 1895 where his homosexual activities were exposed. Despite being born in Dublin, his death in 1900 had not been marked in the city, as people seemed content to forget him. The Gate staged a number of successful productions of Wilde's plays and by the 1930s his work was being recognised, produced and praised once more. *The Importance of Being Earnest* was produced in 1933, and was 'one of their most successful productions ever'. It was restaged in 1935, 1936 and 1938 and toured as far as Egypt in 1937.[46] Orson

Welles made his acting debut in the gate in 1931 when he was just 16 years old.

SEÁN O'CASEY

Despite the Gate's success, the Abbey remained an institution at the forefront of Irish cultural life. One of the most important playwrights to emerge in independent Ireland was Seán O'Casey He was closely associated with the Abbey and he helped to ensure that the theatre remained in the limelight. O'Casey's early plays centred on the guerrilla warfare campaign that had been waged on Dublin streets three years previously, but his plays also dealt with the Dublin's urban working class. Although some commentators felt that O'Casey's plays would not retain their significance, his controversial treatment of historical events ensured that they remain significant to our understanding of Irish politics and society in this period. One of O'Casey's greatest strengths as a playwright was in his portrayal of working-class Dublin, which was informed by his own experiences. He had worked as a labourer from the age of nine, joined a trade union and participated in the 1913 lockout, the largest industrial dispute in Irish history. His socialism drove him to write, and he had contributed articles to the ITGWU paper *The Irish Worker*.[47] Although O'Casey was a nationalist, he was more of a socialist than a republican, and his plays were often critical of republicans. This criticism was difficult for many to swallow, especially in the aftermath of the Civil War, when so many had lost so much. O'Casey's first play, *The Shadow of a Gunman*, was not produced until he was 43, first appearing on the Abbey stage in 1923. It was set in a tenement building in Dublin's Merrion Square and dealt with the War of Independence, as well as the high levels of poverty in the city. O'Casey's next play, *Juno and the Paycock*, was produced in 1924, and centred on a family of tenement dwellers embroiled in the Civil War.

The third play in this trilogy was *The Plough and the Stars*, which opened in the Abbey on 8 February 1926 and was greeted by riots echoing those that greeted *The Playboy* 10 years earlier. One of the main objections was that one of the characters was a prostitute. Many commentators argued that Irish women, good Catholics renowned for their virtue, should not be portrayed as prostitutes. This was an exceptionally blinkered view of both Irish women and Irish society. The Abbey Theatre was a five-minute stroll from 'Monto', the area around Talbot Street, Amiens Street and Montgomery Street that was the city's red-light district. At its peak, from the 1880s to the 1920s, it was believed to be the most densely populated red-light district in the British Empire. The area featured in Joyce's *Ulysses* and in a famous Dublin folk song, 'Monto'. In 1925 the state, lobbied by the Catholic Legion of Mary, successfully moved to shut down prostitution in the area. O'Casey's portrayal of a prostitute was, for many, an uneasy reflection of contemporary Ireland. Christopher Fitz-Simon, former artistic director of the Abbey, says that the 'real reason for the riots were not so much the presence on stage (for example) of a prostitute, or the pastiche of Patrick Pearse's oration at the grave of the Fenian leader O'Donovan Rossa, but more that the Rising was depicted with photographic realism and not as an idealised patriotic print in sepia tones'.[48] The rising had been idealised as a great republican event, and its memory went unsullied in the state. The public did not want O'Casey tampering with that image. O'Casey was attempting to hold a mirror to the events and portray a realistic version of what happened. Irish audiences were not yet ready for such realism. The controversy prompted audiences to flock to the theatre, and O'Casey became an international name. *Juno and the Paycock* was produced in London that summer to critical acclaim. When O'Casey sent his next play, *The Silver Tassie*, to the Abbey it was rejected. The play focused on the Great War, and O'Casey believed it to be his best play to date. But Yeats believed it was impossible to stage. He was also critical of the topic, and he failed to acknowledge the important contribution Irishmen and Irishwomen made in the Great War. Although Gregory had given O'Casey huge support up until then, she backed Yeats on this, showing her 'continuing bond' to him as well as 'her growing remoteness from literary creativity and newer trends'.[49] It was subsequently staged in London to great acclaim. Nevertheless, O'Casey was angered by the Abbey's rejection of the play and he sent his correspondence with the theatre to a London newspaper to publicise the issue.[50] The affair was to greatly damage the Abbey's reputation, with questions being raised over Gregory's and Yeats's direction of the theatre. Gregory was 75 when the *Silver Tassie* argument erupted. She increasingly withdrew from the theatre and died at her beloved estate at Coole, County Galway, on 22 May 1932. Yeats's health was also failing and he spent increasing amounts of time in the Mediterranean.

In 1932, when Éamon de Valera's Fianna Fáil took power, the theatre lost one of their greatest supporters in government, the former minister for finance, Ernest Blythe. He was invited to take a place on the board of the theatre, a position which he held for the next 37 years. An economic downturn in the 1930s meant that the government had to economise, and they reduced the theatre's annual grant to £750. Yeats argued that the subsidy was so small it should be rejected. He felt that accepting any funding from the government meant the theatre could be accused of being a government organ and that it could be susceptible to government censorship. Yeats met with de Valera and they agreed that in all American tour programmes a line should be inserted stating that the government of Ireland accepted no responsibility for the content of the plays.[51] Tours remained important for theatre finances. They also raised the profile of the theatre. In 1932, for example, the Abbey Company actors met the US President Herbert Hoover at the White House.

When Yeats died in 1939, Blythe took up the reigns. In 1941 he became managing director, a position which he held until 1967. He was successful in keeping the theatre financially afloat during very difficult economic times. Nevertheless, his 26 years at the helm of the theatre would lead to artistic stagnation. No new playwrights emerged from the Abbey to challenge the mantle of Synge or O'Casey. Emerging talent seemed to go elsewhere.

THE ABBEY THEATRE FIRE

One of the most challenging events in the history of the theatre occurred on the night of 17–18 July 1951, when the building went on fire. The auditorium, dressing rooms, sets and costumes were destroyed, along with the theatre archive containing hundreds of scripts that had been submitted to the theatre for consideration: 'a merciful end for some of them, it was suggested'.[52] Actors and other staff rushed to the burning building to try to rescue what they could. A number of historic paintings were rescued by staff and actors. Blythe was notified of the fire by an *Irish Times* reporter who was one of the first on the scene.[53] The following night the company performed *The Plough and the Stars* in the Peacock. *The Irish Times* ran with the headline 'Abbey burning did not stop play', and reported that George Dermot Findlater, the chairman of Belfast's Empire Theatre, had opened a subscription fund to rebuild the theatre and had donated the first £250.[54] Blythe was offered, and accepted, the use of Rupert Guinness Hall as a temporary playhouse. The company's play run continued uninterrupted. Blythe later arranged for the use of the Queen's Theatre, by then 'a down-at-heel music hall'.[55] There were some alterations made, and it became home to the Abbey for the next five years. While this solved the immediate problem of a venue, the company was still struggling financially, and Blythe was forced to cut his own salary to that of a non-player.[56] The cost of rebuilding was troublesome. The first Abbey play to be staged in the Queen's was O'Casey's *The Silver Tassie*, which opened on 24 September 1951. The theatre held 760 seats, much smaller then the Abbey itself. This presented staging problems, as the Abbey actors were used to a far smaller stage. It was also difficult to fill the seats, and Blythe was forced to run more commercial plays, 'the Irish equivalent of the light comedies of Broadway and the West End'.[57] This was something that the Abbey had never done before. Indeed it was one of the issues that had forced the Fay brothers to leave. One of the best runs of the 'Queen's Theatre period was Brendan Behan's *The Quare Fellow*. Blythe had turned down an early draft of the play, but after it ran, with great success, at the Pike Theatre Club in 1954, Blythe decided to take the play on.

The Queen's period could be said to mark a nadir in the Abbey's creative history. The four most important Irish plays of the 1950s and 1960s were produced elsewhere. These included John B. Keane's *Sive*, produced in 1959; Tom Murphy's *A Whistle in the Dark* in 1961 (both rejected by Blythe), and, in 1964, Brian Friel's *Philadelphia Here*

I Come! and Eugene McCabe's *King of the Castle*.[58] While the artistic director, Ria Mooney, was blamed for this creative downturn, she hit back, claiming that the Abbey had creative problems beyond her remit. She seemed to be referring to Blythe's continuing pursuit of an Irish-language programme, as well as constant staging of peasant plays.[59] There was not much money for lavish stage props. By the late 1950s there was much pressure on Blythe to reform the way the theatre was run and the players were paid. Mooney retired in 1963, and Blythe gave into pressure, engaging an artistic director who would broaden and modernise the playbill.

IRISH DRAMA COMES INTO CONFLICT WITH THE STATE

In the 1950s it was left to other theatres, and playwrights unconnected with the Abbey, to spark controversy and excite debate. The years 1957 and 1958 were two stormy years in the history of Irish drama and its relationship with the government. In 1957 *The Rose Tattoo* case highlighted the extent to which independent Ireland's conservative Catholic ethos could stymie the theatre. The Pike Theatre Club, run by Alan Simpson and his wife, Caroline Swift, premiered the plays of Behan and Samuel Beckett. Behan's *The Quare Fellow* was staged at the Pike in 1954 and Beckett's *Waiting for Godot* in 1955. *The Irish Times* critic sent to review *Waiting for Godot* seemed unsure about Beckett's play: 'I'm not sure what Mr Beckett deserves—people, as a rule, don't like to be made uncomfortable, and I don't think anybody can see "Godot" without spending at least one restless night asking "why" and "whither"?'[60] Nevertheless, the critic praised Simpson, stating that he 'deserves the thanks of everybody who cares about worth-while, new departures in theatre'.[61] *The Irish Times* also praised Simpson's stage production of Behan's radio play *The Big House* in 1958, stating that it 'has suffered nothing in the transition, it has gained colour and life … thanks to producer Alan Simpson'.[62] He was well-respected in the theatre world for breaking new ground. The Pike staged the European premiere of Tennessee Williams's *The Rose Tattoo* in May 1957 as part of a theatre festival. In the play one of the character's drops a condom on stage. Although the actor merely mimes the act of dropping the condom, Simpson, the founder and manager of the theatre, was prosecuted for indecency and imprisoned for a short while. The arresting officer had purchased and read a copy of the play. He had not been to see the production, but from his reading of the play he considered it to be indecent. Despite Simpson's arrest, his wife continued to stage the play, as well as drawing media attention to the dubious nature of his arrest.[63] Some Catholic groups and individuals picketed the theatre. When Simpson was exonerated in June 1958, the presiding judge, Justice Flynn, admonished the Gardaí, stating that they seemed to have a frontier-like policy in place when making arrests of this nature: 'shoot first then ask questions later'.[64] Despite this victory, Simpson was forced to close the Pike due to his legal bills, a big blow to Irish drama.

Irish playwrights were next to challenge the Irish establishment, in the form of the church. In 1958 the Dublin Theatre Festival, just a year old, had scheduled Seán O'Casey's play, *The Drums of Father Ned*. Archbishop John Charles McQuaid of Dublin refused to say a votive mass for the festival because of O'Casey's presence on the programme. The festival organisers capitulated to McQuaid's demands, removed O'Casey from the billing and had their mass said. O'Casey was so enraged that from that point on he refused to have any of his work produced in Ireland. The Abbey had nothing to do with his play being pulled, but the theatre suffered the most from O'Casey's prohibition. The Abbey did not stage another of his plays for six years.[65] When Beckett heard of the furore over O'Casey's play, he wrote to Simpson: 'As long as such conditions prevail in Ireland I do not wish my work to be performed there, either in festivals or outside them. If no protest is heard they will prevail for ever'.[66] Outraged, Beckett pulled his play from the programme and held his prohibition until 1960, although *Krapp's Last Tape* was performed at the Trinity Players Theatre (now called the Beckett Theatre) in 1959.[67] The festival went ahead in 1958, but embattled playwrights ensured their voices and protests were heard around the world. O'Casey had the last laugh. To mark Ireland's entry to the European Economic Community *The Silver Tassie* was performed by the Abbey Players in Brussels. As part of the Irish delegation, McQuaid was present in the audience.

RETURN TO ABBEY STREET

It was not until 1966 that the Abbey Theatre re-opened on Abbey Street, on an enlarged site. The rebuild cost £725,000.[68] The architectural style of the theatre (which was designed by Michael Scott and Ronald Tallon) received mixed reviews. It is not particularly striking. Casey calls it 'dull in the extreme'.[69] The auditorium, which contains seating for 628, was designed 'in the purest modernist tradition'. The stepped seating layout focuses 'all the room's energies on the stage, forcing its audiences to give the performance their full attention'.[70] It places the stage at the very centre of the room, with little to see in the rest of the auditorium. The fact that the government was prepared to finance a new theatre, and the company's return to its Abbey Street home, proved to the theatre-going public and artistic community that the Abbey could not be done away with easily, and would remain central to Irish cultural life. The first series of plays in the new theatre was performed under the title *Recall the Years* and were a reminder to the public of all the Abbey had achieved and of the literary talent the theatre had given birth to. But the return to Abbey Street did not mark a return to old ways. It marked a reinvigoration of the company. The management and players returned with fresh ideas and enthusiasm. A new team assisted in this revitalisation. Tomás MacAnna became artistic adviser in 1966. Ernest Blythe gained a new assistant, Phil O'Kelly, who had spent years working in the Gaiety and brought his experience of working in that commercially successful theatre. He focused on bringing commercial success to the Abbey as well as spending money on sets and costumes to make Abbey productions more lavish. He became manager in 1967 when Blythe retired. Blythe stayed on the board for a further five years, but his retirement opened the way for a new direction for the theatre.

From the late 1960s the Abbey began to engage more directly with Irish playwrights. It built up strong links with emerging and established writers, and not only produced their plays but took artistic and creative advice from them. The 1960s and 1970s were years of significant social change in Ireland, and this can be seen in the nature of productions at the Abbey. Morash says that the new

Abbey building 'can stand as an image of much that has taken place in Irish culture in the mid-1960s'.[71] Tom Murphy produced four ground-breaking new plays with the Abbey in the late 1960s and early 1970s. P.J. O'Connor's adaptation of Kavanagh's autobiography *Tarry Flynn*, and Frank McMahon's adaptation of Behan's *Borstal Boy* rounded off the period.[72] Some of the theatre's successes later in this period included their production of Beckett's *Waiting for Godot*, his first play to be produced at the Abbey. The theatre commissioned the Tyrone playwright Brian Friel, who was an internationally recognised playwright by the early 1970s, to produce a play. *Freedom of the City* was produced in February 1973, and dealt with the events of 'Bloody Sunday' in Derry in January 1972, when British soldiers shot 26 civil rights protesters, killing 13 of them. Friel himself had taken part in the march. The play acts as a reminder of the importance playwrights have in exposing and exploring injustices and the part the Abbey Theatre played in exploring key events and topics from Irish politics and history.

The atmosphere of the old Abbey could still be felt in the Peacock. This stage was small, and intimate leading many to comment it recreated the feeling of the old Abbey, which had been central to the development of the Abbey acting style. The Peacock was also a space where Irish-language plays, which attracted a far smaller audience, could be staged. The Abbey strived to keep producing them but the audiences were smaller. Between 1966 and 1976 the Abbey produced twenty-one Irish-language plays, and nineteen of them were produced on the Peacock stage.[73] During the 1970s the theatre broadened its artistic horizons further, staging a greater number of non-Irish plays and the works of other companies. This engagement with international drama meant that the Abbey diversified its productions, as 'musicals, revues and pantomimes' became part of the regular bill. In 1976 the Abbey staged Thomas Kilroy's *Tea and Sex and Shakespeare*. Blythe had earlier rejected Kilroy's plays, and this production, along with others, showed a new willingness to produce work that challenged audiences' views and the outlook of the theatre.

Around this time, the company was also bringing new talent on board. A part-time position was created to assess the unsolicited

Modern Abbey Theatre
building designed by
Michael Scott and
reopened on 18 July
1966.

scripts that were sent to the theatre, with a view to engaging writers of promise and returning scripts that were not desirable. In the 1960s, 300 scripts a year were being received, so this was a mammoth task.[75] Internationally recognised Irish playwrights such as Brian Friel, John B Keane, Hugh Leonard, Tom MacIntyre and Tom Murphy worked closely with the theatre and helped to raise its standards and reputation after the nadir of the 1940s and 1950s. The theatre continued to prove its relevance in the 1970s and 1980s, with plays like Graham Reid's *The Death of Humpty Dumpty*, which dealt with sectarian violence in Belfast; Antoine O'Flatharta's *Gaelgeoirí*, which looked at the failure of the government to resurrect the Irish language; and Frank McGuinness's landmark *Observe the Sons of Ulster Marching Towards the Somme*, which has been described as a 'crucial event in Irish playwriting'.[76] The artistic directorship of Joe Dowling was also noteworthy, and he directed Friel's *Aristocrats* and Leonard's *A Life* to great acclaim.

With an increase in productions came an increase in production costs and staff. Eventually, the theatre desperately needed to reduce expenditure. The huge cost of staging plays such as Flann O'Brien's *An Béal Bocht* (*The Poor Mouth*) illustrated this.[77] Poor reviews in the press and spending cuts suggest that the Abbey was going into decline once more. In 1987 a couple of very successful productions created an operating surplus, but not enough to reduce the overall debts of the theatre. As part of a fund-raising drive, the players produced *The Playboy of the Western World* in America. It was a hugely successful tour. While ground-breaking new plays continued to be produced, including a number by Tom Murphy, the deficit loomed over the theatre. In 1989 the government gave a one-time payment of £400,000 to clear the debts. While it carried the flame of great Irish playwrights such as Beckett, Synge and O'Casey into the 1990s and beyond, reaffirming their relevance to new generations, the Abbey also engaged with contemporary Irish playwrights. Brian Friel's *Dancing at Lughnasa* was first produced at the Abbey in 1990, rather than by his own theatre company. Award-winning author and playwright Sebastian Barry also had plays produced for the Abbey. Plays by established writers such as Thomas Kilroy, Tom Murphy and

Frank McGuinness were also regularly produced. These playwrights were all internationally recognised and the productions ensured that the Abbey was seen not merely as a relic of the past but as a cutting-edge national theatre.

Irish drama is at the heart of Irish culture, and forms an important part of the school curriculum today. While Irish school-goers study O'Casey, Synge and other great Irish playwrights, to see a play enacted is to truly experience and understand it. The Abbey keeps these plays alive, and reminds Irish audiences of their social, political and historical importance. While the Abbey's productions declined in the middle of the twentieth century, it re-emerged to reclaim its place as Ireland's national theatre. Fitz-Simon has pointed out that 'almost all of the great plays of the Irish theatre since 1904 originated in the Abbey Theatre, and most of those that did not were later absorbed into its repertoire'.[78] He added that 'a hundred years hence the social commentator will understand the preoccupations, the inconsistencies, the haunting obsessions of Irish life far better from the content of the plays than from any political or demographic studies'.[79] The insight these plays provide, and the history of the theatre that produced these stories, ensure that the Abbey is one of the most important cultural landmarks in Dublin to this day. The theatre seemed to represent the values and policies of the government and challenging the status quo fell outside the theatre's remit. Other voices emerged within the world of theatre to question the social, political and sexual norms in twentieth-century Ireland. This meant that the theatre was left behind for a time. Nevertheless, the theatre re-emerged in the 1970s as one of Ireland's premier theatres and returned to the heart of Irish drama, where it continued to challenge both the Irish public and policy-makers.

10

Croke Park

THE FIRST CHAPTER in this book looked at the oldest cathedral in Dublin, and the last will look at what might be described as a cathedral of the modern era: a sports stadium. Croke Park is no ordinary sports stadium, however. It is the headquarters stadium of the Gaelic Athletic Association (GAA): an organisation at the heart of the Gaelic Revival. Gaelic games were an important and distinctive facet of Irish culture. This was not lost on those Irish nationalists who promoted and used Gaelic football and hurling (amongst other games) to highlight that Irish culture was sophisticated, and different to British culture. Consequently there was a great overlap between membership of the GAA—a nationalist sporting body—and political and militant nationalist groups. When the Irish Free State was established the new Irish government saw the need to develop an Irish identity based on more than politics alone. The sports played at Croke Park, and the stadium itself, became key to the development and promotion of a distinctive Irish culture in an independent Irish state. The historian Tim Carey says that 'if the Abbey Theatre represented the higher end of the Irish cultural landscape', then 'Croke Park, as a manifestation of the GAA, became the most popular feature'.[1] The Tailteann Games, the government's answer to the Olympic Games, whereby Celtic nations and the diaspora of these nations competed against each other in a variety of sports, was hosted in Dublin in the late 1920s, and Croke Park was its home.

Although Croke Park is in Dublin, it is truly an All-Ireland stadium. In chapter one, Christ Church Cathedral showed us how diverse Dublin's origins are. Early Irish Christians, Vikings and Anglo-Normans all played a part in shaping the city. The island as a whole was politically fragmented throughout this period, with Dublin, the centre of colonial power, remaining distinctive and particularly susceptible to external influences. Croke Park, in contrast, could be said to represent the culturally homogenous Ireland that the Irish state sought to portray after 1922. The site might be in Dublin, but it does not belong to Dublin alone. Every summer, people from all over Ireland come to Croke Park to watch the best amateur sportsmen and women fight for the All-Ireland titles in Gaelic football, hurling, and camogie.

GAELIC GAMES IN DUBLIN BEFORE THE GAA

Gaelic games were played in Dublin as early as the fourteenth century. Although the traditional Irish sports of Gaelic football and hurling feature in Irish myths (particularly the epic poem the Táin), the first written reference to a game that might be hurling dates to the seventh and eight centuries. Under Brehon law, a player who sustained injuries during a hurling match should be compensated. The 1366 Statutes of Kilkenny (see chapter two) banned a game called 'horlinge' from being played within the city limits. This 'horlinge' was probably an early version of hurling. This early version of our modern Gaelic games had few, if any, rules. There were also regional variations. Eighteenth-century accounts of hurling matches that took place in Dublin give us some sense of how chaotic these early games could be. A somewhat biased account in the *Freeman's Journal* in the 1770s complained about hurling matches that took place in Phoenix Park every Sunday: 'The Sabbath is abused by permitting a hurling match to be played there every Sunday evening which is productive of blasphemous speaking riot, drunkenness, broken heads, and dislocated bones, among ten thousand of the lower class'.[2] These matches seem to have been played at fixed times among different communities. Nevertheless, they were chaotic with few or no rules, no set number of players and with goalposts that varied in width and location. A football match between the county Dublin villages of Lusk and Swords is recorded in an epic poem from 1721, written by Matthew Concannon, in which the teams have just six players each. It has been suggested, however, that Concannon makes them play six-a-side so that the poem does not become overburdened with names.[3] One account of eighteenth-century hurling matches described how a blow from a hurley could kill a player on the pitch: 'It frequently happened, in pursuit of the ball, that two antagonists came into collision, and in the shock one of them, thrusting the handle of his hurley under his arm, took with the point of it his antagonist in the side, who in some instances fell dead'. Lucky players, however, might get away with 'crushed ribs'. But he recorded that hurling was a rough sport that had 'maimed and disabled [a] man for life'.[4]

THE FOUNDATION OF THE GAA

The formation of the GAA was prompted by two distinct but widespread, late-nineteenth century developments—the growth of spectator sports internationally and, as we shall see further on, the Gaelic Revival in Ireland. In particular, the popularity of sports had increased dramatically across all sectors of British society. An increase in leisure time, as well as the steady advance of the railway, a relatively cheap form of transport, meant that even the working and middle classes had time and money to travel to and from sporting events such as football (soccer) matches. These games had few rules about pitch sizes, points, and even numbers of players. This made it difficult for rival teams to play each other and for local or national competitions to emerge. Overall, sports in the mid-nineteenth century can be described as 'chaotic and disorganised'.[5] Without rules or regulations, games could descend to on-pitch fighting or to teams marching off the pitch. The Victorians began seeking more organised ways of playing sports, and so they started to develop rules and regulations and publishing guidelines to sports, so that teams playing rugby or football throughout the British Isles would begin playing by the same rules. Mike Cronin and Roisin Higgins, both historians of the GAA, note that 'where before there had been local sports and traditions, in their place came a fixed and regulated sense of the rules; games became sports, and everything was defined'.[6] This movement to codify sports spread quite quickly from Britain to Ireland. Irish sports clubs and teams were inaugurated and adopted these British rules. By 1910 clubs had been established for all kinds of sports throughout Ireland. There were 400 clubs for soccer alone.[7] The increased participation in sports was not restricted to Irishmen. Irishwomen enthusiastically embraced the new trend too. By the early twentieth century women in Dublin were playing hockey, tennis, bowls and croquet.

The Gaelic Revival was an important context for the development of the GAA. As we have seen in earlier chapters, many Irish people developed a great interest in aspects of traditional Irish culture including language, literature, history and folklore. This led to a resurgence in interest in Irish games. As part of this broader trend a number of formal associations were founded, such as the Gaelic League, founded in 1893 by Douglas Hyde (a close friend of Michael Cusack, one of the principal founders of the GAA). It hoped to preserve and revive the Irish language. But the GAA had been founded even earlier, in 1884, which shows how ahead of the curve these sportsmen were. Later cultural associations like the Gaelic League and the National Theatre were following a trend that the GAA had initiated; the creation of a formal organisation to protect a cultural pastime.

In 1881 the Dublin-based teacher Michael Cusack encouraged a number of his students to form a Dublin hurling club, which became known as the Metropolitan Hurling Club. Inspired by its success, he began to call on more people to establish clubs and become involved in Irish games. He was supported in this by two nationalist (and arguably Fenian) newspapers, *The United Irishmen* and *The Irishman*. He printed an article in both newspapers on 11 October 1884 headlined 'A word about Irish athletes', in which he called for 'the preservation and cultivation of the national pastime of the people'. Referring to the spread in Ireland of English games such as soccer and cricket, he called them 'corrupting and degrading influences'.[8] They were also seeking freedom from the Amateur Athletic Association of England under whose auspices they had to operate. The farmer and athlete Maurice Davin had a similar interest in the games, and published an article soon after Cusack's, echoing his sentiments. The two men got together and called a meeting with the purpose of drawing together interested sportsmen to play the games, as well as regulating how the games would be played. This meeting took place in Hayes Hotel in Thurles, Co Tipperary, on 1 November 1884, and so the GAA was formed. The seven founders are recorded as Michael Cusack, Maurice Davin, Thomas St George McCarthy, John McKay, John Wyse Power, P.J. O'Ryan and John Bracken. Cusack, who is now credited with being the primary founder of the GAA, had a great interest in Irish games, particularly hurling. Davin became the first president of the association, while Cusack became secretary. Once the GAA was formed, it lost little time in codifying the games. Davin was responsible for drawing up the early rules, with changes being made later. The rules were important in providing an early framework for the association.[9]

Although the movement did not seem political, it became involved in nationalist politics from early on. It had a strong connection with the Home Rule movement, as well as more radical groups such as the IRB. Indeed, the GAA was seen as a recruiting ground for Fenianism, and there was an overlap in membership of both associations. Three of the founding members were also members of the Irish Republican Brotherhood, and although there was no formal connection, the leadership was clearly well-disposed towards the republican movement. Republicans were also keen to be involved in the GAA.[10] Cusack's article of October 1884 gives us a strong idea of his own nationalist beliefs. He referred to soccer, cricket and other games being played in Ireland as 'imported and enforced customs'. He added 'a warlike race' like the Irish 'is ever fond of games requiring skill, strength, and staying power. The best games of such a race are never free from danger'. There is a suggestion here that in reinvigorating Gaelic Games, those involved could be preparing for war. He cited the British colonisation of Ireland as the reason for the decline of Irish culture and sport: 'Foreign and hostile laws and the pernicious influence of a hated and hitherto dominant race drove the Irish people from their trysting [meeting] places at the cross-roads and hurling fields back to their cabins where but for a few short years before famine and fever reigned supreme'.[11] Having an association with such a high number of IRB members had implications for the future. It might seem logical that men and women interested in Irish independence would similarly be interested in Irish cultural pursuits such as hurling, camogie and Gaelic football, but the GAA attracted more Fenians than other cultural groups.

Croke Park as the home of the GAA

From the early years of the association, the All-Ireland finals became the central event in the GAA calendar. They are the most written-about, listened-to and watched games in the Irish sporting calendar. As home to these finals and much of the preceding championship, Croke Park has hosted generations of players and supporters. Indeed, it was through its search for a suitable venue for All-Ireland finals that the GAA actually found its home at Jones' road. During the early years of the association the GAA had no fixed, official home, and finals were played at various sports venues throughout Dublin. In June 1894 the hurling finals were held at the Ashtown Trotting Grounds in the Phoenix Park. These rented venues were not always suitable; in 1894 the players and crowds arrived in Ashtown to discover a pitch that was totally unsuitable. The grass was knee-high and the pitch had no markers or goalposts. The players and crowds were forced to walk to the Phoenix Park, where they found more suitable grounds.

The football final of that year was played at Clonturk stadium in Drumcondra. This game, between Dublin and Cork, ended in a draw and when the referee ordered extra time the Cork team refused to play on. A replay was ordered, this time on more neutral ground. On 21 April 1894 the replay took place in Thurles. This rematch only added to the great Cork—Dublin rivalry. With Cork leading, the crowd invaded the pitch, which led to a halt in play. Dublin refused to play on when the pitch was cleared, and when another replay was ordered Cork refused to play it. The association declared Dublin the champions by default. Pitch invasions were a frequent occurrence in the early games. Spectators had easy access to the pitch, and it was difficult to stop them from interrupting play when they did not like a refereeing decision or what was happening on the pitch. When a large crowd invaded it often took some time to clear the pitch.

The early association could be badly organised, which sometimes led to chaos at the games. The 1895 football final was played in 1896 and was the first final to be played on Jones's Road. There was a large crowd, but unusually no pitch invasions, so the game lasted just sixty-eight minutes. The frequency of pitch invasions meant games could last up to two hours. While Tipperary's Arravale Rovers won, the referee wrote a letter to the *Irish Independent* the next day stating that one of the points scored by them was illegal and that the game should have ended in a draw between them and the Meath team, Navan O'Mahony's. The council decided to let the result stand, but made special medals for the Navan O'Mahony's players.[12] In the early years of the twentieth century, Michael Crowe, a referee, began to address the problem of pitch interruptions, along with discipline, and inconsistencies in the application of regulations.[13]

The rules for games were quite different then from their modern incarnations. For instance, there were initially twenty-one players on a team, which made the pitch very crowded. This was reduced to seventeen players and later to fifteen. In these early days, a goal wiped out the points that your opponent had scored, so points only mattered when no goals were scored. This meant that scores tended to be low. There was no net, and it was often difficult to tell when a point or goal had been scored. Carey tells us that 'wrestling and tripping was allowed', meaning that 'there was more than a passing resemblance to American football or rugby'.[14] A number of changes were introduced at the turn of the century that quickened the pace of games. Nets were introduced, as were the goalposts we are familiar with today. The weight of the sliotar (the leather ball used in hurling) was reduced so the ball could travel further. A goal was given a weighting of five points and later three.

It was not a foregone conclusion that Dublin would become the home of the GAA and All-Ireland finals. Of the first 22 hurling finals played, twelve were outside Dublin, while twelve of the first twenty-three football finals were played outside the capital.[15] The 1892 football final was played in 1893 between Kerry's Laune Rangers and Dublin's Young Irelands (intercounty teams had not yet taken hold). The Dublin crowd were so hostile to the Kerry team that some called for all future finals to be played outside Dublin. This did not happen, however. One reason for this was the importance of the railway in the development of nineteenth-century sport. Stadiums were no use if spectators could not get to them. The spread of railways across the country meant that transportation was not only fast, but cheap too. This allowed the middle and working classes to travel to games on their day off. Many new sports clubs and stadiums were built alongside railway stations in recognition of this. Dublin was the focal point for many lines, and was easy to get to.[16] It was particularly convenient when teams from opposite sides of the country played each other. The number of sports grounds in Dublin also made it a convenient place to hold finals. All of these reasons made the capital seem like an obvious home for the GAA, and in 1909 the association set up headquarters in Dublin, at 68 Upper O'Connell Street.[17]

JONES ROAD BECOMES CROKE PARK

Throughout its history, Croke Park has been remodelled and renovated to suit the needs of each sporting generation. One of the most important figures in the stadium's history is Frank Dineen. He had been an excellent sprinter in his youth, and he worked as a sports journalist for the *Freeman's Journal* and the *Evening Telegraph*. He was elected president of the GAA in 1895 and secretary in 1898, before going on to become the first president of the athletics' council (which later broke away to form its own council). When the stadium was purchased by Dineen in 1908 for £3,250 the grounds were desperately in need of work. The 1905 All-Ireland final, which was played at Jones road, showed up the inadequacies of the grounds. Some 15,000 attended the match. Most people sat on the sidelines rather than in the stands, which were full to capacity. Many gained entry by simply climbing over the wall. There were two pitch invasions which led to long delays in the game.[18] The renovations that Dineen carried out were greatly admired. In May 1909 a journalist in *Sport* said that 'the new proprietor has spared neither expense not architectural skill in laying out the grounds, and as an athletic arena it is now second to none in the Three Kingdoms'. He added that the crowd assembled for the hurling final 'must have felt sincerely proud of the headquarters of Gaelic sport in Ireland'.[19] Jones's Road had become one of the finest stadiums in Ireland. Although the stadium was the main venue for GAA matches, it was not yet the home of the organisation.

In 1913 a memorial tournament was organised across the country to raise funds for a monument to Thomas Croke, Archbishop of Cashel, an important patron of the early GAA. Games were played throughout the country as part of this tournament, and a much-anticipated football match between Louth and Kerry was scheduled for Jones road. Dineen made a number of alterations to the grounds that increased the seating to 10,000.[20] The score was very close throughout the game, with scores level at half-time and again at the final whistle. A rematch was scheduled for June at Jones road. While the teams trained in preparation for the big match, alterations at the stadium allowed for seating for a further 3,000, which would have brought in increased revenue. The match didn't just affect the grounds and surrounding area, however. 21,000 extra people passed through Kingsbridge Station (now Heuston Station) and Amiens Street Station (now Connolly Station) en route to the match. It is estimated that 32,000 people watched the match inside the stadium, with thousands more watching for free from the railway lines which ran adjacent to the grounds. The Home Rule leader John Redmond was in the crowd. As a major celebrity, he was recognised, given a standing ovation and brought to meet the team captains. Kerry won the game 2-4 to 0-5, but the replay was not as exciting as the crowds anticipated.[21]

The gate receipts from the memorial games around Ireland were larger than anticipated: £2,400. Rather then putting up a traditional 'monument', the central council decided that £300 from the funds raised would be put towards purchasing a hall in Thurles, which would be called Croke Hall. Some £2,400 of the GAA's money was put towards purchasing the Jones road stadium from Dineen. The grounds would be called after Archbishop Croke. Dineen, who had invested hugely in the refurbishment of the stadium, had the land valued at £4,000, which was too high an asking price for the GAA. When the association began to investigate a site on the southside of the city, Dineen dropped his asking price to £3,500.[22] Although the first advertised mention of the 'Croke Memorial Park' was for the All-Ireland Football Final on 14 December 1913, the GAA only took formal ownership of the grounds on 22 December 1913. As the GAA was an organisation with no legal basis, and the people who negotiated the stadium purchase were liable for its debts, they became a limited company in 1914. They quickly began to make further alterations to the grounds such as levelling the pitch and demolishing an old timber stand. It installed 1,500 sideline seats at a cost of £115. This was a prudent investment, which brought in an additional £300 in ticket sales for the 1914 final alone. The additions and continual modernisation of the stadium ensured that it was one of the finest in Ireland. The stadium had become the heart of the organisation.

CROKE PARK DURING THE WAR OF INDEPENDENCE

Fighting during the War of Independence had a big impact on the GAA, and on Croke Park in particular. There was an inevitable overlap in membership between the GAA and militant nationalist groups such as the IRB and the Irish Volunteers. Nevertheless, the GAA initially sought to separate itself from the mobilisation of paramilitaries that was occurring throughout the country in 1913–14. The GAA banned the Volunteers from drilling in the stadium, but the 1916 Rising became a turning point for the organisation. After the rising, the GAA became visibly sympathetic to militant nationalism. The annual Volunteer convention was held in Croke Park in 1917. One of the most famous spectator areas of Croke Park today is Hill 16 or Dineen Hill. This terrace was originally a mud embankment, but today it is a concrete terrace that can hold up to 13,000 spectators. The terrace, which is at the railway end of Croke Park, is strongly associated with Dublin fans. Few know that the terrace was originally called 'Hill 60' after a sixty-metre hill that was fought over during the Gallipoli campaign in the First World War; a campaign in which large numbers of Irish troops were killed. The name was given to honour members of the GAA who had fallen fighting for the hill in British uniforms. The name was later changed to Hill 16 in recognition of the 1916 Rising.

Michael Collins at Croke Park in 1919 (National Library of Ireland)

Republican gatherings were held at the stadium, and matches were played to raise money for the republican cause. One such match was that on 6 April 1919 between Tipperary and Wexford. Those in attendance included Éamon de Valera (who threw the football in to start the match) Michael Collins (who threw in the sliotar), Arthur Griffith, Harry Boland (who refereed) and the lord mayor of Dublin, Lorcan Sherlock. The deaths of prominent republican figures were also marked at Croke Park. When Terence MacSwiney died on hunger strike, all matches were cancelled in the stadium for a week as a mark of respect. The war also caused disruptions to scheduled games, just as it had disrupted attendance at the Abbey and many other social events across the city. In July 1918 the British government banned a large number of public meetings in thirteen counties. The ban affected GAA events, but not soccer, rugby or cricket. The government believed that Gaelic games were being used for covert republican meetings, and match permits had to be obtained through the Royal Irish Constabulary, which was often hostile to these events. The GAA refused to apply for the permits, which brought it into direct confrontation with the government. In July 1918 soldiers interrupted a match in Kildare and dismantled the goalposts to ensure the game could not go ahead. Games were halted in Offaly, Down and Cavan. During the 1918 Ulster Championship game between Cavan and Armagh, troops occupied the playing field. The local priest addressed the crowd of 3,000 and asked them to disperse. The game was allowed to take place the following day, but it was overseen by soldiers and the local RIC.[23]

The GAA could also be a protest vehicle against increasingly repressive British rule. On Sunday 4 August 1918, in an attempt to prove it would not be coerced, the GAA played 2,000 games in one afternoon. The exercise was a huge success. GAA historian Eoghan Corry notes that 'parishes and townlands which had not fielded a team for a generation lined out'.[24] The games became a form of mass protest against the interference of the British forces in Irish sport and social life and against their attempts to curb the population's freedom of choice. Corry estimates that 54,000 players took part with many thousands more coming to watch the games. Not only did they peacefully make their protest, but they succeeded in gaining more supporters for the association.

BLOODY SUNDAY, 21 NOVEMBER 1920

This did not bring an end to official hostility towards to the GAA, however. The association continued to support the nationalist cause, and the government continued to view it with suspicion. Indeed, Croke Park was to become the scene of the worst civilian losses during the War of Independence. In November 1920 Dublin challenged Tipperary to a football match at Croke Park, the proceeds of which were to be donated to the Republican Prisoners Fund. These were two of the best football teams of that year, and large crowds were expected.[25] There were rumours among some of the players that some IRA activities were scheduled for the same day as the match, but there were no details about what they were. Collins, as the IRA's director of intelligence, had been provided with information that the British forces had a specialist unit nicknamed the 'Cairo Gang' that was tasked with targeting key figures within the republican movement. Collins was given names and addresses of the alleged members of the gang. He sent a group of his own men, known as 'the squad', to execute these men, who were deemed a huge threat to the republican movement. On the morning of Sunday 21 November the squad killed twelve British officers, presumed to be intelligence agents, in their lodgings. The intelligence officers were unarmed, a highly controversial aspect of the killings. Two RIC officers were also killed. The GAA had been informed about what was planned, but the association had decided not to call off the game in case it would link the IRA with the GAA in the minds of the British.[26]

When news spread of the republican killings, British forces (Auxiliaries and Black and Tans) went looking for the republicans involved. They drove to Jones road, entered the stadium and opened fire on the crowds. The shots resulted in chaos, with terrified spectators rushing for cover. Members of the crowd attempted to exit the stadium, but were prevented from doing so. The shots were aimed at players on the pitch as well as those in the crowd. Players from both teams thought they would be shot. The spectators were individually searched before they were allowed to leave the stadium. The body of Michael Hogan, a Tipperary player who had been shot dead, was left on the pitch throughout these searches. Thirteen other civilians were killed.[27] The youngest was a 14-year-old schoolboy, John Scott, who died of a chest wound. Another of the victims, 26-year-old Jane Boyle, who was shot dead, had been due to be married the Wednesday following the match. As well as the dead, there were large numbers of wounded.

The details surrounding the shooting at Croke Park were contested by both British forces and by spectators. An investigation by the British authorities into the controversial shootings led to the following findings: the government claimed that the match had been organised as cover for the assassinations and that republicans who had carried out the early-morning killings had hidden in the crowds during the game. The British forces that took part in the shooting stated they were pursuing men who had fired shots outside the stadium and who had fled inside when it became apparent that they were being pursued. Finally, the British forces claimed that once they had moved their

The Cairo Gang, the British intelligence officers targeted and killed by Michael
Collins' Squad during Bloody Sunday.

armoured car into the stadium and had occupied the pitch, an officer
had called on the men who had fired shots outside the stadium, and
who had taken part in the morning shootings, to come forward so
they would be arrested, but none had.[28]

This official version of events was contested by eyewitnesses to the
tragedy. The RIC report was contradicted by evidence given by three
officers from the Dublin Metropolitan Police who were stationed at
the Canal Bridge entrance. They said they saw no civilians who looked
threatening, and did not witness anyone shooting first. They reported
seeing up to 15 military lorries arriving at the Canal Bridge entrance
at 3.30 p.m.[29] Furthermore, there does not seem to have been a
warning for republicans to surrender to the officers who had invaded
the stadium. Many historians view the shootings as one of the many
unofficial British reprisals carried out in the War of Independence.
They point to the burning of Cork city in December 1920 and the
sack of Balbriggan in September 1920, both of which were reprisals by
the British for IRA attacks. The scenes at Croke Park did not end the

violence on 21 November; that evening two IRA members, Brigadier Dick McKee and Vice-Brigadier Peadar Clancy, along with a civilan, Conor Clune, all of whom had been detained by British forces the night before, were killed while in custody in Dublin Castle.

Bloody Sunday had a significant legacy within the GAA, as well as in Irish history more broadly. The Tipperary player who was killed, Michael Hogan, has both a stand in the stadium and a championship cup, awarded to the school football champions, named after him. Bloody Sunday is a reminder of how the war affected those who were not directly involved in a political party or paramilitary organisation. It also affected public opinion. The event is widely considered to be the peak of the violence in the War of Independence. The day certainly saw the highest number of fatalities in the war. The idea that British forces could gun down innocent civilians enjoying an afternoon of sport horrified not only the Irish public but also the British public, and the British government began to experience a backlash from a British population that did not have an appetite for another bloody war. It would take a long time for the GAA, the stadium staff and spectators to recover from such a traumatic event. It was difficult for many to return to the stadium afterwards. While club games were played at Croke Park a few weeks after the event, an inter-county event would not be held at the grounds until the Anglo-Irish truce in July 1921. The crowds attending games at the stadium were smaller too. Bloody Sunday had highlighted that during the War of Independence it was dangerous to be associated with the GAA, and even to attend their events.

CROKE PARK IN THE IRISH FREE STATE

The first inter-county match played at Croke Park after the signing of the Anglo-Irish treaty was in February 1922, when a fundraiser was held for the Prisoners Dependents Fund. One unfortunate advertisement seemed to have forgotten the tragedy of 1919 and stated 'desperate shooting at Croke Park (for goals and points)'.[30] The new government quickly recognised the importance of the GAA as a cultural institution. The GAA had run up debts in a stadium refurbishment in 1921. Although the association had run a number of tournaments in 1920 to cover the cost of this work it had fallen short of its intended target. The government cleared the GAA's debts of £1,700 in 1922 and offered a low-interest loan of £6,000. The speed at which this was done is striking when compared with the drawn-out negotiations that the Abbey Theatre had with the government. The GAA had a broad popular appeal, and matches at Croke Park were almost guaranteed to draw a crowd.

In the immediate aftermath of the Civil War, the GAA was seen as an organisation that could help to heal the divisions produced by that conflict. Mike Cronin says that the government party, Cumann na nGaedheal, tried to embrace the process of reconciliation, most obviously in public events and memorials. One of the most significant events the new state held was *Aonach Tailteann*, which took place in Dublin 1924, 1928 and 1932. This was a sporting and artistic festival aimed at 'projecting the positive attributes of the new state'.[31] The *Aonach Tailteann* festival drew on the pre-Norman Gaelic tradition of national games of the same name, and consisted of athletic, gymnastic and equestrian competitions. Storytellers, poets and musicians from all over Ireland would have gathered for the festival too. Cultural and political nationalists had previously become fascinated by the games, and from the 1880s there had been calls for their revival. The idea of re-staging them was finally revived in 1919, with Éamon de Valera being a leading advocate.[32]

The new state was eager to host a cultural celebration of all things Irish, so in 1922 an initial grant of £6,000 had been set aside to fund the games but the outbreak of the Civil War meant that they had to be postponed. They were eventually held in 1924. There had been a political dimension to the original games that would not have been lost on those who organised the 1924 version.[33] 'The original games were held under the terms of a national truce and aimed to celebrate the illustrious dead. The modern games came a year after the ending of a bloody civil war that had resulted in thousands of deaths and the destruction of the Irish infrastructure'.[34] The theme of reconciliation in the aftermath of the Civil War was common in the speeches made at the first games. This would have had a great

Aonach Tailteann 1924, America v. Ireland hurling teams
(National Library of Ireland)

resonance in the country at this time, with the last of the republican prisoners from the war being released. The government was making a clear statement: the games were intended to heal. They were also intended to show the world that Ireland was unified, confident, and, in the aftermath of independence from the British state, reconnecting with its own indiginous culture.

The 1924 games came shortly after the Olympic Games in Paris, the first Olympiad in which an Irish Free State team had attended. The Tailteann games were not just for Irish-born participants, however, and teams were sent from all 'Celtic' nations as well as countries with a large Irish diaspora such as the US, Australia and Canada. Cronin says it 'was essentially a celebration of a single ethnic group'.[35] Although the intention was to celebrate 'Irishness', the games were not limited to Gaelic games. Golf, soccer, swimming, tennis, and motor-car racing were all featured as competitions. International teams did, however, play Irish games and the picture above shows the American soccer team that took on Ireland in a game of hurling at Croke Park. Arts events were also scheduled, including plays, concerts and readings.

Croke Park became the main home for the games. Although not all the events were held at the stadium, it was central to the festival, with the opening and closing games being held there. The elaborately choreographed opening ceremony was watched by 20,000 spectators, and started with the entry of Queen Tailté, queen of the mythical Fir Bolg tribe, and her court into Croke Park. Two large, medieval-style towers were erected at the entrance to the stadium to bring the spectators and athletes back in time to an older Ireland. The ceremony was filled with nationalist symbolism, including two young men who were featured in the opening ceremony, dressed in traditional Irish dress, leading Irish wolfhounds into Croke Park. A parade, dedicated to Irish industry and crafts, was held in the city of centre. The streets were decorated with flowers and bunting, creating a festival feeling throughout the capital. Floats displayed the products and processes involved in creating traditional Irish goods and only Irish goods were included. The parade was very popular.[36] While attendance for the 1924 games as a whole was very good, some of the events 'failed to ignite enthusiasm'. For instance, just 100 people watched the only camogie game of the tournament, which was played in Terenure.[37]

Although there were concerns that the festival would run up a massive debt beyond the £7,500 they had been granted, in the end the government was left with a bill for an additional £3,000—less then was feared—and the games provided a boost to tourist numbers, which was very helpful after the revolutionary years.[38] The games were not only an advertisement for 'Irishness', but they became an advertisement for modernity too. Two of the biggest attended events were motor racing and air racing. Both were new sports and fascinated the audiences. So too did the use of wireless to relay scores to news rooms across the city. One photograph from the games shows three men appearing fascinated by a wireless set.[39]

Although the games were a huge success in their first year, this was not to last. The new state was always torn between wanting to project a proud and positive image and wariness at the costs this would incur.[40] The numbers attending the games dropped in 1928. This led to a backlash in the press. The government was left with a bill of £9,000 for overspending during the 1928 games.[41] In 1932

Aonach Tailteann, opening ceremony 1924 (National Library of Ireland)

the games were given just £1,000 in funding by the new Fianna Fáil government headed by de Valera, which viewed the games as an unwanted legacy of their Cumann na nGaedhal predecessor. Although the games recorded a loss this time of just £12, they were widely criticised as being too parochial. They lacked the 'wow' factor of previous games and attendances were poor, particularly compared to the one million people who packed into the Phoenix Park for the Catholic Eucharistic Congress in the same year.[42] While the games had arguably aided post-Civil War reconciliation in 1924, Cronin points out that the most popular events were the modern games, rather then the traditional Gaelic games: 'The pull of the motor cycle was greater than the pull of the hurley stick'.[43]

THE GROWTH OF THE GAA AND THE DEVELOPMENT OF SPORTING MEDIA

Over the next twenty years GAA stadiums sprang up around the country, and a GAA club could be found in every county and in almost every parish in Ireland. This did not diminish the importance of Croke Park. In fact it made the All-Ireland trip to Croke Park all the more special: only the best players in the country got to play there. In 1925 the GAA made a formal announcement that All-Ireland finals would be played in the stadium. The GAA was 'a pillar of new independent Ireland' and Croke Park was the symbolic heart of the GAA.[44] During this period the All-Ireland finals became 'a national affair', and increased space in newspapers was given over to them. This interest went beyond the teams who played in them.[45] Irish sports journalism began to develop, and newspaper sales increased. The *Irish Press* was launched on All-Ireland hurling final day in 1931 to take advantage for the increased demand for news and commentary that the games created. While the *Irish Independent* and *Irish Times* covered GAA games to some degree, de Valera's *Irish Press* was recognised as having 'boosted Gaelic games coverage'.[46]

The new state radio station, 2RN, also had a part to play in increasing the popularity of the games. The station first broadcast on 1 January 1926. It too intended to project an image of a technologically modern Ireland. In August 1926 the hurling semi-final between Kilkenny and Galway became the first sports game to be broadcast over the radio, not just in Ireland, but in Europe. A dedicated press table was also added to the stadium. The broadcast of games was not greeted enthusiastically by everyone, however. Some within the GAA argued that broadcasting the games would lead to a decline in attendances. In reality the opposite happened. For many it made attendance at the games even more special, as they could soak up the atmosphere. Listening to games over the radio allowed the games to be followed more closely and led to increased popularity. About 25,000 listeners tuned in to each game that was broadcast.[47] This is a significant number considering that radio sets were still luxury items. Nevertheless, they allowed large groups and even whole communities to gather and listen to the matches. In the 1930s a plan of the stadium appeared in newspapers to assist those who were listening to games on the radio.

Other sports quickly followed the GAA's example. Soccer and rugby were soon broadcast by 2RN. In fact the GAA feared that 'the new service would challenge its cultural ascendancy', and complained about other sports results being broadcast on the radio, but were overruled.[48] One of the more controversial rules of the GAA was its ban on members playing or engaging with foreign games. The ban covered soccer, rugby and cricket. While the ban was recognised as important in the early years of the association, when other cultural institutions were bemoaning the decline of Irish pastimes and the ascendancy of British culture, by the 1930s it was seen by many as unnecessary. Many 'ignored and resented' the ban.[49] It seems doubtful in retrospect that engaging in sports such as soccer could undermine such a healthy association. Nevertheless the ban was upheld and taken to ridiculous lengths. In 1938, Douglas Hyde, the president of Ireland and founder of the Gaelic League, was ejected from the GAA for attending an international soccer match between Ireland and Poland at Dalymount Park in his capacity as a head of state (final score was 3-2 to Ireland).[50] Hyde had been a close friend of Michael Cusack and an advocate of the GAA in its early days. This seemed to count for very little in the eyes of the GAA.[51] The most common criticisms of the GAA in the twentieth century concerned this ban.

Sporting drama at Croke Park

Arguably one of the most dramatic hurling finals ever played at Croke Park, and nominated by the sports commentator P.D. Menighan as the greatest hurling match ever played, was the 1939 match between Kilkenny and Cork, which took place on 3 September.[52] The match was played during a thunder storm. The rain was so heavy that the dye from the players' jerseys ran from the fabric and covered their legs and arms. Cork, captained by future Fianna Fáil taoiseach Jack Lynch, were trailing at half time but the two teams were neck and neck in the second half, with Kilkenny scoring the winning point just minutes before the whistle blew.[53] One of the young hurlers on Cork's team, and a rising star of Irish sport, was Christy Ring, one of the finest hurlers to ever play the sport. The GAA commentator Micheál Ó Muircheartaigh says of Ring that his 'unique prowess as a hurler is universally accepted'. He adds that Ring was 'courageous, passionate, obsessive, powerful and inspirational'. He had an 'extraordinary' record of victories that included 'eight All-Ireland's, nine Munster titles, three National Leagues and eighteen Railway Cup medals'.[54] When Ring died in 1979, his funeral was attended by 60,000 people in Cork along with the Taoiseach, Ring's former team-mate Jack Lynch.[55]

In June 1959, on the seventy-fifth anniversary of the foundation of the GAA, the new Hogan Stand was opened. To mark the occasion All-Ireland winners were invited to a special ceremony, presided over by the then-president Seán T. Ó Ceallaigh. More than 900 were to see the new 16,000-seater, two-tier stand officially opened. It cost £250,000.[56] The GAA remained at the cutting edge of stadium architecture in Ireland. With better seating, more diverse events could be held at Croke Park. *The Pageant of Cuchulann* was staged there as part of *An Tostal* (a cultural festival aimed at attracting tourists into Ireland) events in 1957, with *The Pageant of St Patrick* being staged in 1961.[57] The newly refurbished stadium also played a key part in the fiftieth anniversary commemorations of the 1916 Rising in 1966. A special pageant, created by the Abbey Theatre producer Tomas Mac Anna, was staged at the stadium. It involved 800 actors, who re-enacted scenes from Irish history between 1798 and the establishment of the Dáil in 1919.[58] The survivors of the 1916 Rising were also photographed in the stadium in 1966.

While the 1930s and 1940s were hailed as a golden era for the GAA, in the late 1960s and 1970s the association faced a number of challenges. Attendance for finals began to decline to around 70,000, as Croke Park and the GAA felt the impact of modernisation. The GAA was part and parcel of 'traditional' Ireland. The strong association which the GAA had with the Catholic Church was just one way in which this was evident. Senior church figures were patrons of the association. Religious events were held in Croke Park, such as the Golden Jubilee of the Pioneer Total Abstinence Association in 1949. Ten years later, the sixtieth anniversary of the Pioneers was marked in the stadium. The Patrician Year Mass was also held in Croke Park in 1961. Images of Ireland's archbishops parading around the stadium ensured that Catholic Church and the GAA remained closely linked in the minds of the public. While the population of the Republic of

Ireland was still overwhelmingly Catholic, the image reinforced in the minds of Ireland's young that the GAA was part of 'old' Ireland. The GAA had seemed to embrace modernity in the 1920s and 1930s, but that was no longer the case. Youth culture now centred less on the GAA, and more on music, soccer, films and television.

CROKE PARK'S DECLINE

The advent of television had positive and negative effects on the GAA. The first match was televised in August 1962, just a year after the founding of Télefís Éireann: a football semi-final between Kerry and Dublin at Croke Park. In 1966 both Télefís Éireann and BBC Northern Ireland broadcast the games live. People could now view the games at home. While radio broadcasts had made more people want to visit Croke Park, televising the games made people less likely to attend games and crowd numbers at Croke Park fell off. On the other hand, the games could be followed more closely by a larger population, and they were now available to the Irish diaspora in Canada and the United States, giving the games an international dimension.[59] The 1966 and 1970 soccer World Cups were also televised in Ireland, however, and this helped to further popularise that game. The popularity of soccer increased, and this was believed to be damaging to the GAA's younger support base.

With declining numbers attending matches, the GAA realised by the 1970s that they had to make more of an effort to attract an audience to Croke Park. Among the suggestions made in a commission report were a better sound system, more modern toilets, more buses on match days, and better catering and refreshment facilities. Carey says 'the changes envisaged were basic', and 'underlined just how far the main stadium of the GAA had fallen behind the times'.[60] One positive development in the 1970s, however, was that women's football and camogie made more prominent appearances in the GAA's annual programme.

By the 1960s, a growing opposition to the GAA's ban on foreign games had emerged. This opposition seemed to be growing in line with the growing interest in soccer. The ban was eventually dropped in 1971.[61] This opened up the stadium to other sports and created one of the stadium's, and Ireland's, greatest sporting events. On 19 July 1972 Muhammad Ali fought Al 'Blue' Lewis in Croke Park in a comeback match for Ali: 'The fight became the talk of the town and tickets were in scarce supply'.[62] In true Irish style, many blagged or barged their way into the already-packed stadium to see one of the world's most famous sportsmen. Ali defeated Lewis after eleven rounds, in a match that was watched around the world.

REDEVELOPMENT OF CROKE PARK

The stadium experienced issues with crowd control just once, in 1983, when Dublin beat Galway in the football All-Ireland final. The match became known as 'the game of shame'. The stadium was packed to capacity, with 71,988 attending. During the game Dublin had players sent off and were playing with just twelve men by the end of the game. They were later nicknamed the 'dirty dozen' for their rough tactics on the pitch. Rather than waiting to exit the stadium after the game, there was a rush, as 'people slid down the wet banks, often before the people who had gone before them were able to move away'.[63] This led to a crush at the Canal End and at the Hill 16 exits. Clashes between Galway and Dublin fans inside the stadium prompted more spectators to try to rush out of the stadium. One fan was stabbed in a fight, and dozens more were injured in a crush. It is fortunate that no one died. The event highlighted how Croke Park was drastically in need of refurbishment. New guidelines on safety at sports grounds were introduced in 1986 and Croke Park fell short of these standards.[64]

The GAA was hoping to increase the capacity of the stadium to 90,000. The plan stalled until 1989, when the GAA initiated the work again. One of the biggest issues for the redevelopment was safety. There were not enough emergency exits, some had been blocked over the years, signage was poor, the turnstiles allowed several people through at a time and crowd numbers were not adequately counted. The Cusack Stand, in particular, was in a bad condition, being more than fifty years old. A major reconstruction was needed, and it was estimated that this redevelopment would cost £115 million. The design stage was slow as issues such as sight line, ensuring that the pitch can be viewed from every seat in the stadium, were worked out. An application for planning permission was lodged in February 1992, and permission was granted in March 1993.

The redevelopment took fifteen years, and was carried out in four stages so that the stadium could remain open during that time. The Cusack Stand was the first to be demolished, in 1993. The new stand was opened for the Leinster football final in 1994, and now contained 25,000 seats (up from 14,000).[65] It also included corporate boxes and premium seats. The sale of these boxes went towards defraying some of the €44 million that the new stand had cost. Land had to be purchased as well, as the new stand took up far more space then the old one. In 1998 the GAA museum was opened in the Cusack Stand, incorporating a new Hall of Fame. Phase two began in 1997 when the Canal End was demolished. It was re-opened in 2000. In 1999 phase three was started, with the demolition of the Hogan Stand. A new pitch was laid in 2002, for the first time since the 1920s. A redeveloped Hill 16 was completed in 2004. This finished the project. Unusually for an Irish property development, it was completed ahead of schedule. By the end of the project the stadium had cost 250 million euro. Over the 2002 season there were more than 1.3 million visitors to the new stadium, while attendance increased by 5–10,000 people per match. *The Irish Times* said of the new stadium: 'If you grew up in the GAA, the new Croke Park is a dream world. Slow escalators taking people to the sky, great banks of seats making the amphitheatre and a seam of executive boxes making the money'.[66] Croke Park seemed to embody the confidence that Ireland felt during the Celtic Tiger.

In February 2007 Croke Park became the stage for a sort of political and historical healing. Lansdowne Road, the home of Irish soccer and rugby, was in need of major redevelopment. While the stadium was undergoing this work, the Irish Rugby and Football Union (IRFU) needed to find an alternative venue for international matches. It approached the GAA to see if the stadium could be used for games. The only other option was to use a British stadium for home games which was impractical, considering the newly renovated Croke Park was available. Although the GAA had lifted the ban on its members playing foreign games in 1971, Rule 42, which prohibited foreign games being played in GAA stadiums still stood. Rugby and soccer had not been played in the stadium since the GAA had bought the Jones's Road site from Dineen. While some were against the proposal, the GAA decided to allow the IRFU to use the stadium. The first rugby game was played on 11 February 2007 between Ireland and France. The next match was far more momentous, however. On 24 February Ireland played England in the stadium. Members of the GAA and the public had objected to the English anthem 'God save the Queen' being played at the scene of Bloody Sunday, now considered to be the worst example of British brutality during the War of Independence. Nevertheless, the match went ahead, and the playing of the anthem took on a whole new significance. Rather then being viewed as disrespectful to the Bloody Sunday dead, in the aftermath many viewed it as a sign of how far Ireland had come. The GAA had opened its doors to foreign games, had embraced international teams and had moved beyond its own ghosts. While it was certainly an emotional moment, it was also a 'momentous occasion'.[67] The match symbolised that old wounds had healed. This attitude might, of course, have been aided by the fact that Ireland defeated the English side 43–13. In contrast to this, the first soccer game between Ireland and Wales to be played in the stadium passed off with little comment (final score was 1–0 to Ireland).

LEGACY

The symbolism attached to Croke Park was as much political as it was sporting or cultural. Nevertheless, the 2007 rugby game against England seemed to lay this political element of the stadium to rest. Croke Park is an institution with a proud political, social and cultural history, and these aspects have been preserved within the stadium through the GAA museum. Croke Park was at the heart of the GAA from its purchase in 1913, and from there the stadium became an important cultural centre. Croke Park attracted tens of thousands of spectators for most matches. Over the years the stadium has been attended by more of the population than any other Irish cultural institution. Apart from this major cultural significance, the stadium was home to important political events too. The *Aonach Tailteann* games assisted with reconciliation in the aftermath of a turbulent civil war. The stadium hosted some of the largest state commemorative events during the fiftieth anniversary of the 1916 Rising. The religious celebrations that were held in the stadium also reflected crucial aspects of Irish society in the twentieth century. The stadium was full for these events because religion observance remained at the heart of many Irish homes. While the Catholic Church is in decline in twenty-first century Ireland, and it could be argued we have made sports stadiums new cathedrals of a sort, Croke Park remains an important mirror on Irish culture and society.

Epilogue

MANY OF THE FIGURES that funded, designed and built these land-marks set out to create a legacy through the buildings. They were conscious that the buildings they left behind were important historical artefacts, and that they would play a big part in the historical narrative of the city. In the 1570s an inscription to honour Lord Deputy Henry Sidney, who undertook renovations in Dublin Castle (visible in the walls of the Castle in 1680 but now lost), drew on the importance of buildings to our understanding of history.

> Books record the famous deeds of many men,
> And marks of praise stay fixed in documents.
> These stones do truly tell of Sidney's praise,
> For such glory is not enshrined in books alone.
> If books perish, people can remain,
> Should people perish, timber can endure.
> If timber perishes, stone will not therefore perish,
> And should stone perish in time, time itself will be.
> If time perishes, eternity will hardly be consumed,
> Because it exists with a beginning, but without an end.
> While books are flourishing; while people live;
> While stone, with timber, is strong enough to last;
> While time remains, and finally eternity endures,
> Your worthy praise, O Sidney, cannot pass away.[1]

The message is clear: as long as history is being written, Dublin Castle would remain a monument to Sir Henry Sidney's deeds, and those of the English government he served. History cannot be written in books alone, and these buildings act as important signposts, marking where we have come from and how we have progressed. These buildings can also bring us closer to our ancestors; they allow us to learn about the

Dubliners who inhabited the same space as we do now. By visiting, inhabiting and using these buildings, we are creating a sense of historical continuity and we are keeping the traditions and culture of this city alive. One of the most enjoyable aspects of researching the book was visiting each building, looking for details in the stonework and imagining the events staged within the halls, the people who walked the corridors, worked in offices or inhabited the chambers. It was an exciting way to connect with the past. I would encourage the reader, where possible, to do the same.

Endnotes

INTRODUCTION

1. Anngret Simms, 'Origins and early growth', in Joseph Brady & Anngret Simms (eds), *Dublin: Through Space and Time (c. 900–1900)*, (Dublin, 2001), p. 34.
2. Finbar Dwyer, *Witches, Spies and Stockholm Syndrome: Life in Medieval Ireland* (Dublin, New Island Press, 2013), p. 130.
3. Louis Cullen, 'A story of growth and change: Dublin 1560–1800' in Howard B. Clarke (ed.), *Irish Cities* (Cork, 1995), p. 98; Simms, 'Origins and Early Growth', in Brady & Simms, *Dublin*, p. 56.
4. Cullen, 'A story of growth and change', in Clarke (ed.), *Irish Cities*, p. 99.
5. Edel Sheridan, 'Designing the capital city: Dublin *c.*1660–1810', in Brady & Simms, *Dublin*, p. 70.
6. Jacinta Prunty, 'From city slums to city sprawl: Dublin from 1800 to the Present', in Clarke (ed.), *Irish Cities*, p. 109.

CHAPTER ONE: CHRIST CHURCH CATHEDRAL

1. H.B. Clarke, *Dublin: Part I, to 1610*, (Dublin, 2002), p. 2.
2. *Ibid.*, p. 1.
3. Simms, 'Origins and Early Growth', in Brady & Simms, *Dublin*, p. 18.
4. Clarke, *Dublin: Part I*, p. 3.
5. H.B. Clarke, 'Sitriuc Silkbeard', in *Dictionary of Irish Biography* [hereafter *DIB*].
6. Simms, 'Origins and early growth', in Brady & Simms, *Dublin*, p. 19.
7. *Ibid.*, p. 16.
8. *Ibid.*
9. Clarke, 'Sitriuc Silkbeard', in *DIB*.
10. Stuart Kinsella 'From Hiberno-Norse to Anglo-Norman *c.*1030–1300', in Kenneth Milne (ed.), *Christ Church Cathedral, Dublin: A History* (Dublin, Four Courts, 2010), p. 29; Clarke, 'Sitriuc Silkbeard', in *DIB*.

11. Peter Somerville-Large, *Dublin: The Fair City* (London, 1996), p. 3.

12. Kinsella, 'From Hiberno-Norse to Anglo-Norman', in Milne (ed.), *Christ Church Cathedral*, p. 28.

13. *Ibid.*, p. 29.

14. Roger Stalley, 'The construction of the medieval cathedral, *c.* 1030–1250', in Milne (ed.), *Christ Church Cathedral*, p. 55.

15. Somerville-Large, *Dublin*, p. 31.

16. *Ibid.*, p. 32.

17. Mac Shamhráin, Ailbhe 'Ua Tuathail, Lorcán (O'Toole, Laurence)', in *DIB*.

18. Somerville-Large, *Dublin*, pp. 32–33.

19. *Ibid.*, p. 35.

20. *Ibid.*, pp. 34–36.

21. Stalley, 'The medieval sculpture of Christ Church Cathedral, Dublin' in Howard Clarke (ed.), *Medieval Dublin: the Making of a Metropolis* (Dublin, 2012), p. 202.

22. Roger Stalley, 'The construction of the medieval cathedral, *c.* 1030–1250', in Milne (ed.), *Christ Church Cathedral*, pp. 55, 61.

23. *Ibid.*, p. 53.

24. *Ibid.*, p. 59.

25. *Ibid.*, p. 59.

26. *Ibid.*, p. 70.

27. Stuart Kinsella, *Christ Church Cathedral Dublin: Visitor's Guide* (Dublin; Christ Church Cathedral Publications, 2012), p. 1

28. Stalley, 'The construction of the medieval cathedral', in Milne (ed.), *Christ Church Cathedral,* pp. 109–111.

29. *Ibid.*, p. 54.

30. Kinsella, *Christ Church Visitor's Guide*, p. 4.

31. Thomas Drew, 'The Ancient Chapter-House of the Priory of Holy Trinity, Dublin' in Clarke (ed.), *Medieval Dublin*, pp. 181–182.

32. *Ibid.*, p. 175.

33. Douglas Bennett, *The Encyclopaedia of Dublin* (Dublin, 2005), p. 235.

34. Rachel Moss, 'St Patrick's Well' in Yvonne Scott & Rachel Moss (eds), *The Provost's House Stables: Buildings & Environs, Trinity College Dublin* (Dublin, 2008), pp. 73–84.

35. Dublin City Council 'Dublin City Development Plan, Built Heritage, 2011–2017' (http://www.dublincitydevelopmentplan.ie/pdf/BACKGROUND_Built_Heritage.pdf)

36. J.T. Gilbert, *A History of the City of Dublin*, (3 vols, Dublin, 1861), iii, pp. 102, 106.

37. Stalley, 'The construction of the medieval cathedral', in Milne (ed.), *Christ Church Cathedral*, p. 108.

38. Gilbert, *Dublin*, iii, p. 106.

39. Thomas and Valerie Pakenham, *Dublin: A Traveller's Companion* (London, St Edmondsbury Press, 1988), p. 77.

40. *Ibid.*

41. Stalley, 'The construction of the medieval cathedral', in Milne (ed.), *Christ Church Cathedral*, p. 107.

42. Ciaran Diamond, 'The reformation Charter of Christ Church Cathedral Dublin, 1541', in *Archivium Hibernicum*, 53 (1999), p. 20.

43. The bones of Laurence O'Toole were interred in a parish church at Churley, in Lancashire, but were destroyed during the Reformation.

44. *Irish Times*, 3 March 2012.

45. *Irish Times*, 24 August 2012.

46. Kenneth Milne, *The Dublin Liberties, 1600–1850* (Dublin, 2009), p. 7.

47. Raymond Gillespie, 'The shaping of reform, 1558–1625', in Milne (ed.), *Christ Church Cathedral*, p. 189.

48. Stalley, 'The construction of the medieval cathedral', in Milne (ed.), *Christ Church Cathedral*, p. 63.

49. *Ibid.*, p. 63.

50. Stalley, 'The 1562 collapse of the nave and its aftermath', in Milne (ed.), *Christ Church Cathedral*, p. 234.

51. Stalley, 'The construction of the medieval cathedral', in Milne (ed.), *Christ Church Cathedral*, p. 128.

52. Beranger, Gabriel, (ca. 1729–1817), UCD Library Special Collections. Beranger Watercolours, Wat 18. http://digital.ucd.ie/view/ivrla:3509 (accessed 3 June 2014)

53. Bennett, *Encyclopaedia*, p. 124.

54. John L. Robinson, 'Christ Church Cathedral, Dublin, Proctors' Accounts, 1689–90', in *The Journal of the Royal Society of Antiquarians of Ireland*, sixth ser., 1, 3 (Sept. 1911), p. 260.

55. *Ibid.*

56. *Ibid.*, p. 262.

57. *Ibid.*, p. 264.

58. Michael Barry, *Victorian Dublin Revealed: The remarkable legacy of Nineteenth-Century Dublin* (Dublin, 2012), p. 82.

59. *Ibid.*, pp. 86–87.

60. *Ibid.*, p. 82.

61. David Murphy, 'Henry Roe', in *DIB*.

62. David Murphy, 'George Edmund Street', in *DIB*.

63. Kenneth Milne, 'The stripping of the assets, 1830–1960', in Milne (ed.), *Christ Church Cathedral*, p. 323.

64. Murphy, 'Roe', in *DIB*.

65. Milne, 'The stripping of the assets, 1830–1960', in Milne (ed.), *Christ Church Cathedral*, pp. 324–325.

66. Stalley, 'George Edward Street and the restoration of the cathedral', in Milne (ed.), *Christ Church Cathedral*, pp. 362–363.

67. Kinsella, *Christ Church Visitor's Guide*, p. 1; Gillespie, 'The shaping of reform, 1558–1625', in Milne (ed.), *Christ Church Cathedral*, pp. 174–175.

Chapter Two: Dublin Castle

1. Madame de Bovet, *Three Month Tour in Ireland* (London, 1891), p. 16.

2. Patrick Healy, 'The town walls of dublin', in Clark (ed.), *Medieval Dublin*, p. 183.

3. Clarke, *Dublin: Part I*, p. 4.

4. Peter Costello, *Dublin Castle in the life of the Irish Nation* (Dublin, 1999), p. 28.

5. *Ibid.*, p. 31.

6. *Ibid.*, p. 32.

7. Anngret Simms, 'Medieval Dublin in a European Context: from proto-town to chartered town', in Clark (ed.), *Medieval Dublin*, p. 49.

8. Mairead Dunlevy, *Dress in Ireland* (London, 1989), pp. 33–35.

9. *Ibid.*, p. 35.

10. Denis McCarthy, *Dublin Castle: At the heart of Irish History* (Dublin, 2nd ed. 2004), p. 26.

11. McCarthy, *Dublin Castle*, p. 26.

12. Detail from John Derrick, *Image of Irelande* (London, 1581).

13. Pakenham, *A Traveller's Companion*, p. 57.

14. Francis Clark, 'Margaret Ball', in *DIB*.

15. McCarthy, *Dublin Castle*, p. 53.

16. *Ibid.*, p. 54.

17. J.B. Maguire, 'Seventeenth-century plans of Dublin Castle' in Clark (ed.), *Medieval Dublin*, p. 196.

18. Costello, *Dublin Castle*, p. 50

19. McCarthy, *Dublin Castle*, p. 72.

20. From this date it replaced St Werburgh's as the official chapel of the lord lieutenant.

21. Costello, *Dublin Castle*, p. 59.

22. Joseph Robins, *Champagne & Silver Buckles: The Viceregal Court at Dublin Castle 1700–1922* (Dublin, 2001), p. 36.

23. Edward McParland, *Public Architecture in Ireland 1680–1760* (New Haven, 2001), p. 100.

24. Robins, *Champagne & Silver Buckles*, p. 39.

25. Sarah Foster, 'Buying Irish: Consumer nationalism in eighteenth-century Dublin', in *History Today*, 47, 6 (1997).

26. Tomás O'Riordan, 'The theft of the Irish Crown Jewels, 1907' in *History Ireland*, 9 (Winter, 2001), p. 23.

27. McCarthy, *Dublin Castle*, p. 73.

28. Foster, 'Buying Irish'.

29. *Freeman's Journal*, 15 Mar. 1783.

30. *Ibid.*

31. McCarthy, *Dublin Castle*, p. 90.

32. David Hicks, *Irish Country Houses: A Chronicle of Change* (Cork, 2012), p. 84.

33. Patricia Pelly & Andrew Todd (eds), *The Highland Lady in Dublin 1851–1856* (Dublin, 2005), p. 74.

34. *Ibid.*

35. *Ibid.*, p. 326.

36. *Ibid.*, p. 72.

37. *Ibid.*, p. 268.

38. Percy Fitzgerald, *Recollections of Dublin Castle and of Dublin Society* (New York, 1902), pp. 43–44.

39. *Ibid.*, pp. 96–97.

40. Pelly & Todd, *The Highland Lady*, p. 285.

41. *Ibid.*, pp. 61–62.

42. The only monarchs to wear it were Edward VII and Queen Victoria.

43. Myles Dungan, *The Stealing of the Irish Crown Jewels: An Unsolved Crime* (Dublin, 2003), p. 93.

44. *Ibid.*, p. 97.

45. *Ibid.*, p. 96.

46. O'Riordan, 'The theft of the Irish Crown Jewels, 1907', p. 26. *History Ireland*, vol. 9, no. 4 (Winter, 2001), p. 26.

47. *Ibid.*, p. 26. *History Ireland*, vol. 9, no. 4 (Winter, 2001), p. 26.
48. *Freeman's Journal*, 10 Aug. 1907.
49. *Ibid.*, 27 Jan. 1908.
50. Dungan, *Stealing*, pp. 100–101.
51. O'Riordan, 'The theft of the Irish Crown Jewels, 1907', p. 25. *History Ireland*, vol. 9, no. 4 (Winter, 2001), p. 25.
52. Fearghal McGarry, *The Rising: Ireland 1916* (Oxford, 2010), p. 2.
53. *Ibid.*
54. Brian Ó Conchubair (ed.), *Dublin's Fighting Story 1916–1921: Told by the men who made it* (Cork, 2009), pp. 113–114.
55. David Neligan, *The Spy in the Castle* (Dublin, 1999), p. 59.
56. *Ibid.*, p. 63.
57. *Ibid.*, p. 88.
58. *Ibid.*, p. 108.

CHAPTER THREE: TRINITY COLLEGE DUBLIN

1. Colm Lennon, *Sixteenth-Century Ireland: The incomplete conquest* (Dublin, 1994) p. 138.
2. *Ibid.*, p. 143.
3. J.V. Luce, *Trinity College Dublin: The first 400 years* (Dublin, 1992), p. 1
4. *Ibid.*, p. 2
5. *Ibid.*, p. 5.
6. *Ibid.*, p. 12.
7. *Ibid.*, p. 4.
8. *Ibid.*, pp. 2–3.
9. Pakenham, *A Traveller's Companion*, p. 165.
10. *Ibid.*, pp. 165–166.
11. Luce, *Trinity College Dublin*, p. 11.
12. *Ibid.*, p. 22.
13. *Ibid.*, p. 23.
14. John McCafferty, 'James Ussher', in *DIB*.
15. George Otto Simms, 'Early Christian Manuscripts', in Peter Fox (ed.), *Treasures of the Library* (Dublin,1986), p. 48.
16. *Ibid.*, p. 44.
17. McCafferty, 'James Ussher', in *DIB*.
18. Peter Fox, 'They much glory in their library', in Fox (ed.), *Treasures of the Library*, pp. 3–5.

19. Simms, 'Early Christian Manuscripts', in Fox (ed.), pp. 48–49.
20. Muriel McCarthy, *Marsh's Library: All Graduates and Gentlemen* (Dublin, 2003), p. 19.
21. Luce, *Trinity College Dublin*, p. 29.
22. McCarthy, *Marsh's Library*, p. 21.
23. *Ibid.*
24. Fox, 'They much glory in their library', in Fox (ed.), *Treasures of the Library*, p. 5.
25. The first library keeper, who held the post between 1601 and 1605, was Amrbose Ussher, brother of James Ussher.
26. McCarthy, *Marsh's Library*, p. 21.
27. Pakenham, *A Traveller's Companion*, p. 168.
28. *Ibid.*, p. 169.
29. Fox, 'They much glory in their library', in Fox (ed.), *Treasures of the Library*, p. 5.
30. *Ibid.*, p. 5.
31. Luce, *Trinity College Dublin,* pp. 40–41.
32. Patrick Geoghegan, 'Thomas Burgh', in *DIB*.
33. Luce, *Trinity College Dublin*, p. 41
34. Peter Fox, 'The Old Library: *ut erat – ut est – ut esset*', in W.E. Vaughan (ed.), *The Old Library: Trinity College Dublin, 1712–2012* (Dublin, 2013), p. 1.
35. Fox, 'They much glory in their library', in Fox (ed.), *Treasures of the Library*, p. 8.
36. *Ibid.*, p. 10.
37. Luce, *Trinity College Dublin*, p. 41
38. *Ibid.*
39. Fox, 'They much glory in their library', in Fox (ed.), *Treasures of the Library*, p. 27.
40. Luce, *Trinity College Dublin*, p. 51.
41. *Ibid.*, p. 67.
42. *Ibid.*, p. 96.
43. Fox, 'The Old Library', in Vaughan (ed.), *The Old Library*, p. 10.
44. *Irish Independent*, 12 Nov. 1928.
45. Lorcan Collins & Conor Kostick, *A Guide to Dublin in 1916* (Dublin, 2000), p. 37.
46. *Irish Independent*, 12 Nov. 1928.
47. Maurice Craig, *Dublin 1660–1860: The Shaping of a city* (Dublin, 2006), p. 103.

48. *Irish Independent*, 12 November 1928.
49. Craig, *Dublin 1660–1860,* p. 104.
50. Fox, 'The Old Library', in Vaughan (ed.), *The Old Library*, pp. 8, 10.
51. *Ibid.*, p. 17.
52. R.B. McDowell, *McDowell on McDowell: A Memoir* (Dublin, 2008), pp. 73–74.

CHAPTER FOUR: PARLIAMENT HOUSE (NOW BANK OF IRELAND)

1. Christine Casey, *Dublin* (New Haven, 2005), p. 380.
2. Thomas Bartlett, *Ireland: A History* (Cambridge, 2010), p. 143.
3. *Ibid.*
4. Pakenham, *A Traveller's Companion*, p. 184.
5. Gilbert, *Dublin*, iii, p. 57.
6. Casey, *Dublin*, p. 377.
7. Gilbert, *Dublin*, iii, p. 59.
8. *Ibid.*, p. 60.
9. Edith Mary Johnston-Liik, *MPs in Dublin: Companion to the History of the Irish Parliament, 1692–1800* (Belfast, 2009), p. 9.
10. Trinity College, Dublin, 'The Down Survey of Ireland: Mapping a century of change' (http://downsurvey.tcd.ie/); Thomas Bartlett, *The Fall and Rise of the Irish Nation: The Catholic Question, 1690–1830* (Dublin, 1992), p. 47.
11. Bartlett, *Ireland*, p. 145
12. Ian McBride, *Eighteenth Century Ireland: The Isle of Slaves* (Dublin, 2009), p. 198.
13. *Ibid.*, p. 199.
14. Bartlett, *Fall and rise*, p. 47.
15. McBride, *Eighteenth Century Ireland*, p. 199.
16. David Dickson, *New Foundations: Ireland, 1660–1800* (Dublin, 2000), p. 80.
17. McBride, *Eighteenth Century Ireland*, p. 194.
18. Gilbert, *Dublin*, iii, p. 70.
19. *Ibid.*, pp. 72–73.
20. *Ibid.*, p. 73.
21. Edward McParland 'Edward Lovett Pearce and the Parliament House in Dublin' in *The Burlington Magazine*, 131, 1031 (Feb. 1989), p. 91.
22. *Ibid.*, p. 92.
23. McParland, *Public Architecture*, p. 179.

24. Gilbert, *Dublin*, iii, p. 74.
25. *Ibid.*, pp. 77–76.
26. McParland, *Public Architecture*, p. 177.
27. Gilbert, *Dublin*, iii, p. 77.
28. *Ibid.*, p. 78.
29. Casey, *Dublin*, p. 383
30. Gilbert, *Dublin*, iii, p. 78.
31. *Ibid.*, p. 78.
32. Michael MacDonagh 'In the Strangers' Gallery at College Green', in *The Irish Monthly*, 49, 579 (Sept., 1921), p. 355.
33. John Edward Walsh, *Ireland Sixty Years ago* (Dublin; M'Glashan, 1851), pp. 150–151.
34. MacDonagh 'In the Strangers' Gallery at College Green', pp. 355–356.
35. Pakenham, *A Traveller's Companion*, p. 184.
36. Gilbert, *Dublin*, iii, p. 78.
37. *Ibid.*, p. 79.
38. Bartlett, *Ireland*, p. 146.
39. The two professions of barber and surgeon were joined until the late eighteenth century when surgeons began to develop as a distinct profession.
40. *An alphabetical list of the freemen and freeholders that polled at the election of members of parliament to represent the city of Dublin* (Dublin, 1760).
41. Gilbert, *Dublin*, iii, p. 104.
42. *Ibid.*, pp. 104–105.
43. The full Guild title is 'printers, painter-stainers and cutlers guild' or the Guild of St Anne.
44. *Saunder's Newsletter*, 7 Feb. 1782.
45. *Freeman's Journal*, 12 Feb. 1782.
46. *Saunder's Newsletter*, 7 Feb. 1782.
47. Gilbert, *Dublin*, iii, p. 112.
48. *Ibid.*, p. 116.
49. *Ibid.*, p. 117.
50. *Ibid.*, p. 111.
51. Bartlett, *Ireland*, p. 187.
52. Gilbert, *Dublin*, iii, p. 124.
53. *Ibid.*, p. 126.
54. Bartlett, *Fall and rise*, p. 47.
55. It was common for political groups to meet in taverns as well as coffee houses and the Eagle tavern was used by many political clubs.

56. Bartlett (ed.), *Life of Theobald Wolfe Tone* (Dublin, 1998), p. 46.
57. Bartlett, *Ireland*, p. 213.
58. *Ibid.*, p. 224.
59. *Ibid.*, p. 227.
60. *Ibid.*, p. 224.
61. Patrick M. Geoghegan, *The Irish Act of Union* (Dublin, 2001), p. 128.
62. *Ibid.*, p. 129.
63. F.G. Hall, *The Bank of Ireland* (Dublin, 1949), p. 458.
64. Gilbert, *Dublin*, iii, p. 177.
65. David Griffin, 'Parliament house to Bank of Ireland', in *Irish Arts Review* (2002), 28, 4 (Dec. 2011 – Feb. 2012), p. 117.
66. *Ibid.*
67. *Ibid.*, p. 116.
68. Pakenham, *A Traveller's Companion*, p. 196.

Chapter Five: Dublin City Hall

1. Sheridan, 'Designing the capital city: Dublin *c.*1660–1810', in Brady & Simms, *Dublin*, p. 80.
2. *Ibid.*, p. 82.
3. Helen Andrews and John Coleman, 'Luke Gardiner' in *DIB*; Seán J. Murphy 'The Gardiner Family, Dublin, and Mountjoy, County Tyrone', in *Studies in Irish Genealogy and Heraldry* (Windgates 2010), pp. 28–35: (http://homepage.eircom.net/~seanjmurphy/studies/gardiner.pdf).
4. Sheridan, 'Designing the capital city: Dublin *c.*1660–1810', in Brady & Simms, *Dublin*, pp. 87–89.
5. For more information on Merrion Square see Nicola Matthews, 'Merrion Square', in Dublin City Council, *The Georgian Squares of Dublin* (Dublin, 2006), pp. 33–55.
6. Louis Cullen, *Princes and Pirates: The Dublin Chamber of Commerce 1783–1983* (Dublin, 1983), p. 18.
7. Sheridan, 'Designing the capital city: Dublin *c.*1660–1810', in Brady & Simms, *Dublin*, pp. 105–116.
8. Cullen, *Princes and Pirates*, p. 38.
9. 'Fair Minute Book of Commitee of Merchants', Royal Irish Academy (RIA) MS 12. D. 29.
10. Cullen, *Princes and Pirates*, pp. 39–40.
11. 'Fair Minute Book of Commitee of Merchants', RIA MS 12. D. 29.

12. For details on the composition of the freemen in Dublin between 1660 and 1860 as well as details on the guilds see Jacqueline Hill, *From Patriots to Unionists: Dublin Civic Politics and Irish Protestant Patriotism, 1660–1840* (Oxford, 1997). Dublin City Library and Archives have also digitised their extant lists of freemen and guildsmen which can be found here: http://dublinheritage.ie/freemen/ (accessed 3 June 2014).

13. Casey, *Dublin*, p. 362.

14. *Ibid.*, p. 361.

15. Rachel Finnegan (ed.), *Richard Twiss: A Tour in Ireland* (Dublin; University College Dublin Press, 2008), p. 12.

16. Gilbert, *Dublin*, ii, p. 57.

17. Draft Minute Book of Committee of Merchants, 1767–83 (RIA, MS 3. C. 25).

18. Craig, *Dublin 1660–1860*, p. 120.

19. *Ibid.*, p. 263.

20. See William Eden Auckland, *Considerations submitted to the people of Ireland, on their present condition with regard to trade and constitution. In answer to a pamphlet* (Dublin, 1781); Anon. *Considerations on the removal of the Custom-House Humbly submitted to the public* (Dublin, 1781); Anon, *Strictures on a pamphlet lately published, entitled, 'Considerations submitted to the people of Ireland'* (Dublin, 1781).

21. Craig, *Dublin 1660–1860*, p. 264.

22. Casey, *Dublin*, p. 141.

23. Craig, *Dublin 1660–1860*, p. 263.

24. Gilbert, *Dublin*, ii, p. 58.

25. D.J. Kelleher, *The Glamour of Dublin* (Dublin, 1920), pp. 50–51.

26. Gilbert, *Dublin*, ii, p. 59.

27. *Ibid.*

28. Gearóid Ó Tuathaigh, 'Daniel O'Connell', in *DIB*.

29. Virginia Crossman, 'Thomas Drummond' in *DIB*.

30. John Moloney, 'Thomas Davis', in *DIB*.

31. Pól Ó Conghaile, *Secret Dublin: An Unusual Guide* (Versailles, 2013), p. 83.

32. Casey, *Dublin*, p. 361.

CHAPTER SIX: ST JAMES'S GATE BREWERY

1. G. Ivan Morris, *In Dublin's Fair City* (London, 1947), p. 31.

2. Mary Daly, *Dublin: The Deposed Capital: A Social and Economic History, 1860–1914* (Cork, 2011), p. 23.
3. *Ibid.*, p. 26.
4. David Dickson, 'Arthur Guinness', in *DIB*.
5. Edward J. Bourke, *The Guinness Story: The Family, the Business, the Black Stuff* (Dublin, 2009), p. 14
6. David Dickson, 'Arthur Guinness', in *DIB*.
7. Bourke, *The Guinness Story*, p. 14.
8. Dickson, 'Guinness', in *DIB*.
9. Bourke, *The Guinness Story*, p. 52.
10. *Ibid.*, pp. 21–23.
11. Gilbert, *Dublin*, i, p. 151
12. *Ibid.*, p. 153
13. Kevin C. Kearns, *Dublin Pub Life and Lore* (Dublin, 1997), p. 10.
14. Louis Cullen, 'A story of growth and change', in Clarke, *Irish Cities*, p. 99.
15. Gilbert, *Dublin*, i, p. 157.
16. Kearns, *Pub Life*, p. 10.
17. Walsh, *Ireland Sixty Years Ago*, p. 53.
18. George Rudé, *Hanoverian London* (Stroud, 2003), p. 6.
19. *Ibid.*, pp. 4, 70.
20. Details from http://www.guinness-storehouse.com/en/History.aspx.
21. Bourke, *The Guinness Story*, p. 52.
22. *Ibid.*, p. 24.
23. Details from http://www.guinness-storehouse.com/en/History.aspx.
24. Tony Corcoran, *The Goodness of Guinness: The Brewery, Its people and the City of Dublin* (Dublin, 2005), p. 23.
25. Dickson, 'Guinness', in *DIB*.
26. Corcoran, *Goodness of Guinness*, p. 23.
27. *Ibid.*, p. 24.
28. *Ibid.*, p. 25.
29. F.H.A. Aalen, *The Iveagh Trust: The First Hundred Years, 1890–1990* (Dublin, 1990), p. 8
30. *Ibid.*, p. 1; Casey, *Dublin*, p. 652.
31. Aalen, *Iveagh Trust*, p. 39.
32. Casey, *Dublin*, p. 653.
33. Aalen, *Iveagh Trust*, p. 31.
34. Ó Conghaile, *Secret Dublin*, p. 219.
35. Corcoran, *Goodness of Guinness*, p. 45.
36. *Ibid.*, pp. 55–56.

37. Casey, *Dublin*, p. 70.
38. Corcoran, *Goodness of Guinness*, p. 27.
39. *Ibid.*, p. 28.
40. Kearns, *Pub Life*, p. 11.
41. Bourke, *The Guinness Story*, p. 29.
42. Daly, *Deposed Capital*, p. 23.
43. *Ibid.*
44. David Dickson, *Old World Colony: Cork and South Munster 1630–1830* (Cork, 2005), p. 388.
45. *Ibid.*, p. 389.
46. *Ibid.*, p. 388.
47. Bourke, *The Guinness Story*, p. 29.
48. Daly, *Deposed Capital*, pp. 24–25.
49. Casey, *Dublin*, pp. 69–70.
50. Daly, *Deposed Capital*, pp. 24–25.
51. *Ibid.*, p. 24.
52. Dickson, *Old World Colony*, p. 386.
53. Flann O'Brien (1911–1966), the celebrated Irish writer (and drinker), was a pseudonym of Brian O'Nolan. He also wrote for *The Irish Times* under the name Myles Na gCopaleen.
54. Flann O'Brien, *At Swim Two Birds* (London, 2007), p. 70.
55. *Ibid.*, pp. 74–75.
56. Kearns, *Pub Life*, p. 48.
57. *Ibid.*, p. 48.
58. Joseph V. O'Brien, *'Dear, Dirty, Dublin': A city in Distress, 1899–1916* (Berkeley, 1982), p. 188.
59. Kearns, *Pub Life*, p. 22.
60. Donal Fallon, Sam McGrath, & Ciarán Murray, *Come Here To Me! Dublin's other History* (Dublin, 2012), p. 269.
61. Kearns, *Pub Life*, p. 23.
62. O'Brien, *Dear, Dirty, Dublin*, p. 163.
63. Corcoran, *Goodness of Guinness*, pp. 70–71.
64. Collins & Kostick, *Dublin 1916*, p. 107.

CHAPTER SEVEN: KILMAINHAM GAOL

1. Pat Cooke, *A History of Kilmainham Gaol* (Dublin, 2006), p. 5.
2. Bennett, *Encyclopaedia*, p. 144.

3. Gilbert, *Dublin*, i, pp. 257, 264.

4. *Ibid.*, p. 274.

5. *Ibid.*

6. David Dickson, *Arctic Ireland: The Extraordinary Story of the Great Frost and Forgotten Famine of 1740–41* (Belfast, 1998), p. 54.

7. Gilbert, *Dublin*, i, p. 274.

8. Rod Morgan, 'Howard, John (1726?–1790)', *Oxford Dictionary of National Biography* 60 vols (Oxford, 2004).

9. Cooke, *Kilmainham Gaol*, p. 7

10. Niamh O'Sullivan, *Every Dark Hour: A History of Kilmainham Gaol* (Dublin, 2007), pp. 21–22, Cooke, *Kilmainham Gaol*, p. 8.

11. Cooke, *Kilmainham Gaol*, p. 9.

12. O'Sullivan, *Every Dark Hour*, pp. 21–22, Cooke, *Kilmainham Gaol*, p. 8.

13. O'Sullivan, *Every Dark Hour*, p. 204.

14. *Ibid.*, p. 22.

15. *Ibid.*, pp. 22–23.

16. James Kelly, *Gallows Speeches from Eighteenth-Century Ireland* (Dublin, 2001), p. 160.

17. Brian Henry, *Dublin Hanged: Crime, Law Enforcement and Punishment in Late Eighteenth-Century Dublin* (Dublin, Four Courts, 1994), p. 101.

18. O'Sullivan, *Every Dark Hour*, p. 198.

19. *Ibid.*, p. 196.

20. *Ibid.*, pp. 201–202.

21. O'Brien, *Dear, Dirty, Dublin*, pp. 173–174.

22. O'Sullivan, *Every Dark Hour*, p. 194.

23. Daly, *Deposed Capital*, p. 15.

24. David Dickson (ed.), *The Hidden Dublin: the social and sanitary conditions of Dublin's working classes in 1845* (Dublin, 2002), p. 26.

25. O'Brien, *Dear, Dirty, Dublin*, p. 171.

26. *Ibid.*

27. *Ibid.*, p. 171.

28. Dickson (ed.), *Hidden Dublin*, p. 35.

29. *Ibid.*, p. 36.

30. Cooke, *Kilmainham Gaol*, p. 11.

31. O'Sullivan, *Every Dark Hour*, p. 17.

32. *Ibid.*, p. 22.

33. William Smith O'Brien's infant son was baptised in the Jail when he was incarcerated there, something he had to get special permission for. (O'Sullivan, *Every Dark Hour*, p. 62).

34. Cooke, *Kilmainham Gaol*, p. 26.
35. Frank Callanan, 'Charles Stewart Parnell', in *DIB*.
36. *Ibid.*
37. Pakenham, *A Traveller's Companion*, p. 121.
38. *Ibid.*, p. 118.
39. *Ibid.* p. 120.
40. O'Sullivan, *Every Dark Hour*, p. 97.
41. Shane Hegarty & Fintan O'Toole, *The Irish Times Book of the 1916 Rising* (Dublin, 2006), p. 161.
42. *Ibid.*
43. Willie was Patrick Pearse's brother, he was not a senior organiser of the rising but is believed to have been executed because of his brother. During his court martial he made the mistake of pleading guilty.
44. Hegarty & O'Toole, *Irish Times Book of the 1916 Rising*, p. 162.
45. The lord mayor of Dublin wears a ceremonial chain which was presented to the city by the Protestant William of Orange after he had defeated the Catholic King James. Kathleen refused to wear this chain because of its association with King William and instead wore the chain of the President of the Court of Conscience on ceremonial days.
46. Hegarty & O'Toole, *Irish Times Book of the 1916 Rising*, p. 185.
47. *Ibid.*, p. 157.
48. Frances Clark, 'Grace Gifford', in *DIB*.
49. Hegarty & O'Toole, *Irish Times Book of the 1916 Rising*, p. 127.
50. *Ibid.*, p. 128.
51. O'Sullivan, *Every Dark Hour*, p. 137.
52. *Ibid*, p. 157.
53. Sinead McCoole, *No Ordinary Women: Irish Female Activists in the Revolutionary Years 1900–1923* (Dublin, 2003), pp. 117–118.
54. O'Sullivan, *Every Dark Hour*, p. 167.
55. McCoole, *No Ordinary Women*, p. 116.
56. *Ibid.*, pp. 115–116.
57. *Ibid.*, p. 117.
58. Rory O'Dwyer, '"The Wilderness Years": Kilmainham Gaol, 1924–1960', *History Ireland*, 18, 6 (Nov/Dec. 2010), p. 41.
59. *Ibid.*, p. 42.
60. *Ibid.*, p. 43.
61. *Ibid.*

Chapter Eight: The General Post Office (GPO)

1. Casey, *Dublin*, p. 147.
2. Clair Wills, *Dublin 1916: The Siege of the GPO* (London, 2009), p. 79.
3. Stephen Ferguson, *Letter, Lives & Liberty at the An Post Museum* (Dublin, 2011), p. 17.
4. *Dublin Penny Journal*, 6 Dec. 1834.
5. *Ibid.*
6. Micheál Ó Riain, 'Nelson's Pillar: A controversy that ran & ran', *History Ireland*, 6, 4 (Winter 1998), p. 22.
7. Casey, *Dublin*, p. 213.
8. Ó Riain, 'Nelson's Pillar: A controversy that ran & ran', p. 22.
9. Morris, *Dublin's Fair City*, p. 38.
10. Ó Riain, 'Nelson's Pillar: A controversy that ran & ran', p. 23.
11. Yvonne Whelan, 'Symbolising the State – the iconography of O'Connell Street and environs after Independence (1922)', *Irish Geography*, 34, 2 (2001), p. 141.
12. Ó Riain, 'Nelson's Pillar: A controversy that ran & ran', p. 21.
13. Wills, *Dublin 1916*, p. 8.
14. Yvonne Whelan, *Reinventing Modern Dublin: Streetscape, Iconography and the Politics of Identity* (Dublin, 2003), p. 54.
15. *Ibid.*, p. 73.
16. *Ibid.*, p. 64.
17. *Ibid.*, p. 54.
18. *Ibid.*, p. 73.
19. Bartlett, *Ireland*, p. 366.
20. Diarmaid Ferriter, *The Transformation of Ireland 1900–2000* (London, 2004), p. 118.
21. Bartlett, *Ireland*, p. 371.
22. McGarry, *The Rising*, p. 45.
23. *Ibid.*, pp. 62–63.
24. *Ibid.*, p. 85.
25. *Ibid.*, p. 92.
26. *Ibid.*, p. 96.
27. *Ibid.*, p. 103.
28. *Ibid.*, p. 103.
29. *Ibid.*, p. 222.
30. Liberty Hall was the headquarters of the Irish Transport and General Workers Union (ITGWU).
31. John O'Connor, *The 1916 Proclamation* (Dublin, 1999), p. 28

32. *Ibid.*, p. 29.
33. McGarry, *The Rising*, p. 124.
34. Wills, *Dublin 1916*, pp. 5–6.
35. Pakenham, *A Traveller's Companion*, pp. 284–285.
36. Wills, *Dublin 1916*, p. 37.
37. Pakenham, *A Traveller's Companion*, pp. 284–285.
38. Adrian and Sally Warwick-Haller (ed.), *Letters from Dublin, Easter 1916 Alfred Fannin's Diary of the Rising* (Dublin, Irish Academic Press, 1995), p. 27.
39. Wills, *Dublin 1916*, p. 49.
40. Pakenham, *A Traveller's Companion*, pp. 286, 289.
41. Wills, *Dublin 1916*, p. 50.
42. *Ibid.*, p. 52.
43. O'Connor, *The 1916 Proclamation*, p. 49.
44. *Ibid.*, p. 49.
45. *Ibid.*, p. 50.
46. Wills, *Dublin 1916*, p. 51.
47. McGarry, *The Rising*, pp. 172–174.
48. *Ibid.*, p. 192
49. *Ibid.*, p. 193.
50. Charlie McGuire, 'Seán McLoughlin: The Boy Commandant of 1916' in *History Ireland*, 14, 3 (Mar.–Apr. 2006), p. 27.
51. Wills, *Dublin 1916*, p. 37.
52. *Ibid.*, p. 76.
53. *Ibid.*, p. 79.
54. *Ibid.*, p. 81.
55. Warwick-Haller, *Letters from Dublin*, p. 19.
56. Ferriter, *Transformation of Ireland*, pp. 153–154.
57. Wills, *Dublin 1916*, p. 100.
58. Ó Riain, 'Nelson's Pillar: A controversy that ran & ran', p. 21.
59. Casey, *Dublin*, p. 371.
60. Brian Hanley, 'The forgotten massacres: responses to the Dublin and Monaghan bombings', *History Ireland*, 22, 3 (May/June 2014), p. 47.

Chapter Nine: The Abbey Theatre

1. Ferriter, *Transformation of Ireland*, p. 376.
2. Christopher Morash, *A History of Irish Theatre* (Cambridge, 2002), p. 107.

3. Morash, *Irish Theatre*, p. 110.
4. Brendan Lynch, *City of Writers* (Dublin, 2013), p. 203.
5. Morash, *Irish Theatre*, p. 112.
6. *Ibid.*
7. *Ibid.*, p. 113.
8. *Ibid.*, p. 114.
9. *Ibid.*
10. *Ibid.*, p. 110.
11. *Ibid.*, p. 104.
12. Lady Augusta Gregory, *Our Irish Theatre: A Chapter of Autobiography* (Gloucestershire, 2008), p. 3.
13. *Ibid.*, p. 3.
14. *Ibid.*, p. 5.
15. Morash, *Irish Theatre*, p. 117.
16. Gregory, *Our Irish Theatre*, pp. 4–5.
17. *Ibid.*, p. 10.
18. *Ibid.*, p. 16.
19. Ferriter, Diarmaid 'William Fay', in *DIB*.
20. *Ibid.*
21. Gregory, *Our Irish Theatre*, p. 19.
22. *Ibid.*
23. *Ibid.*
24. Casey, *Dublin*, p. 175.
25. Christopher Fitz-Simon, *The Abbey Theatre* (London, 2003), p. 19.
26. Gregory, *Our Irish Theatre*, p. 24.
27. Fitz-Simon, *The Abbey Theatre*, p. 21.
28. Maume, Patrick, 'Augusta Gregory', in *DIB*.
29. Fitz-Simon, *The Abbey Theatre*, p. 30.
30. Morash, *Irish Theatre*, p. 144.
31. *Ibid.*, p. 145.
32. Gregory, *Our Irish Theatre*, p. 25.
33. Morash, *Irish Theatre*, p. 119.
34. Ferriter, *Transformation of Ireland*, p. 94.
35. *Ibid.*, p. 145.
36. Gregory, *Our Irish Theatre*, p. 29.
37. Fitz-Simon, *The Abbey Theatre*, p. 30.
38. Ferriter, *Transformation of Ireland*, p. 95.
39. Ferriter, 'Fay', in *DIB*.
40. Fitz-Simon, *The Abbey Theatre*, p. 57.

41. Morash, *Irish Theatre*, p. 160.

42. Fitz-Simon, *The Abbey Theatre*, p. 57.

43. *Ibid.*, p. 58.

44. Morash, *Irish Theatre,* p. 189.

45. *Ibid.*, p. 176.

46. *Ibid.*, p. 183.

47. Lynch, *City of Writers*, p. 160.

48. Fitz-Simon, *The Abbey Theatre*, pp. 58–59.

49. Maume, 'Gregory', in *DIB*.

50. Ferriter, 'Fay', in *DIB*.

51. Fitz-Simon, *The Abbey Theatre*, p. 74.

52. *Irish Times*, 18 July 1951, Fitz-Simon, *The Abbey Theatre*, p. 101.

53. *Irish Times*, 18 July 1951.

54. *Irish Times*, 19 July 1951.

55. Fitz-Simon, *The Abbey Theatre*, p. 101.

56. *Ibid.*

57. *Ibid.*, p. 102.

58. *Ibid.*

59. *Ibid.*

60. *Irish Times*, 29 Oct. 1955

61. *Ibid.*

62. *Irish Times*, 15 Apr. 1958

63. *Irish Times*, 24 May 1957.

64. *Irish Times*, 10 Jun. 1958.

65. Fitz-Simon, *The Abbey Theatre*, p. 103.

66. Morash, *Irish Theatre*, p. 219.

67. *Ibid.*, p. 220.

68. Bennett, *Encyclopaedia*, p. 2.

69. Casey, *Dublin*, p. 176.

70. Morash, *Irish Theatre*, p. 226.

71. *Ibid.*, p. 226

72. Fitz-Simon, *The Abbey Theatre*, p. 118.

73. *Ibid.*, p. 136.

74. *Ibid.*

75. *Ibid.*, p. 153.

75. *Ibid.*, p. 154.

77. *Ibid.*, p. 167.

78. *Ibid.*, p. 177.

79. *Ibid.*

Chapter Ten: Croke Park

1. Tim Carey, *Croke Park: A History* (Cork, 2007), p. 72
2. Pakenham, *A Traveller's Companion*, p. 100.
3. Earnán P. Blythe, 'The First Decade of the GAA in Dublin', *Dublin Historical Record*, 19, 1 (Dec. 1963), p. 17.
4. Walsh, *Ireland Sixty Years Ago*, p. 34.
5. Mike Cronin & Roisín Higgins, *Places We Play: Ireland's Sporting Heritage* (Cork, 2011), p. 17.
6. Cronin & Higgins, *Places We Play*, p. 19.
7. Ferriter, *Transformation of Ireland*, p. 102.
8. *The United Irishmen; The Irishman*, 11 Oct. 1884.
9. Eoghan Corry, *An Illustrated History of the GAA* (Dublin, 2006), p. 13.
10. *Ibid.*, p. 17.
11. *The United Irishmen; The Irishman*, 11 Oct. 1884.
12. Carey, *Croke Park*, p. 23.
13. *Ibid.*, p. 24.
14. *Ibid.*, p. 25
15. *Ibid.*, pp. 31–32.
16. Corry, *History of the GAA*, p. 57.
17. Carey, *Croke Park*, p. 32.
18. *Ibid.*, p. 29.
19. *Ibid.*, p. 33.
20. *Ibid.*, p. 34.
21. *Ibid.*, p. 37.
22. *Ibid.*, p. 38.
23. Corry, *History of the GAA*, pp. 49–50.
24. *Ibid.*, p. 50.
25. Carey, *Croke Park*, p. 47.
26. *Ibid.*, p. 48.
27. Carey, *Croke Park*, pp. 51–53.
28. Tim Carey and Marcus de Búrca, 'Bloody Sunday 1920: New evidence' in *History Ireland*, 11, 2 (Summer 2003), p. 15.
29. Carey, *Croke Park*, p. 49.
30. *Ibid.*, p. 56.
31. Mike Cronin, 'Protecting the nation through sport and culture: Ireland, Aonach Tailteann and the Irish Free State, 1924–32', *Journal of Contemporary History*, 38, 3 (July 2003), p. 396.
32. *Ibid.*, pp. 397–399.
33. *Ibid.*, pp. 397–398.
34. *Ibid.*, p. 400.

35. *Ibid.*, p. 404.
36. *Ibid.*, p. 402.
37. *Ibid.*, p. 405.
38. *Ibid.*, pp. 406–407
39. *Ibid.*, p. 406.
40. *Ibid.*, p. 397.
41. *Ibid.*, pp. 408–409.
42. *Ibid.*, p. 410.
43. *Ibid.*, p. 411.
44. Carey, *Croke Park*, p. 72
45. *Ibid.*, p. 77
46. Corry, *History of the GAA*, p. 66
47. *Ibid.*
48. *Ibid.*, p. 67.
49. Ferriter, *Transformation of Ireland*, p. 427.
50. *Ibid.*, p. 427.
51. Micheál Ó Muircheartaigh, *Micheál's GAA Odyssey: A Celebration of Gaelic Games* (Edinburgh, 2009), p. 66.
52. Corry, *History of the GAA*, p. 67.
53. Ó Muircheartaigh, *Micheál's GAA Odyssey*, p. 15.
54. *Ibid.*, p. 28.
55. *Ibid.*, p. 96.
56. Carey, *Croke Park*, p. 127.
57. *Ibid.*, p. 112.
58. *Ibid.*
59. *Ibid.*, p. 135.
60. *Ibid.*, p. 139.
61. Ferriter, *Transformation of Ireland*, p. 606.
62. Ó Muircheartaigh, *Micheál's GAA Odyssey*, p. 81.
63. Carey, *Croke Park*, p. 152
64. *Ibid.*, p. 154.
65. *Ibid.*, p. 162.
66. *Ibid.*, p. 171.
67. *Ibid.*, p. 190.

Epilogue

1. J.B. Maguire, 'Seventeenth-century plans of Dublin Castle', in Clark (ed.), *Medieval Dublin*, p. 201.

Select bibliography

PRIMARY SOURCES

Newspapers
Dublin Journal
Dublin Penny Journal
Freeman's Journal
Irish Times
Irish Independent
Saunder's Newsletter

Contemporary works and editions of texts

Agnew, Jean (ed.) *Drennan-McTier Letters, vol. 2 1794–1801* (Dublin, Irish Manuscripts Commission, 1999)

An alphabetical list of the freemen and freeholders that polled at the election of members of parliament to represent the city of Dublin (Dublin, 1760)

Bartlett, Thomas (ed.), *Life of Theobald Wolfe Tone* (Dublin, Lilliput, 1998)

Bovet, Madam de, *Three Month Tour in Ireland* (London, Chapman & Hall, 1891)

Finnegan, Rachel (ed.), *Richard Twiss: A Tour in Ireland in 1775* (Dublin, UCD Press, 2008)

Fitzgerald, Percy, *Recollections of Dublin Castle and of Dublin Society* (New York, Brentanto's, 1902)

Gamble, John, *Sketches of history, politics and manners in Dublin and Northern Ireland* (London, 1810)

Gregory, Lady Augusta, *Our Irish Theatre: A Chapter of Autobiography* (Gloucestershire, Dodo Press, 2008)

Kelleher, D.J., *The Glamour of Dublin* (Dublin, The Talbot Press, 1920)

Kelly, James, *Gallow Speeches from Eighteenth-Century Ireland* (Dublin, Four Courts Press, 2001)

Pakenham, Thomas and Valerie, *Dublin: A Traveller's Companion* (London, St Edmondsbury Press, 1988)

Pelly, Patricia & Todd, Andrew (eds), *The Highland Lady in Dublin 1851–1856* (Dublin, New Island, 2005)

McDowell, R.B., *McDowell on McDowell: A Memoir* (Dublin, Lilliput Press, 2008)

Morris, G. Ivan, *In Dublin's Fair City* (London, Home & Van Thal, Ltd., 1947)

Neligan, David, *The Spy in the Castle* (Dublin, Prenderville Publishing, 1999)

Walsh, John Edward, *Sketches of Ireland Sixty Years Ago* (Dublin, J. M'Glashan, 1851)

Warwick-Haller, Adrian and Sally (ed.), *Letters from Dublin, Easter 1916 Alfred Fannin's Diary of the Rising* (Dublin, Irish Academic Press, 1995)

SECONDARY SOURCES

Aalen, F.H.A., *The Iveagh Trust: The First Hundred Years, 1890–1990* (Dublin, Iveagh Trust, 1990)

Barry, Michael, *Victorian Dublin Reveleaed: The remarkable legacy of Nineteenth-Century Dublin* (Dublin, Andalus Press, 2012)

Bartlett, Thomas, *Ireland: A History* (Cambridge, Cambridge University Press, 2010)

—, *The Fall and Rise of the Irish Nation* (Dublin, Gill & Macmillan, 1992)

Bennett, Douglas, *The Encyclopaedia of Dublin* (Dublin, Gill & Macmillan, 2005)

Blythe, Earnán P., 'The First Decade of the GAA in Dublin', *Dublin Historical Record*, vol. 19, 1 (Dec. 1963).

Bourke, Edward J., *The Guinness Story: The family, the Business, the Black Stuff* (Dublin, O'Brien Press, 2009)

Boyd, Gary A, *Dublin, 1745–1920: Hospitals, Spectacle and Vice* (Dublin, Four Courts Press, 2005).

Brady, Joseph & Simms, Anngret (eds), *Dublin: Through Space and Time (c. 900–1900)*, (Dublin, Four Courts Press, 2001)

Carey, Tim, *Croke Park: A History* (Cork, The Collins Press, 2007)

Casey, Christine, *Dublin* (New Haven & London, Yale University Press, 2005)

Collins, Lorcan & Kostick, Conor, *A Guide to Dublin in 1916* (Dublin, O'Brien Press, 2000)

Cooke, Pat, *A History of Kilmainham Gaol* (Dublin Office of Public Works, 2007)

Corcoran, Tony, *The Goodness of Guinness: The Brewery, Its people and the City of Dublin* (Dublin, Liberties Press, 2005)

Corry, Eoghan, *An Illustrated History of the GAA* (Dublin, Gill & Macmillan, 2006)

Costello, Peter, *Dublin Castle in the Life of the Irish Nation* (Dublin, Wolfhound Press, 1999)

Clarke, Howard, *Dublin: Part I, to 1610* (Dublin, Royal Irish Academy, 2002)

— (ed.), *Medieval Dublin: The Making of a Metropolis* (Dublin, Irish Academic Press, 2nd ed, 2010)

— (ed.), *Irish Cities* (Cork, Mercier Press, 1995)

Craig, Julie, *See Dublin on Foot: An Architectural Guide* (Dublin, Dublin Civic Trust, 2001)

Craig, Maurice, *Dublin 1660–1860: The Shaping of a city* (Dublin; Liberties Press 2006)

Cronin, Mike, 'Protecting the Nation through Sport and Culture: Ireland, Aonach Tailteann and the Irish Free State, 1924–32', *Journal of Contemporary History*, 38, 3 (Jul, 2003)

—, Murphy, William & Rouse, Paul (eds), *The Gaelic Athletic Association* (Dublin, Irish Academic Press, 2009)

— & Higgins, Roisín, *Places We Play: Ireland's Sporting Heritage* (Cork, The Collins Press, 2011)

Cullen Louis, *Princes and Pirates: The Dublin Chamber of Commerce 1783–1983* (Dublin, Dublin Chamber of Commerce, 1983)

Daly, Mary, *Dublin: The Deposed Capital: A Social and Economic History 1860–1914* (Cork, Cork University Press, 2011)

Diamond, Ciaran, 'The Reformation Charter of Christ Church Cathedral Dublin, 1541', *Archivium Hibernicum*, 53 (1999)

Dickson, David (ed.), *The Gorgeous Mask: Dublin 1700–1850* (Dublin, Trinity Workshop, 1987)

—, *New Foundations: Ireland, 1660–1800* (Dublin; Irish Academic Press, 2000)

—, *Arctic Ireland: The extraordinary story of the Great Frost and Forgotten Famine of 1740–41* (Belfast, White Row Press, 1998)

—, *The Hidden Dublin: The Social and Sanitary Conditions of Dublin's Working Classes in 1845* (Dublin, A & A Farmar, 2002)

—, *Old World Colony: Cork and South Munster, 1630–1830* (Cork, Cork University Press, 2005)

Dublin City Council (ed.), *The Georgian Squares of Dublin* (Dublin; Dublin City Council, 2006)

Dungan, Myles, *The Stealing of the Irish Crown Jewels: An Unsolved Crime* (Dublin, Town House, 2003)

Dunlevy, Mairead, *Dress in Ireland* (London, Batsford Ltd, 1989)

—, *Dublin Barracks: A Brief History of Collins Barracks, Dublin* (Dublin, Office of Public Works, 2002).

Dwyer, Finbar, *Witches, Spies and Stockholm Syndrome: Life in Medieval Ireland* (Dublin, New Island Press, 2013)

Ferguson, Stephen, *Letters, Lives & Liberty at the An Post Museum* (Dublin, An Post, 2011),

Fallon, Donal, McGrath, Sam, & Murray, Ciarán, *Come Here To Me! Dublin's Other History* (Dublin, New Island, 2012)

Ferriter, Diarmaid, *The Transformation of Ireland 1900–2000* (London, Profile Books, 2004)

Christopher Fitz-Simon, *The Abbey Theatre* (London, Themes & Hudson, 2003)

Fox, Peter, (ed.), *Treasures of the Library* (Dublin, Royal Irish Academy, 1986)

Foster, Sarah, 'Buying Irish: Consumer Nationalism in 18th century Dublin', *History Today*, 47, 6 (1997)

Geoghegan, Patrick M., *The Irish Act of Union* (Dublin, Gill & Macmillan, 2001)

Gilbert, J.T., *A History of the City of Dublin* (3 vols, Dublin, James Duffy, 1861)

Griffin, David, 'Parliament house to Bank of Ireland' *Irish Arts Review* (2002), 28, 4 (Dec. 2011–Feb. 2012)

Hegarty, Shane & O'Toole, Fintan, *The Irish Times Book of the 1916 Rising* (Dublin, Gill & Macmillan, 2006),

Hall, F.G., *The Bank of Ireland* (Dublin, Hodges Figgis, 1949).

Henry, Brian, *Dublin Hanged: Crime, Law Enforcement and Punishment in Late Eighteenth-Century Dublin* (Dublin, Four Courts, 1994)

Hicks, David, *Irish Country Houses: A Chronicle of Change* (Cork, The Collins Press, 2012)

Hill, Jacqueline, *From Patriots to Unionists: Dublin Civic Politics and Irish Protestant Patriotism* (Oxford, Oxford University Press, 1997)

Kautt, W.H., 'Ambushes in the War of Independence: Kilmichael reconsidered', *History Ireland*, 18, 2 (March–April 2010)

Kearns, Kevin C., *Dublin Tenement Life: An Oral History* (Dublin, Gill & Macmillan, 1994)

—, *Dublin Pub Life and Lore* (Dublin, Gill & Macmillan, 1997)

Kelly, James, *The Liberty and Ormond Boys: Factional Riot in Eighteenth-Century Dublin* (Dublin, Four Courts Press, 2005)

Kinsella, Stuart, *Christ Church Cathedral Dublin: Visitor's Guide* (Dublin, Christ Church Cathedral Publications, 2012)

Laffan, William (ed), *The Cries of Dublin: Drawn from the Life by Hugh Douglas Hamilton, 1760* (Dublin, Irish Georgian Society, 2003)

Lennon, Colm (eds), *Dublin: 1610–1756* (Dublin, Royal Irish Academy, 2008)

—, *Sixteenth Century Ireland: The Incomplete Conquest* (Dublin, Gill & Macmillan, 2005)

Lynch, Brendan, *City of Writers* (Dublin, The Liffey Press, 2013)

Luce, J.V., *Trinity College Dublin: The First 400 years* (Dublin, Trinity College Dublin Press, 1992)

McBride, Ian, *Eighteenth Century Ireland: The Isle of Slaves* (Dublin, Gill & Macmillan, 2009)

McCarthy, Denis, *Dublin Castle: At the Heart of Irish History* (Dublin, Government Publications Office, 2004).

McCarthy, Muriel, *Marsh's Library: All Graduates and Gentlemen* (Dublin, Four Courts Press, 2003)

McCoole, Sinead, *No Ordinary Women: Irish Female Activists in the Revolutionary Years 1900–1923* (Dublin, O'Brien Press, 2003)

McCullough Niall, *Dublin An Urban History: The Plan of the city* (Dublin, Lilliput, 2007)

MacDonagh, Michael, 'In the Strangers' Gallery at College Green', *The Irish Monthly*, 49, 579 (Sept. 1921)

McGarry, Fearghal, *The Rising: Ireland 1916* (Oxford, Oxford University Press, 2010)

McGuire, James & Quinn James (eds), *Dictionary of Irish Biography*, (9 vols, Cambridge, Cambridge University press, 2009)

McGuire, Charlie, 'Seán McLoughlin: The Boy Commandant of 1916', *History Ireland*, 14, 3 (March–April 2006)

McGuinne, Dermot, *Irish Type Design: A History of Printing Types in the Irish Character* (Dublin, National Print Museum, 2010)

McParland, Edward, *Public Architecture in Ireland 1680–1760* (New Haven & London, Yale University Press, 2001)

—, 'Edward Lovett Pearce and the Parliament House in Dublin' in *The Burlington Magazine*, 131, 1031 (Feb. 1989)

Milne, Kenneth, *The Dublin Liberties, 1600–1850* (Dublin, Four Courts Press, 2009)

— (ed.), *Christ Church Cathedral, Dublin: A History* (Dublin, Four Courts Press, 2010)

Morash, Christopher, *A History of Irish Theatre* (Cambridge, Cambridge University Press, 2002)

Moss, Rachel & Scott, Yvonne (eds), *The Provost's House Stables: Buildings & Environs, Trinity College Dublin* (Dublin, Associated editions; 2008)

O'Brien, J.V., *'Dear, Dirty, Dublin': A City in Distress, 1899–1916* (Berkeley, University of California Press, 1982)

Ó Conghaile, Pól, *Secret Dublin: An Unusual Guide* (Versailles, Jonglez, 2013)

O'Connor, John, *The 1916 Proclamation* (Dublin, Anvil Books, 1999)

Ó Conchubhair, Brian (ed), *Dublins' Fighting Story, 1916–1921: Told by the Men who made it* (Cork, Mercier Press, 2009),

O'Dwyer, Rory, '"The Wilderness Years": Kilmainham Gaol, 1924–1960', *History Ireland*, 18, 6 (Nov.–Dec. 2010)

Muircheartaigh, Micheál Ó, *Micheál's GAA Odyssey: A Celebration of Gaelic Games* (Edinburgh, Mainstream Publishing, 2009)

O'Riordan, Tomás, 'The Theft of the Irish Crown Jewels, 1907' *History Ireland*, 9, 4 (2001)

Ó Riain, Micheál, 'Nelson's Pillar: A Controversy That Ran & Ran', *History Ireland*, 6, 4 (1998)

O'Sullivan, Niamh, *Every Dark Hour: A History of Kilmainham Jail* (Dublin, Liberties Press, 2007)

Pollard, Mary, *Dictionary of Members of the Dublin Book Trade: 1550–1800* (London, Bibliographical Society, 2000)

Robins, Joseph, *Champagne & Silver Buckles: The Viceregal Court at Dublin Castle, 1700–1922* (Dublin, Lilliput Press, 2001)

Robinson, John L., 'Christ Church Cathedral, Dublin, Proctors' Accounts, 1689–90', *Journal of the Royal Society of Antiquarians of Ireland*, sixth series, 1, 3 (Sept. 1911)

Rude, George, *Hanoverian London* (Stroud, Sutton publishing, 2003)

Somerville-Large, Peter *Dublin: The Fair City* (London, Sinclair Sevenson, 1996)

Vaughan, W.E. (ed), *The Old Library: Trinity College Dublin 1712–2012* (Dublin; Four Courts Press, 2013)

Wills, Clair, *Dublin 1916: The Siege of the GPO* (London, Profile Books, 2009)

Whelan, Yvonne, 'Symbolising the State: The iconography of O'Connell Street and Environs after Independence (1922)', *Irish Geography*, 34, 2 (2001)

—, *Reinventing Modern Dublin: Streetscape, Iconography and the Politics of Identity* (Dublin, UCD Press, 2003)

Index

Note: illustrations are indicated by page numbers in **bold**.